Understanding Identity

For Steve, Richard, Tamsin,
Jack and Sophie and my sister Sarah

Understanding Identity

Kath Woodward

A member of the Hodder Headline Group
LONDON
Distributed in the USA by Oxford University Press, New York

First published in Great Britain in 2002
Arnold, a member of the Hodder Headline Group
333 Euston Road, London NW1 3BH

http://www.arnoldpublishers.com

Distributed in the United States of America by
Oxford University Press Inc.,
198 Madison Avenue, New York, NY 10016

British Library Cataloguing in Publication Data
A catalogue record for this book is available from the British Library

Library of Congress Cataloging-in-Publication Data
A catalog record for this book is available from the Library of Congress

ISBN 0 340 80849 7 (hb)
ISBN 0 340 80850 0 (pb)

1 2 3 4 5 6 7 8 9 10

Typeset in 11/13 pt Minion and produced by Gray Publishing, Tunbridge Wells, Kent
Printed and bound in Great Britain by MPG Books Ltd, Bodmin, Cornwall

What do you think about this book? Or any other Hodder/Arnold title?
Please send your comments to feedback.arnold@hodder.co.uk

Contents

Introduction

Who am I? It looks like a question that cannot be answered without some reference to you, us and them; to the other people with whom I have contact. Who I am is closely interwoven with ideas about the society in which I live and the views of others who also inhabit that same social context. Ideas about who I am and possible answers to the opening question demand acknowledgement of the social as well as the personal. Identity involves personal investment, often on a massive scale, to the extent that people are willing to die to claim or protect their own identities, but it is always socially located. Identity matters, but how and why it matters depends on time and place and on specific historical, social and material circumstances. This book addresses the importance of identity as a concept in the social sciences and as part of the experience of everyday lives. My aim is to outline some of the paths that the concept has travelled and to look at the ways in which understanding identity can contribute to understanding social relations and social change. However, before we start thinking about the routes that the concept has travelled, we must have some idea of what it is that we are talking about.

Identity offers a way of thinking about the links between the personal and the social; of the meeting place of the psychological and the social, of the psyche and the society. It is the embodiment and location of the psycho-social. As we shall see, at different historical moments and in different places greater or lesser emphasis has been given to one side of the personal/social equation. Some historical moments have greater resonance than others and provide a particular focus on the meaning of identity.

On 11 September 2001, with the destruction of the twin towers of the World Trade Center in New York and of part of the Pentagon in Washington, the United States was plunged into a state of war against an enemy who could not be immediately identified. More alarming even than the devastation and destruction of life on US soil was the immediate uncertainty about who had committed the atrocity and thus the uncertainty about the action which should be taken. What was certain is that the USA, its way of life and what it embodied, had been attacked. The US president George W Bush declared,

> Freedom itself was attacked this morning and I assure you freedom will be defended. Make no mistake. The United States will hunt down and pursue those responsible for these cowardly acts.

In his address to the American people on 15 September he described the conflict in the following terms:

> This is a conflict without battlefields or beachheads, a conflict with opponents who believe they are invisible … Those who make war against the United States have chosen their own destruction … We are planning a broad and sustained campaign to secure our country and eradicate the evil of terrorism. Americans of all faiths and backgrounds are committed to this goal.

> Yesterday I visited the site of the destruction in New York City and saw an amazing spirit of sacrifice, patriotism and defiance. I met with rescuers who have worked past exhaustion, who cheered our country and the great cause we have entered … A terrorist attack designed to tear us apart has instead bound us together as a nation. Over the past few days, we have learnt much about American courage. In the past week, we have seen the American people at their very best. Citizens have come together to pray, to give blood to fly our country's flag. Great tragedy has come to us, and we are meeting it with the best that is in our country, with courage and concern for others. Because this is America. This is what our enemies hate and have attacked. (*The Observer*, 16 September, 2001: 3)

What does this rhetoric tell us about what we mean by identity? This is the rhetoric of war that has an immediacy that gives expression to strongly held feelings. Thousands of people had lost their lives in this most surprising of attacks, and as president, Bush had to give voice to the shock but also to galvanize the people of the USA in response to an enemy he cannot as yet name. Hence, in this instance oppositions are expressed as abstract nouns, such as 'freedom', which is set against 'terrorism'.

Identity is about difference; it is about marking out 'us' and 'them', and what is understood as war is a time when this distinction must be clearly marked in a most conflictual manner. This difference is also marked through direct oppositions, which exaggerate the dualisms that so often characterize identity formation. Identity requires a classificatory system that picks out those who share an identity and distinguish them from those who do not. However, identity also involves the management of difference. Each of us has to manage different selves even on an occasion such as this, when oppositions are emphasized, there has to be an acknowledgement of heterogeneity even among 'the American people'; especially among the American people, with their diverse faiths and cultures.

Identity also involves an understanding of agency and of rational choice. In this scenario, and in Bush's speech rationality is the prerogative of the US subject. The USA and her allies are rational, whereas this rationality is set in opposition to the lack of rationality of the enemy, according to this conceptualization. This raises matters of both agency and rationality and invokes questions that relate to difference. Whose agency and which rationality? How do we define what is rational and might one person's rational decision be another person's mindless folly?

Identity is marked through symbols, notably the symbol of the flag, which has particular resonance in the USA, where allegiance to the flag is a requirement of citizenship and of loyalty. Following the events of 11 September, not only was the US flag displayed most prominently by patriotic Americans, it was also burnt in some other parts of the world as a symbol of some people's hatred of the Americans. Symbolic systems mark the difference and provide the means of signifying identities.

Identity formation involves setting boundaries. These boundaries locate the parameters of difference and of sameness. Those with whom we share an identity are marked out as the same, in contrast to those who are different. Sameness is featured by the use of 'we' and 'us' and 'our' pronouns which draw in those with whom the identity is shared and exclude those who are characterized as 'other'. 'Us' is the USA, the American people, but in this instance, sameness also has to embrace difference, people of 'every faith and background' are included. However, securing identity includes managing different selves. Boundaries are not as secure as might at first be thought, especially in the context of political rhetoric. Establishing secure boundaries includes naming those who are included and those who are excluded. Laying claim to an identity involves being named; the American people are named, on several occasions in this speech and national unity is invoked. The problem in this case is that 'the enemy' cannot as yet be named in the conventional discourse of war. The enemy is referred to as 'terrorist' but as yet has no name. Even when Osama bin Laden was named as the most likely suspect and his Al Quaeda group cited as the most likely instigators of the attacks, the 'enemy' could not be identified as a nation state or group of nations. In the case of Pearl Harbor, with which the events of 11 September 2001 were compared, an enemy was immediately identified that conformed to a set of expectations about the form that such an enemy could take. It is possible to declare war against a nation, which has a distinct national identity and a geographical location with clear boundaries. It is much more difficult to wage war against an enemy whose identity seems to defy location and all the attributes of nation. This might be an enemy that knows no boundaries, as well as an enemy that transgresses one's own boundaries, those that might have appeared to be secure.

However, the 'enemy' does have an identity even if it cannot be defined in terms of nation state or even a specific geographical location. It is characterized as 'terrorist' here. In order to emphasize the 'otherness' of the enemy in Bush's rhetoric here, that enemy is described both as 'cowardly' and as 'evil'. Oppositions are brought into play; whereas the enemy is cowardly, the people of the USA display 'courage'. 'We' are defiant and patriotic, whilst the enemy is evil. The people of America stand together and support their nation patriotically, while the enemy does not even have a nation. Very soon after the destruction of the World Trade Center buildings, images of Osama bin Laden were used to signify the 'other' and the terrorist threat to the USA, and indeed, as characterized by Bush, the threat to the western world. Perhaps even more frighteningly it also illustrates the extent of commitment to a cause, even one that is called 'terrorist'. These people are willing to die; to kill themselves in suicide attacks for whatever it is they believe in. The outcomes of people willing to identify with such a cause are massive and have tragic, global implications as has also been illustrated in the Middle East with Palestinians committing suicide in defence of their people and in the assertion of Palestinian identity. The ways in which people espouse such identities that demand such aggressive action have material, social and economic consequences as well as arising from material inequality and social circumstances. Identity clearly matters, and in order to make sense of identity and to begin to address the question of why people take up the identity positions they do, we have to interrogate the material, social circumstances and the symbolic and psychic processes that are involved. The process of identification demands psychic investment as well as having social and material contexts.

The above example illustrates well the historical specificity of the importance of identity. It also offers some examples of the ways in which identities are constructed, through the marking of difference, which is both social and symbolic. Identities are formed through processes of identification and there has to be psychic investment in the identity that is adopted. The example of those who are willing to die for that identity as in the case of the suicide attacks on the USA, is an extreme instance of this process. People from the USA and her coalition allies are also willing to die for the protection of their own identities, which may be expressed as the defence of democracy and freedom. There has to be some element of agency, of the person actively engaging with an identity as well as the social roles that are imposed upon people. The emphasis in the 11 September example is on collective identities, none more so than Bush's appeal to the collectivity of the 'American people', but the identity of 'the other' that is only negatively constructed here and not explored, is both a collective identity and a personal identity. In the president's rhetoric there is a call for personal commitment to that collective identity, again indicating the necessity of personal investment in an identity position. There is clearly overlap between what has been called collective identity and that which has been classified as 'personal', as we shall see later in the book.

It may be that, as Kobena Mercer has claimed, 'identity only becomes an issue when it is in crisis' (1990: 4) and war has to be an example of crisis. However, it is not only at times of such extremes that identity requires both unity and certainty. Identity gives us a sense of who are and to some extent satisfies a demand for some degree of stability and of security. Crises occur when an identity position is challenged or becomes insecure, whether at the level of the individual or at the level of the state. The events of 11 September and the bombing of Afghanistan that followed were described as a crisis on a global scale. The suicide attacks on the USA were called threats to freedom and civilization, as well as heralding the possible destruction of global capital. The experience of what may be perceived as a threat or challenge to stability may well provoke examples of both hyperbole in the rhetoric and appeals to resist the threat through reinstating stability and order. In the case of identity this stability is often sought through appeals to unity and to an essentialism which 'we' share. Times of threat are not moments that can tolerate fragmentation and diversity. The time of threat is one when people need greater certainty. That certainty may be afforded through essentialist claims, to tradition, to the past, to a shared history and to what is essentially unchanging. In other instances it is the material body that carries the essential features of identity (Woodward, 1997a). This question of the tension between essentialist and non-essentialist interpretations of identity is one that informs much of the discussion in this book. Framing questions about the extent to which it is possible to assert an identity, to invest in an identity position, and to retain some certainty without making appeals to the grounding of essentialism, underpin much of the debate about identity which are explored in the discussion that follows. While this has exercised recent commentators, it has also informed earlier academic discussion. The debate about essentialism is also linked, in the quest for certainty, to the debate about the extent to which people are able to shape their own identities. This tension, implicated in the interrelationship between agency and structure, addresses the extent to which identity formation is influenced or even determined by structural factors, which may take the form of external constraints or the limitations of the bodies we inhabit.

I have attempted to pick out some of the key features of identity and to indicate its importance as a means of understanding social relations. Identity has to be socially located because it is though the concept of identity that the personal and the social are connected. Identity occupies that interstitial space between the personal and the social.

- Identity provides links between the personal and the social, self and society, the psychic and the social.
- Identity is relational, being constructed through relations of difference, such as 'us' and 'them'.
- Identity also has to accommodate and manage difference.
- The formation and establishment of identity involves both locating and transgressing boundaries; there is a constant attempt to establish boundaries which may be impossible to secure.
- Identity is historically specific; it can be seen as fluid, contingent and changing over time.
- Uncertainty about identity may lead people to lay claim to essential truths in their search for security and stability.
- Identity involves identification and thus the exercise of some agency on the part of those who identify with a particular identity position.
- Identities are marked symbolically and are reproduced through representational systems.
- Identity has material bases, including social, economic and political bases as well as those that are linked to the material body.

Chapter 1 traces some of the academic identity narratives that have been concerned with establishing ways of thinking about identity. Identity became a hot topic at the end of the twentieth century, with huge numbers of academic texts being devoted to the subject, in fact to the subject of the subject, although the term identity has dominated much of the literature. However, it is not so new, and Chapter 1 explores some of the background to more recent interest.

Chapter 2 engages with notions of narratives of the self and the stories which we tell in trying to make sense of who we are. There are personal, autobiographical stories which locate the individual within the framework of the public stories which produce different meanings about identity. Psychoanalytic theories offer one of the public stories through which private stories of the self are told. The contemporary western world can be seen as very involved in the exploration of personal identity through self-discovery, and psychoanalytic perspectives offer a route into such personal identity journeys.

Chapter 3 extends the notion of stories of the self and applies it to the broader landscape of mapping the self in relation to other journeys that we take. This encompasses some of the contemporary debates about notions of belonging and longing and the place of 'home' in a globalizing and globalized world.

Chapter 4 shifts the emphasis onto the role of representation in the formation and presentation of identity and examines the importance of symbolic systems and discursive fields as sites of contestation in debates about identity. Difference and sameness are marked through systems of representation which give meaning to how we see ourselves and how others see us.

Chapter 5 takes up what is also a site for the representation of identity by focusing on the notion of embodiment. Embodied selves present both limitations and possibilities for the presentation of identity and embodiment is foregrounded in debates about essentialism and the fixing and fluidity of the self. The body offers a mark of visible difference which can be read in various, differently inflected ways. The body also presents a site upon which meanings are inscribed and a discursive field which highlights the inter-relationship between gender and identity in much of the literature.

Chapter 6 focuses on the debate about essentialism and non-essentialism by exploring the meanings that are attached to the idea of roots and routes. The discussion addresses the difficulties of accommodating the notion of belonging outside the constraints of essentialist readings of identity and the advantages, as well as some of the problems associated with the idea of routes and the more contingent, hybrid fluid understandings of identity.

Acknowledgements

The author and publishers would like to thank the following for permission to reproduce copyright illustrations in this book: Ashmolean Museum, Oxford page 130; Curtis Brown Group Ltd. Estate of Dame Laura Knight page 95; Empics, Nottingham pages 82, 122 and 123.

The author and publishers would also like to thank Macmillan, London for permission to use an extract from *Trumpet* by Jackie Kay used on page 102.

My thanks to Sylvia Lay-Flurrie for all her help with the typing.

1 Knowing me, knowing you

Identity: the story so far

Identity has a history. The concept is one that has been deployed and developed through a number of different stories, academic stories as well as those of individuals, communities, peoples and nations. The identity story is one that has been told around different relationships, such as those between the personal and the social and those between self and others. Any study of identity involves exploring these relationships and the others that underpin ideas about identity, not only in the present, but also in their formulation, conceptualization and reproduction across time. What is a relationship can also be construed as a tension, or even an opposition. I have used 'relationship' to allow for the interconnections that are a focus of this book, as well as the oppositions that form part of the tradition of thinking about identity.

Our understanding of identity has been constructed and reproduced around different relationships. However, while debates have addressed the connections and differences in the personal and the social in identity formation, the equation has been differently weighted at different times. Indeed, an overemphasis on one aspect, leading to claims of 'oversocialization' (Wrong, 1961), has led to attempts to redress the balance. These have often been couched in terms of the need to reinstate a greater degree of human agency, so that it is possible to accord higher status to the responsibility that human beings have for their own actions, in shaping the sort of people they want to be. This raises another of the relationships upon which theories of identity have been based, that between what has been called agency and structure. This has included questions about the extent to which human beings are able to shape their own identities, make choices and take responsibility, as opposed to what people become and who they are, are influenced or even determined by other factors, outside their control. Such factors include economic, social, cultural and political matters.

The bodies we inhabit also offer boundaries and structural constraints as well as being sites for the presentation of identities. Notions of who we are and the relationship between the individual and the personal, and the societies that we live in are always located within the parameters of embodiment. The body might appear to set the boundaries of the self and create the specific site at which identity is formed. The body presents the unique location for the development of the self and for notions of continuity. This is a source of another relationship, that between the body and the mind or the body and the self. It has been articulated in different ways at different historical times, but the nature/culture divide gives expression to the traditional distinction. The relationship between nature and culture has been described as a binary opposition, one that at particular moments has been very unevenly weighted. More recently the nature/culture dualism has been expressed in terms of the relative weighting accorded to genetic as opposed to social factors. Tensions have been expressed between the influence of our genetic inheritance and the societies in which we live, in shaping who we are. Again the opposition is challenged by arguments that point to the ways in which knowledge about genes is also socially constructed; nature is also subject to social and cultural interpretation. A central premise of this book is that there are interrelationships between these different dimensions in the formation of identity, but it is an important part of the identity story that it is based on dualistic thinking, and it is one that it is valuable to trace.

Self, subject, identity

Notions of reforming the self and taking responsibility for our own actions are part of theological and philosophical debates which have been explored over a period lasting at least two and a half thousand years. The claim that reflective self-identity is a new, strictly modern phenomenon may tell us more about contemporary self-indulgence and introspection, than about historical detail. Concerns with knowing the self, more specifically the 'true self' and distinguishing between self-knowledge and self-deception, are the cornerstones of much religious teaching. However, my aim here is to locate the discussion of identity in the context of more recent debates within the social sciences, in particular. The discussion does not always focus on identity per se; at least not always using the term. In some instances 'self' and 'identity' are interchangeable, or the term 'social self' is used. The words 'subject' and 'self' are also often used interchangeably in cultural studies and in social and political theory. Preference for one or other of these terms is often indicated by the distinction between a 'subject' which is produced and controlled by social institutions and discourses and a self which has particular desires, anxieties and needs. Michel Foucault uses 'subject' to suggest someone who is subject to someone else and in his later work suggests the notion of a self who is tied to 'his' (probably his rather than hers, or theirs in Foucault's analysis) own identity by self-knowledge. However, a distinction is not usually made explicitly between subject and self.

Zygmunt Bauman distinguishes between self, identity and agent over time, but argues that differences have limited significance in contemporary society (1992). Bauman, along with Anthony Giddens (1991) however, stresses the autonomy of the self as an agent is largely about producing accounts of oneself. Giddens argues that the processes of social change that have taken place through the late twentieth and into the twenty-first centuries have heightened people's sense of risk and anxiety but have at the same time increased ideas of creative ability to construct ourselves.

> Where large areas of a person's life are no longer set by pre-existing patterns and habits, the individual is continually obliged to negotiate life-style options. Moreover – and this is crucial – such choices are not just 'external' or marginal aspects of the individual's attitudes, but define who the individual 'is'. In other words, life-style choices are constitutive of a reflective self (1992: 75).

Such an account uses self and 'self-identity' to refute other contemporary arguments about a subject who is only socially constructed. Thus there is sometimes a distinction between the 'self' as agent and the subject who is subject to social forces. However, subject and subjectivity also carry contradictory meanings and include a sense of agency and the notion that the subject can also be an agent. The subject encompasses both subjection to outside forces, even to the extent of being determined by such structures in some accounts, and the possibility of agency. The subject may also be a person who exercises some control and creative agency, for example as expressed in the first person singular 'I', who is the subject of the sentence and can be seen as initiating action.

There is clearly overlap between the terms self, subject and identity although in some instances the choice of term may indicate more or less emphasis on the degree of agency that it is possible to exercise. The term identity can be preferred for its accommodation of the interrelationship between the personal and the social and the complex possibilities of an interplay between agency and social construction or even constraint. One of the key debates within contested theories of identity, and a problem which such theories have to address, is the extent to which people, whether as individuals or within collectivities, participate actively in shaping their identities. Some recent theories, such as that of Anthony Giddens, have framed the debate in terms of the tension between structure and agency. Giddens (1991) has stressed the extent to which identity had become so transformed in the late twentieth century that external influences and constraints provided by others, notably those that are rooted in notions of obligation and duty, were replaced by the reflexive project of managing the self. Thus high priority is afforded to the self-constructing self, a self that is what it makes of itself. The projects with which this self engages are transformative and reflexive at the level of the individual, although Giddens also maps the social and cultural changes that have both been conducive to these changes in the construction of the self, and resulted from these shifts.

The debate does not have to be framed in terms of agency and structure as occupying dichotomous or oppositional positions. It is my concern to explore the interrelationships in this book and also to consider alternative conceptualizations which include the political dimensions of the self. The notion of collective agency as a political project draws on the Marxist notion of class action and, while recent debates have sought to move on from determinist notions of selfhood as entirely the product of socio-economic class position, the interplay between structure and agency is formulated within the Marxist paradigm through the vehicle of class consciousness. Marx made the distinction between a class that exists in itself and one that exists for itself. The class in itself describes those people who have a common relationship to the means of production, for example as workers who sell their labour or as capitalists who own the means of production. The class for itself has experienced the generation of a consciousness of common interests, for example of oppression and exploitation in the case of the working class. Class-consciousness, that is the process of becoming a class for itself, is the collective process whereby a collective class grouping has the consciousness upon which to act. In this sense action equates with the political activity that arises from consciousness. The Marxist contribution to the debate rests largely on collective identity and in particular on class identity rather than any notion of a reflective self. Much of the late twentieth debates about identity depended on an engagement with Marxism in some sense. This took the form of developments broadly within Marxism or reactions to its perceived emphasis on supposedly objective structures, especially economic and class structures at the expense of the individual and subjectivity or of other social divisions as well as class. Poststructuralist and postmodernist theories have moved away from class based analyses, focusing instead on diverse individual and group identities and fragmentation rather than cohesion. The question of how identity can be seen to make space for political engagement, exercising and challenging power through political action and active involvement is usefully addressed within this aspect of the Marxist critique, but it is an element that has been lost from some of the accounts that followed. The particular strength of the Marxist understanding of the class for itself is that it accommodates political action, rather than focusing only on the tension between agency and structure.

It is matters of coherence, wholeness and unity that have been most at issue in sociological accounts of identity. Conceptualizations of identity have been classified as the 'sociological subject' (Hall, 1992: 275) in order to distinguish it from its predecessor the 'Enlightenment subject', but this is a useful starting point. Hall stresses the coherence and unity of the 'Enlightenment subject', although other commentators have made more of the rationality of this understanding of subjectivity and it is important to hold onto these elements as well as the notion of unity. What Stuart Hall calls the 'postmodern subject' takes up much of the discussion within this book, but his focus on the 'sociological subject' as making a departure from Enlightenment thinking, is an important moment in the identity story. This was very influential in many twentieth century debates and provides the background to postmodernist critiques.

Setting the scene: some of the big questions

So what are the traditions which inform current thinking about identity? Where do our ideas come from? The established sociological and psychological literature on identity goes back to the late nineteenth century. However, the philosophical and the theological traditions go back much further. As early as 1690, English empiricist philosopher John Locke included a chapter on 'Identity and diversity' with a section on personal identity, in his *Essay concerning human understanding*.

Locke's work was influential in defining the individual as having an identity that stayed the same and was continuous with its subject. It is consciousness (rather than the body) that unites all the different actions an individual has performed and makes a personal self who is the same person today as 40 years ago – as yesterday (1964: 213). This notion, allied to other developments of liberalism has led to our understanding of the 'sovereign individual', a very important concept in EuroAmerican thought and practice, and has achieved some dominance in western thought.

[Throughout this book I have largely used the term 'west' to include Europe, North America, Australia and New Zealand, although I am aware of the problems associated with such terminology. The 'west' is shorthand for these societies and cultures, although the association of particular ways of thinking with geographical locations implies considerable homogeneity. It does not mean specific people in these places but refers to traditions of thought and practice and an historical trajectory. Other writers prefer terms such as

'Euro-North American' (Jamieson, 1998), but I think this term is even more spatially located. There are problems, of which I am aware, in the oppositions that are constructed between 'east' and 'west', in the use of these terms, as are expounded in the work of Edward Said (1978) referred to in Chapter 6, but I merely wish to present some recognition that, despite the difficulties, the word 'west' is used here for practical purposes.]

The understanding of identity as formulated within the thinking of the historical period of the Enlightenment in Europe was characterized by the emergence of individualism in René Descartes' (1596–1650) 'I think therefore I am' (*cogito ergo sum*) which made the basis of knowledge different for each person. The starting point for identity formation was that individual person's existence, not that of other individuals, nor of the whole community. Descartes' claim was that, whatever uncertainties may beset us and however influential the assertions of sceptics, there is one thing of which each of us can be certain, which is that I am thinking (*cogito*). Descartes went on to deduce existence (*ergo sum*) from this indubitable awareness of thought. His influence has been great, to the extent that his conceptualization of the conscious, rational, individual subject has come to be known as the Cartesian subject. Descartes put considerable emphasis on consciousness and distinguished between mind and body in this process. Thus the Cartesian subject is one who is conscious of bodily states through a consciousness that is clearly demarcated from the body of which it is conscious.

It was this Cartesian subject along with the Lockian 'sovereign individual' which has become enmeshed with the individual entrepreneur of liberal economics based on Adam Smith's *Wealth of Nations*, published in 1776, which formed the backdrop to the 'sociological' concept of identity, developed from the nineteenth century. The notion of an individualized self is a relatively new phenomenon in western history. As Foucault argued, the western European understanding of the subject as an individual with social, legal, economic and moral aspects, has only been constructed in the last two centuries (1977). Prior to this ordinary people were largely undifferentiated, indistinguishable as individuals and categorized as members of class, kinship or occupational groups.

What distinguished developments within social philosophical theories in the late nineteenth and early twentieth centuries was their emphasis on experience as the source of knowledge about the self, rather than transcendental, universal principles. Most of these critiques and analyses assume a male subject. In spite of claims to empirical specificity most accounts generalize around a self that is called 'man'. Whereas early, classical accounts are explicit about the male subject, or even address gender difference, as Plato and Aristotle do, albeit in accounts which are somewhat unfavourable in their conceptualization of women's subjectivity, in the nineteenth and first half of the twentieth centuries, masculinity is assumed to embrace humanity.

By the twentieth century identity was understood as involving organiza-tion of the self, as coherent and responsible (Garfinkel, 1967). If individuals are responsible for shaping the identities they present to the world and each individual can be characterized by the ways in which they do this, what does this mean for the interrogation of identity within the social sciences? As Harold Garfinkel pointed out, in the twentieth century, it required detailed investigation into everyday practices and the lives of individuals. This approach, which is dependent on conceptualizations of the individual as taking responsibility for their own identities and being distinguishable from others, has an earlier history.

At one possible nineteenth century starting point for the identity story, it is the language of the everyday, of pronouns such as I, me, you, them and us, which marks out what is to be included under the umbrella of identity. This is the focus of the work of writers such as Charles Horton Cooley and George Herbert Mead. Andrew Feffer argues that the American pragmatist theory of truth claims that knowledge is relative to social, behavioural situations, rather than being universal (1993: 3) although gender differences do not seem to form part of that empirical specificity. The pragmatists' version of the identity story constitutes an important contribution to the 'sociological' concept which grounds identity in the here and now and challenges a transcendental basis of the self.

The looking-glass self

Charles Cooley's 'looking-glass self' is typical of this approach. This self is rooted in the everyday and in language, especially in the language of personal pronouns. This is a self that can be known through observation rather than through metaphysical investigation. Cooley builds on the ideas of William James ([1892] 1961) who in stressing the reflective nature of the self and the fact that whenever I am thinking I am aware that I *am* thinking, not just aware of what I am thinking about, may appear resonant of Descartes' *cogito*. How-ever, James stressed the everyday *empirical* features of this process. His was a pragmatic rather than a transcendental view. As Cooley says, 'it is well to say at the outset that by the word "self" in this discussion is meant simply that which is designated in common speech by the pronouns of the first person singular' (1964: 168). Cooley identifies what he means by the self and goes on to stress that this is an empirical self, which has to be observed in the social context. These are actual people who acknowledge and appropriate their own actions and their presence in the world. While rooting this sense of self in the human species, in an almost Darwinian sense, the self is formed in the context of social interaction. In many ways Cooley presents a common sense view of the self, as being familiar, and part of everyday experience. This self operates through the imagination, notably through Cooley's notion of the 'looking-glass self'. We imagine how we appear to others and also imagine the other person's judgement of us. The third element of this self is the feelings or emotion that a person has, what Cooley calls 'some sort of self-feeling, such as pride or mortification' (p. 184). This dimension of selfhood is crucial to social life, to the adjustment of the self to others. Cooley also focuses on the internalization of collective norms by individuals.

This perspective on the self not only stresses the importance of how we think of ourselves, or how we imagine other people see us, but also retains a strong element of instinct and of a shared human legacy. In the very influential approach of the social philosopher, G.H. Mead, the self becomes more socially interactive and less instinctive.

The 'I' and the 'Me'

Mead gives priority to social interaction and to the intellectual process, 'the internalization and inner dramatization by the individual, of what is happening outside which constitute ... [the] chief mode of interaction with other individuals belonging to the same society' (1934: 173). Mead's 'self' does not exist before the process of communication, it is an integral part of the whole process. The self is part of the communicative process, which reflects upon itself.

> The essence of the self, as we have said is cognitive: it lies in the internalized conversation of gestures which constitute thinking, or in terms of which thought or reflection proceeds. And hence the origin and foundations of the self, like those of thinking, are social (p. 173).

Mead, along with James and Cooley uses language as part of the foundation of his understanding of the self. Mead is probably most famous for his discussion of the 'I' and the 'me'. 'The "I" reacts to the self which arises through the taking of the attitudes of others. Through taking those attitudes we have introduced the "me" and we react to it as an "I" ... The "I" is the response of the organism to others: the "me" is the organized set of attitudes of others which one himself [sic.] assumes' (pp. 174, 175). For Mead it is self-consciousness that provides the core of the self, through the thinking or intellectual process, although consciousness alone is not enough. We have to be conscious of something. Again he notes, 'the internalization and inner dramatization, by the individual of the external conversation of significant gestures which constitutes his [sic.] chief mode of interaction with other individuals belonging to the same society' (p. 173).

This is the process that links the 'I' and the 'me', and which produces the self through the interactions between the internal and the external. Thus 'I' understand myself through imagining how I am understood by others – as 'me'. Consciousness alone is insufficient; one has to be conscious of something. 'I' only exists in relation to the 'me' upon whom I reflect. Mead's interactive, reflective self is a part of the society which provides the meaning, based on experience, which is the substance of reflection.

Mead's self has multiple identities, because in the course of our social lives, in everyday life we are required to present different selves. The self is created in the context of different social circumstances which require different responses. Mead's self, or rather selves, are produced through the process of imagination. For example children learn to form their own identities through play. Mead suggests that children, when they play games, for example with imaginary others, act out imaginary adult roles and practise the selves which they will later adopt. While Mead's approach is rooted in experience and hence qualifies for membership of the philosophical category of pragmatism, his emphasis on the role of the imagination adds a very important dimension to our understanding of identity formation. Mead presents an empirical self, but one which is reflective, and conscious of the positioning of that self within the broad framework of social relations through the operation of the imagination. Mead's self is a social self but one which is constituted through processes of imagination which connect the personal and the social. Through the operation of conscious reflexivity, this is a self which is capable of exercising some agency in the process of identity formation. It is also a self which permits some exploration of some of the processes of the mind in the experience of the internal/external dialectic, even if Mead's external social world seems rather consensual and homogeneous, and he does not interrogate that external world in any detail.

Acting the self

Erving Goffman offers a development of Mead's understanding of roles, which does focus on the external social world. Mead's symbolic interactionist focus was on role taking, for example where children develop understanding of the self by imaginatively taking the roles of others such as teachers or parents. Individuals go on to use role taking throughout their lives in order to work out their own sense of self. Each role involves interaction with other roles, such as teacher or pupil so that people modify their own roles in relation to their expectations of other, related roles. Goffman developed Mead's analysis of role taking in a sophisticated critique of everyday interactions, still focusing on the importance of the symbolic, but extending the understanding of role to include how roles are performed.

Goffman's work is of crucial importance in theorizing identity, even though he focuses on the self and on the idea of roles, rather than employing the word identity as such. Goffman takes the self into the social world, onto the stage of social relations in fact, with his dramaturgical model (1959), Goffman's self is not only a social self, it is a self who takes account of the social situation, the everyday dramas of our lives, and develops from and responds to those social situations. As he argued in *Presentation of self in everyday life*,

> The perspective employed in this report is that of theatrical performance; the principles delivered are dramaturgical ones. I shall consider the way in which the individual in ordinary work situations presents himself [*sic.*] and his activity to others, the ways in which he guides and controls the impression they form of him, and the kinds of things he may not do while sustaining his performance before them (1959: xi).

Thus the self is analogous to the actor playing a part, acting out a role. The script may be written, but there is scope for negotiation, for choice, for interpretation and even for improvisation.

The self has to be presented, the self is engaged actively in performance and the self is committed to this interactive performance. For Goffman, encounters and everyday interactions involve impression management (1961). However, public displays of the self involve presenting information which is both given and, as Goffman suggests, 'given off'. There is the information that is supplied directly and that which may be revealed inadvertently, for example through gestures, actions and ways of speaking. Such practices are resonant of Freudian slips of the tongue, whereby, as Freud observed, we often reveal more of ourselves through what we do not mean to say than through the words that pass from our lips intentionally (Freud, 1905).

Goffman's analysis shifted from stages to film sets, retaining the focus on the performative aspects of social interaction, but incorporating the idea of 'frames' (1974). A frame is a single shot, one of the myriad moments in the making of a film. Everyday life becomes a series of frames, of frozen moments, stills through which individuals pass, presenting themselves within each frame within the expectations and boundaries of that frame.

Goffman's development of a self that is negotiated and re-presented through social encounters is important to the progression of theories of identity, arising from the approaches of symbolic interactionism developed earlier in the work of Mead. Goffman's approach opens up further explanation of the implications of performing the self through exploring analogies between everyday life and theatre. While Goffman's sociological emphasis is on performance, his work makes possible more recent developments, notably in the work of Judith Butler, on performativity, in generating poststructuralist discursive and psychoanalytic critiques.

Another significant aspect of Goffman's contribution to the identity debate is his focus on the multiple selves which are dramatically realized through the diverse performances in which each self is engaged. As James Holstein and Jaber Gubruim argue, 'Goffman reveals that each and every one of us has many selves, pertinent to the purposes of daily living, always part of, yet also reflexively separate from the moral orders we share with others' (2000: 23). Goffman focuses on the ways in which the self is produced and performed in everyday exchanges. This requires a methodological focus on the minutiae of daily routines and encounters. This emphasis on the everyday is also a feature of the work of Harold Garfinkel and the ethnomethodologists.

Ethnomethodological accounts of the self

The work of Garfinkel and the ethnomethodologists is included here because it has had some impact of later developments in theories of identity, although ethnomethodology itself is seldom cited now as a key sociological school of thought. Garfinkel drew on different philosophical strands to produce a particular approach to interrogating social action and relationships. In part, his work derives from phenomenological accounts which have the advantage of focusing on the direct observation of social phenomena, that is things, events and people who are as they appear to the observer. The role of the observer is thus not to interpret these phenomena but to report and record them. Ethnomethodologists used this philosophical tradition to develop his approach to examining the ways in which social actors produce meanings. Garfinkel, whose work can be seen as part of the 'linguistic turn' in the social sciences, also drew on the ideas of the philosopher Ludvig Wittgenstein in his later work, *The Philosophical Investigations* ([1953] 1973), on language games. In his later philosophy, Wittegenstein argued against his earlier view that there was one perfect language which had the sole task of describing the world, and claimed that language was an infinite set of social activities. Each of these sets was called a game, and we learn to play these games in childhood. There are language games which describe the world but there are many others too. For example, there are a host of everyday games – wishing, hoping, thanking, greeting, praying as well as the language games of science and of philosophy. Sometimes we get confused and think that one view, that of describing 'reality', serves the purpose of all language. For example that wishing or hoping describes our mental state and talk as though all we have to do is define a hope or a wish as if it were a psychic process. The task of the philosopher is to reflect on these games within the contexts in which they are 'played' and to alleviate the puzzlement that derives from confusion about how language games operate. Wittgenstein did not seek to develop a theory or an explanatory doctrine, only to remind us of what is on the surface of everyday life. As he said of philosophy, it '… simply puts everything before us, and neither explains nor deduces anything … Since everything is open to view there is nothing to explain … The aspects of things that are most important for us are hidden because of their simplicity and familiarity' ([1953] 1973, paragraphs 126 and 129). This is what the ethnomethodologists sought to do within sociology. Conventional sociology took meanings as unproblematic and failed to engage with the ways in which meanings are produced and interpreted, they argued. Their aim was to elucidate and describe the obvious and the familiar, but not to provide a theory that highlighted reasons and explanations. While Wittgenstein focused on language those who were influenced by his approach in sociology have embraced a wider range of practices, but linguistic competence and performance still retain a high profile in such approaches.

Garfinkel's approach is more radically empiricist than the work of earlier pragmatists, in that he does not take any pre-given meanings for granted. His concern was to describe how people organize and make sense of their lives and how their identities are produced, presented and managed. He did not aim to provide an explanatory framework, but it is the focus on the everyday and on the process of meaning making that makes his contribution interesting and relevant to later explorations of the management of the self, and of the stories we tell about ourselves. There is no unified coherent self to start off, the self is produced through these social interactive processes. For Garfinkel, social actors possess practical linguistic skills, through which the features of everyday life, which can be observed and understood, are meaningfully produced. Thus people create and manage their sense of objective reality. Rather than assuming that actors share meanings of themselves and their situations however, Garfinkel sought to show what was happening; to address the *how* rather than the *why* or *what* of identity. This approach has, of course, been the subject of critical comment, not the least because it fails to take a position and merely describes what we largely know already. The big political and social issues at the macro level are beyond its scope. However, Garfinkel's work has influenced many later writers, including Anthony Giddens who goes further than the ethnomethodological claim that the social world is produced through everyday exchanges and conversations, although he does acknowledge the insights of the approach in relation to an interrogation of the taken for granted rules of talk and action.

There are multiple narratives and an emphasis on the social performance of identity, but in Garfinkel's account as in Goffman's, there is a moral dimension to selfhood. As Goffman argued, 'we must not overlook the crucial fact that any projected definition of the situation also has a distinctive moral character' (Goffman, 1959: 13). However, the issue of morality and how it is articulated in the construction of the self, especially in the relationship between the individual self and the society that self inhabits is deeply problematic. The problems relate to the kind of self that is being constructed and understood. Is this a self that exercises agency and takes responsibility, under the pressure of social and economic change? Under which circumstances does the self operate?

Troubled selves

Morality has always been an aspect of identity in relation to the degree of responsibility born by individuals for their own actions in constructing the self. This issue is well illustrated at particular historical moments when specific circumstances and social changes are seen to pose dilemmas for individuals. It may be periods of time which are characterized as alienating, or as overturning hitherto securely held values. Such an era may even be characterized by great affluence when questions of morality are posed in relation to the breakdown of communication and an increased emphasis on individualism, personal introspection and competition between shared interests and community support. Social and economic change operating at the macro level can be seen as having led to interconnected micro-level shifts in the daily lives of social actors. At the centre of contemporary debates about identity is the perception that recent social and economic changes have made the autonomous self, as a self that is increasingly independent of material and cultural structures, more important than ever before. Some of these issues are explored in more detail in Chapter 2. What has been called the 'Risk Society' (Beck, 1992) has led to an ever greater concern with introspection and concern with personal identity. Peter Berger has explored the links between the distinctive features of modernity and the construction of the self as both 'peculiarly reflective' and peculiarly individuated (Berger *et al.*, 1973: 78–9). Berger argued that identity is particularly subject to crisis in modernity because of the complex relationship between the plurality of selves and the wider society, in which 'identity is part and parcel of a specific constructive of consciousness' (p. 76). These current debates have resonance with earlier concerns too. Such concerns have focused on the problems of negotiating individualism in the contemporary west. This has been a particular feature of North American thinking. Robert Bellah and his collaborators have argued that empirical research reveals the extent to which success is linked to personal chance within individualism in the USA. The problem which they pose as 'how are we Americans to think about the nature of success, the meaning of freedom and the requirements of justice in the modern world?' (1985: 22) is at the root of their exploration of the relationship between economic success and the achievement of a successful public and private life. While acknowledging the constraints to self-fulfilment and the exercise of choice, imposed by poverty and economic disadvantage, Bellah argues that ideas of choice and individual freedom are the core of the American notion of the self. However, this Lockian *tabula rasa* selfhood which exercises choice on the basis of personal needs and wants is contradictory and unsustainable. As Bellah claims, this 'presumes the existence of an absolutely empty unencumbered and improvisational self. It obscures personal reality, social reality and particularly the moral reality, that links person and society' (1985: 80). This is not just a blank sheet upon which the social world inscribes meaning, it is an empty self, created, according to Bellah and his colleagues, by an overemphasis on freedom expressed in terms of financial success and independence, and allied to a psychological ideal of self-control. This, they argued, led to the impossibility of re-creating the solidarity of successful communication.

Charles Taylor, writing within a philosophical framework, developed his own perspective on contemporary western, especially US, individualism by placing it within the wider context of the specific moral context of the ethical outlook of modernity. In this increasingly secular culture, even within religion in the west, there has been much greater emphasis on the notion that rights are rooted in the individual self rather than in the community (1989). In such a culture it becomes apparent that it is through the exercise of individual agency that social good can be achieved. Taylor acknowledges the instrumentalism, of economic individualism, based on the assumption that economic success on the larger scale is achieved through individuals pursuing their own, personal economic interest. However, he is more interested in the 'expressive' individuality which may also characterize modernity. Taylor argues that contemporary, western understandings of identity, whereby social good is widely implicated in an understanding of the self, are expressive. Within his conceptualization of expressivism, for which Taylor draws on eighteenth century Romanticism, with nature as a source, he includes the obligation that each person has to live up to the originality that each of us has. This originality includes creativity, vision and the unique qualities of the individual person. The idea that each person is unique and that each of us has a personal destiny for which we can take responsibility has resonance within western civilization, tied up with idealized notions of freedom, including the freedom to follow your own path in constructing an identity. Taylor argues that this expressive individualism enables people to be different from others in following their own paths, shaping their own identities. The good life for one person is not the same as for another. He extends the analogy to national cultures, whereby different peoples and nations have different ways of expressing their own national identities (1989). Taylor challenges Bellah's more negative interpretation of individualism in the USA as trivializing what he claims to be a new, fuller individuation through which a real sense of community can be achieved, for example through activities as diverse as ecological and environmentalist movements and those promoting distinctive regional and national cultures. However, Bellah's analysis was not the only one and reflects a trend within a movement in the USA.

This more troubled view of the self, located in the specific context of the USA, arising out of Bellah's work in the 1970s and 1980s, is prefigured by earlier post-war concerns with changing times and changing identities. An even bleaker picture of the American self had been drawn by David Riesman in *The lonely crowd: a study of the changing American character* (1950). *The lonely crowd* purports to address the question of 'national character types' but the book's major concern is with the ways in which social conditions produce different selves – or different character types.

Riesman addresses the issue of 'character' rather than explicitly engaging with discussion about self or identity. However, at this point it is apparent that the debate upon which he focuses is very much an identity matter. What he calls 'character', specifically the 'American character' concerns the relationship between the personal and the social at a particular historical movement and within what could be seen as a particular spatial context. Riesman's idea of character is 'the more or less permanent socially and historically conditioned organization of an individual's drives and satisfactions the kind of "set" with which he [*sic.*] approaches the world and people' (1950: 4). This project was to explore the relationship between what is called 'social character' and society in the context of what he calls the transition to the 'second revolution' in social conformity, characterized by the shift from 'an age of production to an age of consumption' (p. 6). The first revolution, which emerged from the Renaissance and Reformation, led to 'inner direction' as the new mode of securing social conformity, accompanied by the growth of capitalism and increased personal mobility.

The 'other directed' character was seen by Riesman to have emerged more recently in the west, especially in the large cities of the USA, and in the mid-twentieth century to be a feature of the new rather than the traditional middle classes – salaried employees, service sector workers and bureaucrats,

> *what is common to all the other-directed people is that their contemporaries are the source of direction for the individual – either those known to him [sic.] or those with whom he is indirectly acquainted, through friends and through the mass media. This source is of course "internalized" in the sense that depend-ence on it for guidance: it is only the process of striving itself and the process of paying close attention to the signals from others that remain unaltered through life* (p. 21, emphasis in original).

Although the sources of the other directed character (like the inner directed) are social, the other directed person is more fluid, changing across the life course in response to diverse social elements. Such characters require approval and may indeed be too keen to respond to and reflect the social context in which they operate.

The north American mid-twentieth century emphasis on independence and individual achievement led to a most negative focus on the most superficial, narcissistic concerns with consumption. What consumers value as superior and desirable, are what others value and determine. There is no sign of Taylor's expressive individualism in this depressing scenario of identities formed through bland conformity, where individuals seek 'approval not fame' (p. 282). Riesman presents a gloomy picture of identities lacking autonomy and independence, in a sense victims of historical circumstances. This is an over-socialized self, which nonetheless has *internalized* its own conformity. Riesman acknowledges this aspect of the process but accords limited space to the exploration of the psychic processes through which conformity is achieved, or through which resistance *might* be achieved. Mead and Cooley were much more concerned with these material processes but this is the element in the formation of identity which has largely been underplayed in the identity stories so far related. Identity cannot be secured, even temporarily and contradictorily without some psychic investment. Identity occupies the interface between the personal and the social, the psychic and the social. The operation of the psychic process in this relationship is what has concerned the psychoanalytic theories which have been developed from the work of Sigmund Freud. Psychoanalysis extends the scope for the interrogation of troubled selves and, importantly, for the deeper, darker recesses of the self.

Identity and the unconscious

While psychoanalytic theories play a significant part in the investigation of identity at many different points in the story, Freud's conceptualization of the unconscious provides an important starting point. Identity involves the inter-relationship between the personal and the social; between what I feel inside and what is known about me from the outside. Some theories, several of which are discussed above, focus more on the external, social processes involved in identity formation. Psychoanalytic theories concern the internal psychic processes and engage with that inner space that constitutes the psyche. Such theories include interaction between inner and outer worlds, but address most specifically the impact of the social upon the internal formation and experi-ence of the self. A separation between 'inside' and 'outside' is deeply trouble-some and the whole notion of a dichotomy has been challenged, but it is employed here to indicate a different focus. In order to understand identity it is possible to focus on external matters or, as Freud did, to concentrate upon subjective experience and upon the internal psychic processes that might be involved. It is through an understanding of the workings of the unconscious that psychoanalytic theories are able to offer an additional contribution to our understanding of identity and, in particular to the process of identification. Identification involves 'a psychological process whereby the subject assimilates an aspect, property or attribute of the other and is transformed, wholly or partly, after the model the other provides' (Laplanche and Pontalis, 1973: 203). Identity is constituted through a series of identifications.

The Freudian model of the psyche with its interrelated components of id, ego and superego, provides a useful means of interrogating the processes that are involved in the attempted resolution of conflict between the personal needs and desires of the id and the social elements expressed in the superego. The unconscious is made up of ideas and repressed desires that may be unacceptable, because they threaten either the individual or the wider society. The id is seen as the source of such desires which demand attention – and satisfaction. The unconscious is made up of powerful desires, often unmet, which have arisen because of the intrusion of the father into the child's relationship with the mother. Jacques Lacan followed Freud in giving primacy to this notion of the unconscious, although Lacan's radical reworking of Freud's theories stressed the symbolic and the role of language in the formation of identities. Lacan developed a linguistic model of reflexivity. This is illustrated by the way in which Lacan prioritizes language in the formation of subjectivity. 'It is not a question of knowing whether I speak of myself in a way that conforms to what I am, but rather of knowing whether I am the same as that which I speak' (1977: 165). Lacan offers an explanation of why we invest in particular subject positions and come to 'be spoken' by the identities which are available within culture. Thus we use the pronoun 'I', although we claim it as our own, the pronoun in language is separate from the I who speaks. In this sense, the first person pronoun is secondhand; it exists in language before I use it and there is a gap between the I who speaks and the 'I' of language.

In Lacan's account there is the understanding that identity is never fixed. There is a gap, a sense that there is something missing, which haunts us, as a desire that can never quite be fulfilled.

The unconscious is seen as working according to its own laws and to a different logic from the conscious thought processes of the rational subject. The conscious mind demands coherence, unity and intelligibility which are not characteristics of the unconscious. For example the unconscious may be revealed through dreams. As Freud argued, a dream is 'not more careless, more irrational, more incomplete than waking thought; it is completely different from it qualitatively and for that reason not immediately comparable with it.

It does not think, calculate or judge in any way at all; it restricts itself to giving things in a new form. ... In the attention that is paid to the logical relationships between thoughts' (Freud, [1900] 1965: 545).

Conscious thought, on the other hand is powered by what Freud calls the secondary processes, which involve the imposition of inflexible logical structures that are both calculating and judgemental. In contrast, the unconscious expressed through dreams is a fluid, free-flowing psychic energy. The unconscious may be contradictory with very different rules of time and space, all of which counter the pursuit of clarity and meaningful precision of the primary process of the conscious mind. The unconscious operates on its own mode of time and has its own currency and logic. The ego endeavours to resolve conflict and to attain control of both inner and outer worlds. This tension is resonant of the desire for certainty and fixity in the formation of identity and the need to stabilize and secure a sense of who we are in a world increasingly characterized by risk, uncertainty and change. Psychoanalytic theories addressing psychic conflict and the operation of the unconscious offer a means of explaining the contradiction, and irrationality of identity. For example, subjects may invest in identity positions which are unacceptable to others, or even to the conscious minds of those involved, that is to themselves. People may fall in love with someone and have a relationship that is clearly not in their interests and appear to be unconsciously committed to a relationship that they may even be conscious is detrimental and even damaging. The unconscious involves mental conflict and has its own dynamic. Freudian psychoanalysis presents a focus on ambivalence and conflict by tracing irrational investment in identities back to the repression of unconscious needs and desires. The self is not a unified whole. The psyche comprises the unconscious id, the superego which acts like a social conscience and the ego which attempts a resolution of conflict. It is thus in a state of flux, never quite fixed and unified.

However, the subject desires a unitary self. This desire may be expressed through identification. In psychoanalytic theory identification goes far beyond imitation and is the expression of a deep longing for unity. According to Lacan, the first step in identity formation is the moment when infants realize that they are separate from the mother (1977). The child realizes that the primitive union with the mother is disrupted, at the point of entry into language. Lacan uses the 'mirror' stage to describe the moment when the infant constructs a self based on a reflection, either actually seen in a mirror or mirrored through the eyes of others. This perception of a bounded self, as seen in the mirror, sets the scene for future identification. During the first few months of life the infant lacks bodily co-ordination and a developed sense of what is inside and what is outside. However, at about eighteen months of age the infant is said to identify with its own mirror image. This image is highly beguiling and offers a wonderful sense of wholeness, which counteracts the anxiety of the actual experience of disunity. We have a sense of who we are, through seeing ourselves reflected back in an illusion of unity. Identity depends on something outside itself and its unity is thus an expression of lack based on identification through which we seek some unified sense of ourselves. For Lacan the mirror phase in the first point at which the infant makes a conscious recognition of a distinction between his or her body and the outside world. Thus this image provides the infant with a first glimpse of wholeness or unity. However, as Lacan points out, this unity is based on an illusion. He calls this illusion 'imaginary'. There is a gap between the ideal of the image and the infant's fragmented psychic state. The mirror, which could be seen as the reflection of the child in the mother's eyes is metaphorical, but it provides a point outside the self through which the self is recognized. Thus the imaginary comes from outside, from the infant's misapprehension of unity. This means that, for Lacan, although his focus appears to be on internal processes and the psyche, the source of meaning is external and lies outside the individual. The mirror also provides the first experience of unity, albeit an illusory one. This is the stage at which the infant is introduced to an order of imaginary representations, when the infant is given an imaginary experience of what it would be like to be whole.

The metaphor of the mirror has enormous resonance across a wide area of cultural experience. The Lacanian focus on the psychic experience of identification expressed through a desire for unity permits an explanation of the formation of identity which is more complex as well as drawing on deeply held feelings and those that focus on mainly social or behavioural aspects.

The mirror phase marks the beginning of the process through which identities are formed. This process is completed in Lacanian thinking by the entry into the symbolic order; initially construed as being language, although later followers of Lacan have included other representational systems. At this point the infant is compelled to abandon the illusion of unity and to identify with the subject positions that are available within the symbolic order. These cultural forms, that is the symbolic order, exist outside us, so they are not a means of accessing the 'real me'. They are 'borrowed', that is from culture, and not fixed or innate. Thus we are recruited into the symbolic order and take up subject positions that are already there. These subject positions are however gender inflected in very particular ways within the Lacanian (and the Freudian) framework. Gender identity is highlighted in Lacanian and the Freudian accounts, with gender identity forming the basis of identification. Sexual differentiation, whereby infants come to identify as either female or male is fundamental to Lacan's account, with a strong emphasis on male authority and the supremacy of masculinity in the symbolic order. While there are clearly problems with so patriarchal and phallocentric an account, not least for women, Lacan's approach can be seen as emphasizing the symbolic order and the *cultural* supremacy that men hold. This is a cultural power and not one that is unchanging and unchangeable.

Psychoanalytic theories offer the advantage of focusing on the importance of both gender and sexuality in the formation of identity. They have been strongly challenged from different positions, both within psychoanalysis and from those who reject its claims altogether. Within psychoanalytic theory there have been challenges from Object Relations theorists and analysts who reject the focus on the power of the father, preferring to focus on the mother–child relationship, and from feminists who seek to theorize the unconscious within prioritizing the status of the phallus as the key signifier of cultural meanings. There are omissions in many other theories. The psychoanalytic theorists' contribution to our understanding of the unconscious is significant, but it is at a price, as we shall see. There are both strengths and weaknesses in the conceptualization of both gender and sexuality in psychoanalytic approaches.

Psychoanalytic theories have an important part to play in explaining the links between the psychic aspects of the personal and the social. This is not, of course, to say that such theories are without problems, especially in relation to this apparently universal claim made for psychic processes, which seem to operate outside specific social and historical circumstances in some accounts.

Conclusion

I have selected some of the key moments in the identity story; notably those points at which the distinguishing features – and problems – of identity have been addressed. This has not been a linear narrative, but rather one which has offered some brief coverage of background to the debate about identity, which is to be explained in more detail in this book. Identity has a long history, but there are key debates which emerge for consideration of contemporary illustration and from the historical development of identity stories.

Much of the debate has centred on the construction of the self and the extent to which the self can be seen to shape its own destiny and be an active agent in the production of identities. Identity necessarily involves interrelationship between the 'inside' and the 'outside', the personal and the social, but this relationship is very differently inflected in different accounts.

These debates can be presented along an historical storyline which sees the self as moving from a unified subject, whether assumed or explicitly defined as unique and distinctive, to more sociological accounts which present the self as constituted more collectively, in relation to others and the modern society. The notion of the sovereign individual is a relatively recent idea historically, but it has had enormous impact and very different manifestations in thinking about identity. The unified subject is one who largely has responsibility for actions that are carried out, and exercises individual agency, whereas in the west with the development of capitalist industrialization came more complex and collective groupings of identity which could be seen as subject to social, structural forces. Economic, cultural and social changes, which have become embedded in institutions and practices, involve changing constructions of the self. However, the post-Enlightenment self is a complex, rational self, not one that is simply subject to external forces. While Marxist analyses attempted to bring together the subjective and objective dimensions of class consciousness, the emphasis remained on economic aspects of identity and focused on socio-economic class at the expense of other elements of social division and differentiation. The Marxist paradigm is seen as one of the grand theories or meta-narratives of modernism, which presents an all-embracing theoretical framework for understanding social relations, based more on overarching theoretical analyses than on empirical detail. Postmodernism challenged the encompassing nature of the grand theories of modernity and suggested that the notion of a unified self, at the heart of social relations could not be sustained. Fragmentation and disunity was a key feature of identity, as illustrated by the psychoanalytic accounts mentioned above.

One of the major challenges to earlier accounts of the self and of identity has been the questioning of the dualisms through which identity has been characterized. This has been illustrated by the distinction that has been drawn between mind and body. More recent accounts, as are explored in Chapter 5, also draw on phenomenological accounts, mentioned in the work of ethnomethodologists, to develop the notion of embodiment, rather than a mind/body split. Embodiment as developed by Merleau-Ponty (1962) uses the idea of embodiment to allude to interconnectedness, where the body is a 'grouping of lived through meanings which moves towards its equilibrium' (p. 153).

The self reflects the complexity of relationships between the personal and the social in the twentieth century. As developed in the work of Mead and Cooley, this was an interactive self whereby identities were produced through the interaction between self, through an internal–external dialectical process, and society. It is through the internalization of social and cultural meanings that individuals are able to occupy their identities and match up the 'subjective' feelings that they bring to the 'objective' places they inhabit. The shift to the social dimensions of identity and the social roles that are performed is developed in Goffman's dramaturgical theories.

Another component in the identity story is the move away from theory towards more empirical concerns, as heralded by the work of pragmatists and developed in interactionist approaches and in Goffman's dramaturgical model of the study of everyday life. This has involved methodological shifts as well as theoretical ones, for example Garfinkel's ethnomethodological analysis, with its emphasis on observation of the practices of everyday life. Garfinkel's understanding of the self is one who negotiates through everyday language, exchanges and routines, through which identities are constructed. This is not a socially determined self, but one who is responsible and actively engaged in the interpretative work of daily life and social interaction. For the ethnomethodologists social structures do not determine action. They, like the self are self-generating, practical accomplishments (1967).

The twentieth century was also characterized by increasing concerns with social, economic and cultural change and by a need to theorize the impact of social change and of the 'outside' on the 'inside'. In the middle of the twentieth century this concern produced expressions of anxiety at the excessive impact of the social on the personal and of the high degree of conformity, for example as expressed in David Riesman's work. Collective identities and the ways in which these can be expressed in the context of the interrelationship between the personal and the social and between sameness and difference have occupied social theorists who have engaged with identity debates.

In the latter part of the twentieth century the focus moved onto concerns with the particularly disruptive aspects of social change in terms of dislocation, displacement, risk and fragmentation. In the discussion so far the notion of fragmentation has been introduced through one of the twentieth century's major contributions to the understanding of conflict in the construction of the self, based on internal, psychic conflict, namely the work of psychoanalysis. Far from assuming a rational subject, psychoanalysis explores the possibilities of irrationality and the illusion of unity in the formation of the self. Whatever their shortcomings, psychoanalytic theories have had considerable impact in exploring and developing understandings of identity which subvert unity and address the possibilities of uncertainty and fragmentation. Psychoanalytic theories can be seen to inform some later work that has focused on the 'decentered subject', that is the fragmented self which is produced through and is subject to, changing social, cultural fields, some of which have been characterized as postmodernist. This focus on fluidity also offers a challenge to the claims, especially the more universalist claims of psychoanalytic theories, a challenge presented for example, in the work of Michael Foucault, whose contributions to the debate are explained in more detail in later chapters in this book. Foucault's critique engages with the ways in which identities are produced through discourse. Discourses include a whole range of practices, ways of speaking, writing, interacting and thinking, that is, broadly how meanings are produced within culture. This approach is historically specific, located in time and space and explores the myriad ways in which identities are produced and reproduced.

The notion of social change, even of crisis which challenges some forms of certainty about who we are and where we belong, has also been introduced by the case study with which the book began. This example posed many of the questions which are raised by matters of identity at a time of uncertainty, movement and change. What is involved in laying claim to an identity position at a particular historical moment? What is the relationship between the personal and the social? Is it possible to stabilize identity – are there any sources of fixity and certainty? How can identity be theorized outside and beyond the polarities and dualisms that have so often characterized the debates? These are the questions which this book addresses.

In the next chapter, we will begin at the beginning, and start with some of the stories we tell.

2   Stories we tell

I was 40 when I found out that my father was a glass jar with a blob of
sperm in it. My father doesn't have a face or a name and he wasn't even a
one night stand. If my mum had had an affair at least there would have
been sex and lust, something human rather than something so cold, scientific and clinical. My parents never even met. I still feel like a freak, a
fake I don't feel I know who I am any more (in Braid, 2002).

This is how Christine Whipp, a woman of 46 living in the UK, described finding out at the age of 40, that she had been conceived by artificial insemination by donor. Such practice has been increasingly popular as a solution to
the problems of infertile heterosexual couples, gay and lesbian couples and
single women. It has been the received wisdom that anonymity was desirable
and in the interests of all parties concerned. However, Christine's statement,
quoted here suggests that this can be read as a betrayal and as a source of
extreme anxiety. The anxiety that is expressed here relates to identity. An adult
woman's sense of who she is has been subverted by the discovery that, not only
is her father not who she thought he was, but he is not named and in a sense
he has no identity. To be without a face or a name suggests that you do not
exist. The woman in turn feels this means that she does not really exist, or at
least that she is a 'fake'; her identity is a false one. If identity is made up of the
ways in which we see ourselves and how others see us, and the links between
ourselves and the social world that we inhabit, why is this discovery so disconcerting? This adult woman has a place in the world, she has relationships
with others, for example as a mother and a grandmother, but she is particularly disturbed by two absences. The first is a key component of identity, the
sense that we have roots, we have origins and a past that it would be possible
to uncover, to give us some sense of the place that we occupy along the life
course continuum. At her attempt to discover her own family roots in relation to knowing who her father was, this woman draws a blank. He has no

name and no known identity. The absence here is the story of source, of family location. The second absence relates to the science fiction scenario of being produced in the test tube. The personal loss in this instance that leads to anxiety and insecurity is the apparent lack of human contact and affection (even if it might only have been lust). Both of these absences highlight a vital element of the identity story; the need to tell a story that has a beginning, that is located within a chronology, with a past that can be revealed and used to position ourselves in the present. This discussion is linked to that of roots, which is the main concern of Chapter 6, but my focus here in this chapter is on personal identity stories and the ways in which these appeal to sources of security in the biographies of individuals. We tell stories about ourselves in order to make sense of who we are.

The idea of roots is associated with the primacy of naming. The woman whose father has no name cannot specify her paternal roots; without a name her father does not exist for her, so in a sense she has no father. Naming is a vital part of identity. We turn round when we hear our name called out. Louis Althusser uses the example of someone calling out your name to illustrate his theory of interpellation (1971), whereby we are recruited into an identity because it seems to fit. We are hailed or interpellated by an identity that appears to be who we want to be and how we see ourselves. At the level of the unconscious we think 'Yes, that's me' and what better way of thinking 'that's me' than through the recognition of one's personal name. It is irritating and insulting when others misspell our name, making it seem as if we do not matter in their eyes. Mistakes over names can indicate ethnocentricity or even racism. It matters if someone gets your name wrong. It matters if you are addressed inappropriately, for example by only your last name. This can seem impersonal. The use of your first name by strangers can be inappropriately familiar or render an adult infantile. ID cards carry our names, as do passports and all the official documents such as birth – and death – certificates, all the means through which we are classified, legitimized and identified (Woodward, 2000a). We may have a number, such as a personal identity number to access a bank account or state benefits through national insurance or health care, but naming makes it personal. Although such cards and documents may increasingly employ a range of methods of identification, with bar codes and personal identification numbers, as well as drawing on DNA testing to ascertain who we are, having a personal name is a very important aspect of placing an individual, of knowing who he or she is. Names are also important in constructing narratives about ourselves; not only our own names, but the names of the key protagonists within our life stories. Stories of origins require some naming of our roots.

The lack of a named father in the case of Christine Whipp is made a more likely scenario by the development of assisted reproductive technologies.

Frequently anonymity is permitted and even required in the case of sperm donors. The interventions of technoscience, for example through reproductive technologies, may assist conception and make it possible for children to be born, who would, without intervention, have never been conceived. The science fiction scenario of assisted reproductive technologies is not necessarily associated with the lack of a name. The case of Diane Blood, an English woman who was eventually granted the right to use sperm donated by her husband who had died of meningitis several years earlier, illustrates the need which people express and feel to secure identity, in this case of the identities of their children. In this instance the father, although dead is named and paternal identity is secured through the interventions of technoscience. Diane Blood, who fought a two year court battle for the right to have her late husband's child, was able to do so because of the facility of using her husband's frozen sperm through artificial insemination at a clinic in Brussels. In spite of losing her legal battle with the HFEA (Human Fertilization and Embryology Authority) in the UK, Diane Blood was able to benefit from EU rulings. Her child, born in 1998 and the second child she later conceived by the same method, will have a named father at least in the stories the children's mother is able to tell them about their family origin. This is a story of struggle to use the advances of technology to secure an identity story for her children and for herself as a mother. Technoscience offers the means, but the motivation is linked to human expressions of love for a real, named person. This story carries the human, affective dimension that the story of the unnamed father in the Christine Whipp story sadly does not.

Hi-tech stories

Technoscience is increasingly employed as a means of securing some certainty in relation to identity. Technoscience offers public stories that can be used to structure and secure personal stories. Not only can assisted reproductive technologies secure parenthood, in some cases, for those who would otherwise be denied the possibility, new technologies such as DNA testing can confirm or deny the identity of a child's father. At least genetic inheritance can be confirmed or denied. Such claims to certainty merely state or counter the existence of biological connections. They give no clues as to the substance of any genetic inheritance in shaping identity. As in the examples of the two women mentioned in this chapter, the interventions of technoscience are contradictory. They can be read positively or negatively. New technologies provide security and some degree of certainty or they can subvert all sense of stability and challenge certainties. Social meanings are attached to new technoscientific inventions and it is social, cultural and political and economic factors which make, for example, assisted reproductive technologies available to some women, but deny access to others. For example in some situations access to reproductive technologies may be much more possible for white heterosexual, middle class women than for women in other socio-economic and ethnic groups and with different sexual identities (Woodward, 2000b).

Reproductive technologies provide the possibility of overturning what might have been held as certainties about parenthood, especially motherhood, which are rooted in biology. No longer is it the case that the woman who conceives and carries a child to term is simply the child's mother. One woman may be the genetic mother by donating an egg, another carries the fertilized egg and another woman cares for the child. The law, which has often lagged behind technoscience, is the source of security (or not) rather than biology. In some instances it may be biology which is invoked to support legal judgements which lay behind changes in social practice, such as in the case of the 2002 Scottish court case which failed to recognize the parental status of both partners in a same sex relationship. In this case the court awarded parental rights to the man who was the biological father of a child through sperm donation, overriding the wishes of the child's mother and her lesbian partner (*The Guardian*, 8 March 2002). In many other cases the law has difficulty disentangling biology, technologies, culture and practice, in making decisions about the status of mothers and fathers and identities in relation to parenthood and origins.

This could become even more problematic as cloning opens up new possibilities for challenging the shifting grounds of certainty in tracing the roots of identity. Cloning might be an example of the fruits of technoscience which could disrupt expectations about genealogical and gender identities and especially about difference (Woodward, 2000b). As Adam Phillips points out there is some significance in the irony that the first animal to be cloned was a sheep. Sheep are creatures not renowned for their individuality and uniqueness (2001). Too much sameness and homogeneity might have severe psychological as well as political consequences. Phillips, as a psychologist, points to the disruption that could result from this challenge of the individual project of establishing identity through difference. The whole pattern of psychoanalysis in assisting individuals to establish some understanding of self through tracing the roots of identity back to childhood and linking the self back to experiences of the relationship with parents and to the repression of sexuality, would be rendered meaningless as would, even more alarmingly, the assertion of difference (Phillips, 2000). Human cloning might offer a story replete with threats of monstrosity, but it is one example of the subversive interventions of technoscience (even if human cloning is not yet permissible by law in most of the world and not technically possible, certainly without severe dangers to the health of those so produced), it is an example of a public story in all its uncertainties that shapes and reflects an understanding of identity. Assisted reproductive technologies, as examples of technoscience, offer public 'stories' which are intimately linked to the personal stories through which people construct their own identities.

Storied lives

Lyn Jamieson uses the term 'stories' to describe different accounts of social change (1998). She includes the stories of everyday life told by 'ordinary people' as well as the accounts, told in a more public forum, by academic researchers as well as by politicians, scientists, religious leaders and other public figures. She expresses a preference for the word 'story' because it retains a structure and a coherence without requiring a hierarchical distinction between different kinds of accounts, those of the 'experts' or those in power, and those of 'ordinary' people! However, 'stories' might be somewhat misleading, suggesting fabrication.

We all tell stories about our lives. We tell ourselves stories and we relate them to others, as a means of making sense of ourselves. As Henrietta Moore suggests 'narrative is a strategy for placing us within a historically constituted world … If narrative makes the world intelligible, it also makes ourselves intelligible' (1994: 119). In this sense a story is what provides coherence. It is not important whether our stories can be verified or disproved, so much as how we construct these narratives, how we put them together to make sense of ourselves. This is what is relevant to the exploration of identity.

The production of identities through narratives is a dynamic process.

> We achieve our personal identities and self-concept through the use of narrative configuration, and make our existence into a whole by understanding it as an expression of a single unfolding and developing story. We are in the middle of our stories and cannot be sure how they will end; we are constantly having to revise the plot as new events are added to our lives. Self then, is not a static thing or a substance, but a configuring of personal events into an historical unity which includes not only what one has been but also anticipations of what one will be (Polkinghorne, 1988: 150).

The stories may change and adapt to circumstances; there is fluidity in these narratives of identity, yet there remains the desire for unity.

In telling stories about ourselves we are endeavouring to make sense of experience by putting together the often disjointed and fragmented pieces of everyday life, including the crises and traumas as well as the banal aspects of routine, into some kind of structure. This involves reconstructing the past, through the lens of the present as in the example at the beginning of this chapter. The past includes the memories and dreams, which Carolyn Steedman argues, reshape our lives and the identities that we take up 'again and again; the story we tell of our life is reshaped around them. ... The past is re-used through the agency of social information, and that interpretation of it can only be made with what people know of a social world and their place within it' (1986: 5).

This 'social information' indicates the wider context in which personal stories are told. As Paul Ricoeur argues these stories enable us to make sense of our lives but they are linked to the wider narrative, to the social context (1991). We do not have complete control, because as Ricoeur suggests, we may be the heroes of our stories but we are not the authors (1991). One aspect of the way in which people endeavour to synthesize the disparate components of their experience to produce a more coherent story is the way in which we draw on the more public stories that have currency at the time. Personal stories link us to the broader social framework in which more public stories are told. In this sense narrative can be used to explore the interrelationship between the personal and the social that forms the basis of identity. Christine Whipp, in the account of who she is, draws not only on revelations made of the past in the present, but on wider disclosure about the significance of reproductive technologies such as artificial insemination by donor. She has drawn on a particular story which sets assisted reproductive technology in opposition to more traditional sexual reproduction involving the contact of two bodies, however briefly. However, Diane Blood's personal story draws on a very different reading of the public stories of reproductive technologies. In this case the individual has reconstructed a more heroic narrative of her struggle to benefit from the advantages offered by technoscience, in order to create a meaningful identity for herself and subsequently for her children. She is using the public story in order to secure an identity and interestingly, ensure that her children will be able to construct and reclaim named roots of origin in their own identity stories.

Holstein and Gubrium offer an account of storying the self that focuses on everyday life. They draw on Harold Garfinkel's model of the social order as constructed by how ordinary people view themselves and construct meanings in the practices of everyday life through the linguistic and interpretative skills they possess. This is a practical approach, which is in many ways in the tradition of pragmatism, in that it pays careful attention to the details of talk and interaction and everyday exchanges and conversations. Holstein and Gubrium are attracted by what they call 'practical, interactionally crafted identity' (2000: 89). Garfinkel's notion of reflexivity suggests that we make sense of who we are through talk and conversation. Although we may think of ourselves as describing what exists around us, through our talk we are creating the order of that world, by making sense (1967). This provides a focus on the everyday stories we tell and through which we construct ourselves. Holstein and Gubrium offer illustration from conversational analysis but seek to incorporate Foucauldian discourse analysis into their theory of the narrativization of identity. They suggest that Foucault's approach, which, however, focuses on a broader social, political, cultural and historical landscape is complementary to Garfinkel's. The operation of power operates diffusely, at different sites and through myriad routines, as well as through the activities of the state and legislation, within Foucault's understanding of the discursive production of knowledge.

In developing his theories of how the subject is, which are discussed in more detail in Chapter 5, Foucault explored the idea of 'technologies of the self' in his later work (1988). These demonstrate how the subject is not only subjected to discourse and produced by knowledge, subjects also actively constitute themselves, through engaging in the cultural practices of everyday life. Holstein and Gubrium draw on these ideas and use arguments about the specific practices through which identities are constructed and the intersection of social matters, such as race, class, gender, sexuality and regional location modalities, to support their claims for the idea of 'shared selves' and their focus on narratives of the self. They argue that while stories 'reflect their sources and circumstances ... they also take shape through their active narration' (2000: 106). It is through the construction of autobiographical stories that people give coherence and diversity to their lives. 'Individuals *compose* their accounts ... while broader narrative formats offer familiar or conventional guidelines for how stories might unfold, they do not determine storylines. Who and what we are, are not frozen in available discourses of subjectivity' (p. 107). Thus according to Holstein and Gubrium a 'shared self' permits agency while acknowledging the impact of social and structural constraints. This self can accommodate *both* diversity and coherence, thus providing an alternative to the uncertainties of the fragmented postmodern self.

Traditionally stories have a structure or form that provides a framework for understanding what is said. This may take the form of a linear narrative with a beginning, a middle and an end. Stories may start at the end or in the middle and work backwards, reconstructing the past and offering some explanation of how the present has been reached. Homer's great epic *The Odyssey* starts in the middle, and has Odysseus relating his adventures to date, before embarking on the latter part of his journey home. However, all stories have a beginning, even if they are not always told chronologically. The story offers a means of piecing together the action and of organizing what has happened into narrative. Folk stories can be seen to reflect and reconstruct the ways in which people attempt to make sense of their own lives. Traditionally, for example as in the Greek myths that have such resonance within western culture, not least within the narratives of psychoanalysis, a physical journey accompanies an identity journey through which the hero's self emerges and unfolds. Myths and the folk stories that become part of popular culture often include the aspect of the life story that relates to roots and origins. These can be linked to childhood.

An identity story may reveal truths about the hero's real parentage, none more powerfully than the Oedipus story. This story has most often been read as an expression of jealousy of the father and desire for the mother on the part of the son. This is hardly surprising due to the primacy given to this reading in Freudian psychoanalysis and the extent to which the notion of an 'Oedipus complex' has been absorbed into western popular culture, informing myriad cultural products, films, plays, poems and songs as well as humour, not to mention psychoanalysis and its popular psychotherapeutic offshoots in magazines, on television and in other media.

In the Oedipus myth which is multiplied in so many forms out of Sophocles' play, one aspect of Oedipus's identity story is the crucial importance of his roots, notably his parentage. Pivotal points in the story focus on knowledge of a belief about who Oedipus really is in relation to his birth parents. When Oedipus is informed by the Oracle that it will be his destiny to kill his father and marry his mother, Oedipus assumes this refers to the man and woman who reared him as their son. These were in fact the parents who adopted him, his own birth parents having already been apprised of this dire prophesy about their infant son. When Oedipus receives the warning of his fate from the Oracle he leaves and reaches a crossroads, at which he decides not to return to the parents who have looked after him, but to take a new road, to a place he has never been to before, thus tragically fulfilling the prophecy. At the crossroads he kills a man who, unbeknown to Oedipus, is his 'real' father and then proceeds to marry a woman who again, unbeknown to him, is his birth. The whole identity story rests on the crucial importance of the authenticity of the birth parents – the 'real' father and mother. The identity story developed by Oedipus in this mythical tale is one that has resonance for other productions of an authentic narrative of self based on the quest for roots of origin. The most common journey in myths and folk stories is that which takes the hero home. Home can be constructed in relation to kinship and especially parentage. The journeys may take many different forms but whatever adventures may befall the hero of the narrative there is commonly a construction of identity through the telling of the life story.

Madan Sarup argues that this process does not only apply to myths and folk stories. He suggests that we are all 'detectives looking for clues, little pieces of the jigsaw puzzle (stories, memories, and photographs) about our parents and our childhood. The story gradually unfolds. But it does not only unfold; to some extent we construct our story, and hence our identity' (1996: 16). Through telling and retelling our life stories we select key moments, respect what seems important or troubling to us and exclude other points. Absences are also significant in the construction of identity through narrative. The narrative involves interpretation both by the teller of the story and by those who listen. As Sarup suggests 'listening to people's biographical narratives is in many ways similar to the work of psychoanalysis' (p. 16).

Sarup cites the example of an autobiography which illustrates his points quite explicitly. He chooses an autobiography which focuses on the individual, linking the personal to the social but incorporating quite specific coverage of psychoanalysis, notably through accounts of the author's own experience of psychoanalysis. It is only through the experience of analysis that the author is able to make sense of this past and to write about it. Analysis legitimizes the experience and enables him to give voice to it. Ronald Fraser's *In search of a past* (1984) offers a good example of an autobiographical work of an upper class English family life at a particular historical moment. It provides a self-conscious narrative of parallel accounts of Fraser's experience of his interviews with staff employed at his parents' estate in England in the 1930s and 1940s, conversations with his mother and father and of his encounters with his analyst. Fraser builds up an understanding of his own identity through the process of psychoanalysis that enables him to reconstruct himself through this childhood and into adulthood. The social context is a privileged class-based one which illustrates well a material and very specific historical positioning; a biography traced through exploration of personal experience and feelings within an historically specific location.

The book starts with a focus on the self, with the author as an adult describing his childhood home to his analyst. The scene setting is social and material as well as personal. He describes the Manor House at Amnersfield and the domestic organization which involved staff, including the nanny and the children of the household occupying separate quarters from his parents. Interview material reveals much about Fraser's relationship with his parents. For example the nanny is reported as saying that there was no physical contact between the boy and his mother, even when he was very young. This she attributes to the English fear of experiencing feelings, and especially of touching (1984: 62).

A picture is built up of the young Fraser's childhood as privileged and well off, but lonely, without much contact with other children and without any physical expression of love and affection from his parents. In analysis he comes to realize that as a person of his class and time he had two mothers, his natural mother who was his 'real' mother but was in effect inoperative, and the nanny, Ilse, who was a surrogate but operative mother, and the object of his affection.

The narrative of the self expands through the encounter of analysis, to explore and reconstruct Fraser's relationship with his father. We learn that, at the outbreak of the Second World War, Fraser's father insisted that his beloved nanny return to her country of origin – Germany. Fraser expresses his loss and the pain of his experience of separation. 'I can still feel the pain, the loss and the fear. My father was to blame' (1984: 123).

The book brings out some of the basic principles of the process of psychoanalysis, through the exploration of childhood experience, relationships with parents and the experience of loss in particular in relation to the mother. This account is especially useful in illustrating some of the distinctive features of psychoanalysis and of the experience of such analysis in relation to identity. As Fraser records in the book, 'Psychoanalysis … doesn't set out to dispose of the past but to understand it. By understanding it one has a choice of how to deal with it' (p. 90).

Sarup also argues that Fraser's story is particularly useful in that it locates identity so precisely in space and time (1996: 23). This autobiographical account indicates the primacy of the search for the roots of identity through revisiting childhood experience. In this specific instance the narrative is retold through returning to the relationship with his parents, the somewhat austere, threatening father, the absent mother and feelings of loss, all key points and pivotal moments in the psychoanalytic account of the self, reproduced and re-presented in psychoanalysis. Fraser's story illustrates one person's attempt to use analysis to recover and reinterpret past experience in order to understand the identities that are taken up in the present and to provide ways of working through loss experienced in the past, in the future. This focus on understanding and even on possible solutions and remedies makes psychoanalysis and associated psychotherapies attractive to many people and may account for their increasing popularity in many areas of life in the west. Psychoanalysis occupies the space between conscious and unconscious selves, and calls up the dreams, desires and fantasies which are brought into play in identity creation, through subjectivization and resistance. Psychoanalysis connects some of these disparate desires into a story; offering a way of thinking about identity that has in many ways passed on to everyday discourse in the west. According to Ricoeur it is one of the ways in which people's lives become intelligible and 'emplotted' (1991).

> The patient who addresses the psychoanalyst brings him [*sic.*] the scattered fragments of lived stories, dreams, 'primal scenes', conflictual episodes. One can legitimately say with respect to analytic sessions that their aim and their effect is to allow the analysand to draw out of these story-fragments a narrative which would be at once more bearable and more intelligible (1991: 30).

The self in psychotherapy

The story of the self which is reproduced within the sphere of psychotherapy that is based on psychoanalytic approaches lends weight to a notion of the self that is constituted in childhood. In a sense this re-creates the notion of a linear narrative. The story starts at the beginning. This process focuses on the mother–child relationship, although it does also include father–child interaction and, in most Freudian psychoanalytic theories, the role of the father is paramount. Adulthood is seen as an effect of childhood. In this sense adult identities are derived from childhood experience and an understanding of choices made in adulthood. Conflicts within the self are best understood through retelling stories of childhood, and especially of relationships with family members. It is often the experiences of childhood and adolescence and especially the unmet desires of these stages in biographies that produce the often incomprehensible feelings which emerge from the unconscious to which they were earlier repressed, at a later point in the life story.

Psychotherapy produces expert knowledge across a range of professional sites, including those of the 'caring professions' but this knowledge is also re-iterated and reproduced in many different fields. Nicholas Rose argues that the psychotherapeutic narrativization of the self, which constitutes 'psy discourse' belongs not only in the professional or formal therapeutic encounter but also on television, on radio, in women's magazines, on the internet and in popular publications such as child care and relationship advice guides (1991). 'Psy knowledges' inform the work of a range of professionals as well as the growth market in Europe and the USA especially of self-help literature and 'personal growth' advice. These knowledges inform reflection on the self, the relationship of the self to itself through 'the unceasing reflexive gaze of our own psychologically educated self-scrutiny' (Rose, 1991: 208). In this sense, the self, like the body becomes a project to be 'worked on' and improved. In the case of the self this may well involve pursuit of a 'real' 'true' self – the 'real me'. Rose argues that so ubiquitous are 'psy knowledges' that 'it has become impossible to conceive of personhood to experience one's own or another's personhood, or to govern oneself or others without "psy" ' (1996: 139). It is worth noting that Rose is presenting a critical analysis of 'psy discourses' from a particular Foucauldian perspective which sees them as producing knowledge about the self rather than the means by which one might gain access to truth about who one really is; that is to say revealing the truth nonetheless. His account of the ubiquity of such narratives is very useful and makes relevant comment on contemporary western life, whatever critical position is adopted.

What kind of stories of the self is involved in psychotherapeutic narratives? How might such stories be useful in framing an account of identity formation? In order to address the first question it is possible to look at a vast range of stories that are produced in the context of personal and couple therapy as well as group counselling. One example which bridges professional and more popular therapy and shows the evolution of psychoanalysis from a treatment of mental illness to a developmental theory of the workings of the human psyche with wide ranging application to everyday life, is relationship counselling. An example of the way in which counselling and therapy have developed new, accessible forms of 'expertise' can be seen in the UK organization 'Relate', which currently deals with 100,000 couples a year (France, 2002). The organization was formerly known as Marriage Guidance and the change in nomenclature indicates very clearly the shifts in attitudes towards different forms of domestic living and patterns of relationships that have emerged in the last 20 years. Relate is a registered charity set up in 1938 which charges for its counselling services. Only half of Relate's counsellors, of whom there were 2000 in 2002, are paid. The organization began with volunteers and relies heavily on volunteer support. Counsellors have to undergo a two-year training scheme and 240 hours of supervised counselling before they qualify. Such practice crosses the boundaries between professional and volunteer, between expert and amateur, producing new public stories and new narratives of the self. What might in the past have been taken for granted as part of the life course, perhaps drawing in friends and family for advice, has become something to be worked at with trained guides who are part of a whole set of knowledge production about selfhood and relationships.

An example

A heterosexual couple visits the Relate counsellor for weekly consultations. He is 73 and has children from a previous relationship. She is 41 and has no children. Both have, or in his case had, successful careers. They have been together for six years but have reached a rocky patch. They quarrel frequently.

> The sessions are fractious. [He] sometimes takes notebooks so he can read the comments that [she] has made during the week … they interrupt each other … things are misheard, misinterpreted. The Counsellor … is hard pressed to contain the emotions in the room sometimes. She has to coax them to imagine a different way of communicating (France, 2002: 22).

The counsellor comments that difficult feelings have to be expressed and brought out into the open. 'It's my job to facilitate conversation, explore different ways of communicating. I can't tell them what to do. All I can do is help them come to the conclusions they want to make' (p. 24). These practices involve those in receipt of counselling internalizing these narratives of the self, what in the discourse of Relate counselling might be called taking responsibility. Thus they are not directed, or even advised, they take care of themselves although the techniques are practised at the counselling sessions. The counsellor suggests separate sessions for the two people. In this case this allows the woman to express her resentment, which later enables her to voice these feelings to her partner. She has much of the burden of domestic work to bear. The situation is exacerbated by her partner's increasing age, which has also brought about other changes in their relationship. The age difference between the two has begun to matter much more in recent years. They are encouraged to recover past aspirations and hopes as well as experiences. A key feature of the sessions is recovery of the past. The final verdict of this couple is that the counselling has helped but they would both have liked more direction, more explicit guidance from the counsellor. However, direct, explicit advice is not really what is on offer. The emphasis is on facilitating and enabling couples to come to their own conclusions and take their own actions.

What does this tell us about identity formation in this particular context? Identity is clearly developed in relation to others and in specific material and social circumstances. Identity is embedded in social change. These changes brought about by generational factors and the ageing process also matter. Identities are embodied and they are formed in time and space. Gendered patterns of domestic activity, involving the separation of the public and private spheres operate to produce particular expectations about who does what. Ageing has material outcomes, which are renegotiated in relation to others through the life course.

The role of the counsellor or psychotherapist is to legitimize and facilitate the decisions which the clients make. Individuals have to take responsibility for their own actions and for the shaping of their own identities. Counselling assumes a high degree of agency on the part of individual in shaping their own identities. Yet counselling is also part of the process of the construction of knowledge about the self, which necessitates the attribution of agency and responsibility to individuals. The narrative of counselling constructs and establishes agency even though those in receipt of counselling might prefer it if the counsellor took responsibility. As in the autobiographical narrative, in counselling or in therapy, identities in the present are constructed through telling and retelling the story of the past. Pivotal moments in the life course are identified as significant and accorded greater status through being legitimized by the 'expert'.

Psychoanalytic approaches

Psychotherapeutic practice is informed by developments within psychoanalysis often arising from Freudian and post-Freudian ideas, as well as those of object relations theories. The primacy given to childhood experience and to gender and sexual identities has led to Freudian psychoanalysis playing a key role in the development and practice of psychotherapy. Freud placed sexuality at the centre of his theory of psychological development and saw the libido, which encompassed a person's struggle to come to terms with sexuality and life energy, as involved in every aspect of human activity, often sublimated and repressed into the unconscious. Freud's emphasis on sexuality, including infant sexuality was historically important and somewhat radical, appearing at a time of apparent repression and denial of sexuality, especially in childhood.

In the late nineteenth and early twentieth century Freud's ideas about mental life going through a series of stages, oral, anal and genital, from birth onwards and culminating in the Oedipal phase in early childhood at about the age of four, both focused on sexuality in the formalities of identity and endeavoured to accommodate embodied sexuality. In Freud's account, based on his evidence delivered from the process of psychoanalysis with his own patients, the libido centred in different parts of the body at each developmental stage. Psychopathology and damaged adult identities could result from fixation at any particular stage with neurosis arising from libidinal arrest at any point. The aim of psychotherapy was to unpack and deconstruct these points of libidinal arrest so that the individual psyche could move on through the necessary stages in development to reach a mature personality. Notably, in Freud's account this maturity is configured around gender identity and sexuality.

The Oedipus complex presented the pinnacle of developmental stages for Freud. This was the point at which sexual identity became fixed, and for Freud appropriate sexual identity was heterosexual. The Oedipal stage is a very gendered moment in Freudian psychoanalysis. This has the advantage of offering recognition of the importance of gender in the formation of identity. While there are social categories of gender, most frequently the two of female and male, and social organization is constituted around these categories, identification with gender will be an important dimension of selfhood. However, the particular version in Freud's account has considerable limitations especially for women. Both boys and girls must separate from the mother at this point. For boys this means that they must detach their sexual feelings for the mother so that they can later attach these feelings to another woman. This happens just at the point when boys see their fathers as rivals for their mother's love. According to Freud, the boy wishes – or fantasizes about the castration of his father and as a result fears castration himself. This fear leads the boy to relinquish his sexual attraction for his mother by repressing his desire and identifying with his father. For girls the process is even more complex. The resolution of the Oedipal complex results from a recognition that they are not male. As a result of realizing that she does not have a penis, the signifier of masculinity in Lacan's account, but rather more embodied in Freud's, the little girl blames the mother for what she thinks is her own castration and turns away from the mother, attaching herself to her father (who has a penis). She eventually gives up the desire for a penis, recognizing she can never have one and replaces this wish with the desire for a child. With that wish in mind the girl takes her father as her love object.

Freud's critique and his explanation of the development of mature sexuality and of gendered identity were based on clinical findings; on his observations of the people – mainly women – who presented as patients. Freud constructed a theory of sexuality which has been adapted but still informs much psychotherapeutic practice, in spite of its very specific, historically located patriarchal view of women's sexuality. His understanding of women's fantasy and the claim that women desire a baby as a substitute for the penis they can never have has been reinterpreted symbolically as a desire for male power in a patriarchal society (Mitchell, 1975). Lacanian emphases on the symbolic power of the phallus as the master signifier, giving meaning to the whole system of representations, and prioritizing the entry into language as key in the confirmation of identity, have been more important in cultural studies than in psychotherapy. It is still difficult not to see the phallus, however symbolic and illusory its powers, as consonant with male anatomy and the possession of male rather than female bodies. Freud's heterosexist bias and his historical specificity which has been translated into universal principles have also been extensively criticized by practitioners within psychotherapy counselling and even psychoanalysis (Eichenbaum and Orbach, 1982). The notion of the unconscious and the repression of desires remain powerful concepts upon which much analysis has been built and developed and psychoanalysis provides a very significant component of the theoretical underpinnings of psychotherapeutic practice.

Post-Freudian developments have followed different paths but have retained the focus on the unconscious. The Oedipus complex has become almost unrecognizable in later work following Freud. It has been questioned for its universal claims, its inadequate account of symbolic meanings and by Melanie Klein and her followers for the timing and excessive emphasis afforded to this stage by Freud. Kleinians stress the pre-Oedipus stage of development. Rather than seeing the father as the bearer of authority, it seems more logical and empirically supported to focus on the relationship between the infant and the mother. Social practices most frequently involve mothers or at least women as carers of babies and very young children. The child's entry into the social world is more likely to be mediated by a woman than a man or even the father or another male relative, who may be absent or play only a minor role in rearing the baby and small child.

Wilhelm Reich was the first psychoanalyst to link individual psychology explicitly to the social world (1970). Reich argued that the family as a particular form of social domestic living creates a particular psychology. He showed that the family was an economic unit of production and consumption which served the social function of protecting women and children who were deprived of economic and sexual rights and the political function of supporting fathers/men as exponents of the authority of the state through the family (1951). Reich indicated the psychic consequences of this form of social and familial organization. This work was influential in the field of psychotherapy in areas where therapists sought to unite the social and psychological worlds.

The recognition that identity necessarily combines personal and social worlds is more explicit in some accounts than others. Erik Erikson's psychosocial theories of identity makes the interconnections more explicit than most psychoanalytic approaches. According to Erikson, identity is made up of 'a conscious striving for continuity ... a solidarity with a group's ideals' (1968: 208). In Erikson's analysis identity requires both stability and identification with the wider social group so that identity provides some sense of continuity with the past and a future trajectory with a core identity that locates each of us as individuals within the social world. When there is a reasonable amount of social stability and consensus, identity is not problematic and there is not a feeling that identity is in any way in crisis. However, at times of social upheaval, the most extreme of which would be war time, identity crises become central to social life. Erikson's own work was carried out at times of major global conflict and his clinical work with veterans of the Second World War led him to argue that at such historical moments identity cannot be taken for granted. In fact he went on to suggest that life in the twentieth century was beset by conflicts which, being common to most people, were typical rather than unusual, constituting normative crises. This meant that life involved the resolution of conflicts between social demands and individual needs. These conflicts were deemed to be more acute at some points in the life course than others. Erikson identified the problems encountered in development in late adolescence as involving a peak period of identity crises. The nature of the identity crises depends on the social context and the society in which the young person is living. In western societies the identity crises of adolescence typically take the form of engaging in illegal or quasi-illegal activities or of drifting between a variety of social roles and occupations. Erikson pointed to other stages in the individual biography, where identity is configured in relation to different experiences of the social world, which of course vary historically, but adolescence is the stage at which, he argued, identity crises appear to be inevitable. He is probably most well known for his development of the concept of 'identity crisis', but his work is noted here for his contribution to the exploration of the psychosocial approach to understanding identity, arising from his acknowledgement of the importance of the social context in which identities are formed and negotiated.

Object relations

Object relations theories, as developed initially in the UK, put the relationship between mother and infant in the first year of life at the centre. This view sees the infant, from birth, as engaging with 'objects', which are perceived as separate from itself. The mother is the focus of this approach. The mother is central, as the main 'object' through which the infant self develops. This is in contrast to the centrality of the father in Freud's Oedipus complex and the primacy afforded to the phallus. Object relations theory can be said to derive from the work of Melanie Klein who based her theory on observation of children and play therapy.

Klein presented strong arguments for the conception of an 'inner world' that recognizes the necessity of conflicting fantasies. These fantasies arise from the anxieties that are inherent in the intense closeness and intimacy of early childhood dependency and love. Individuals unconsciously use the objects in the external world to represent aspects of their own inner world. Klein (1986) redefined Freudian drives by emphasizing impulses and their attachment to objects. For Klein the ego was the centre of the child's world and the child's drives or instincts sought objects as their aim, rather than pleasure as Freud argued. These 'objects' were internal rather than images of actual people in the child's life. When a drive arose in the child so too did an image of an object to satisfy it. Real people served the role of screens upon which the child could project its internal fantasies.

Experience of people, notably the mother, in the child's world confirmed its experience of internal objects relations. Klein retained Freud's two crucial drives of the life force and the death force, but saw these as meeting in the individual's psyche, forming the battleground on which the ego developed. Klein redefined Freud's dual drive theory by foregrounding destructive impulses and their attachment to objects, in particular the prototype object, the breast. At the beginning of life the baby takes into itself, through interjection, the good experience at the breast, and then, through projection, projects onto the breast the bad experiences. In this way the mother's breast, and later the whole person of the mother, becomes both the good and the bad object. Similarly in adult life people intimately connected with the person become a projection for the maternal objects of the individual's psyche. Internal objects are the representations of others. (They are not identical to those others.) These internal objects have the capacity to achieve relative autonomy. They can be creative or destructive. They are destructive when splitting or projection overwhelms the ability we have to distinguish between the different worlds of the internal and the external. Object relations offers a means of locating uniqueness in the individuals who thereby have the capacity to create their own inner worlds and to generate new meanings, not simply to reflect or respond to the external social world. Object relations based therapy aims to enlarge this inner world, while helping the patient to recognize the boundaries.

The inner world is not, of course, separate from or unrelated to the external social world. Object relations theories have been applied to the manifestation of social identities which clearly derive from social, structural relations and specific historical, political practices. For example, Frantz Fanon's famous *Black skins, white masks* (1956) highlights the destructive and most painful effects of racism on the personalities of its victims. He uses his own experience as a psychoanalyst as well as social and cultural observations to explain how the colonial subject is made to suffer and feel inadequate on being immersed in a white world. Although at home the black person has already internalized a white value system that creates white dominance and superiority, it is only upon arrival in the colonial country that people have to confront themselves as having a new identity, that of the 'negro'. Fanon uses the word negro, which is why I have cited it here, as historically specific in this context. He uses the example of black people arriving in France from Algeria to illustrate this moment of awareness of a black identity. Fanon cites the specific mechanisms of projection onto the black man, unlike the Jewish man, he argues, as arising from corporeal, mostly genital and sexual fixations. In Fanon's work the negro represents the repressed sexual desires of the white man. In a different context, Michael Rustin has used a Kleinian perspective to endeavour to explain the inner world of the racist individual (1991). In a provocative paper he points to the need to offer a psychodynamic account of the personal investment made in racism and the primitive ideas which it evokes. Inner worlds can be interrogated to elucidate the operation of social and political ideological perspectives as well as taking the starting point of the individual psyche and the personal problems of maintaining a stable identity.

Nancy Chodorow is a self-proclaimed object relations theorist in the USA who argues against the essentialism of Lacanian psychoanalytic theory and the drive theory of both Freud and even Klein. Chodorow is a feminist sociologist who has more recently become a trained, practising psychoanalyst. The focus of her work has been the development of the gendered self through relationships with others, and the unconscious and conscious experience of negotiating separation and connection. Chodorow's work has privileged the pre-Oedipal relationship between mother and child in contrast to the Freudian focus on the Oedipal stage and the primacy of the phallus. Chodorow is best known for her account of the ways in which women's universal responsibility for mothering creates an imbalance of relational capacities in girls and boys (1978). It is because girls are noticed by a woman, that is a person of the same gender as themselves, they develop the more fluid ego boundaries than boys. A girl's sense of self is thus continuous with others. This is used by Chodorow to explain women's desire to mother. This explanation has much to recommend it and the Freudian notion of penis envy as the source of women's desire to have a child. It also extends the understanding of mothering to aspects of women's relational capacities and emotional lives, beyond the more limited definition of mothering as having a child.

By contrast, according to Chodorow, boys develop their sense of self in opposition to the mother, by establishing more rigid ego boundaries, by separating in such a way that they often denigrate that which is associated with what is feminine and connected to the mother. Hence the fear of losing their sense of masculinity is more concerned with fear of the pre-Oedipal mother than with Freudian fear of castration.

Although Chodorow's work has been criticized as overly deterministic and failing to identify differences among women and the diverse cultural arrangements involved in child rearing, it has its strengths. She is able to link the social and the psychic very effectively in specific socio-cultural contexts. Her work has been popular with feminist psychotherapists and occupies an important place in feminist thinking in the USA. Chodorow's version of the development of the gendered self is more clearly acknowledged as taking place within specific social circumstances than Freudian accounts which infer universal structures from very specific data. She foregrounds motherhood in the process of the development of gender identities, thus giving recognition to what has been called the hidden 'dark continent' of human relations (Irigaray, 1985, see Chapter 5 of this book).

Chodorow went on to develop her work through the practice of psychoanalysis. She uses her own clinical data to explore the ways in which gender can be seen not only as social and cultural but also as requiring personal, individual meanings. This account attempts to put personal meaning into more sociological versions of the identity story, such as those that were addressed in Chapter 1. Chodorow aims to use the notion of personal meaning to accommodate differences among women, and thus to remedy some of the criticisms of her earlier work. As she argues, 'there are individual, psychological processes in addition to, and in a different register from, culture, language and power relations that construct gender for the individual. Meaning ... is always psychologically particular to the individual' (1995: 217). Thus for Chodorow gender identity is a melding of 'personally created (emotionally and through unconscious fantasy) and cultural meaning' (p. 217). This is a very different position from the Foucauldian readings of psychoanalysis as a discursive field which produces its own meanings, as expressed in the governmentality of Nicholas Rose's 'psy discourse'. It could appear that Chodorow might want to have it both ways; to retain the social and invest the psychic without having to lay claim to the 'truth' of personal individual extra discursive meanings. However, what she claims is that 'perception and meaning are psychologically created ... people use available cultural meanings and images, but they experience them emotionally and through fantasy, as well as in particular interpersonal contexts. Individuals thereby create new meanings in terms of their own unique biographies and histories of intra-psychic strategies and practices' (p. 217). This is a view which resists Foucauldian, performative (see Chapter 5) totally social constructionist accounts, and seeks to challenge the universalism of cultural and even social and economic domination. She also challenges the universalism of developmental accounts of the construction of the self as well as the universalism of Freudian psychoanalysis. However, Chodorow's source of difference and of heterogeneity lies in the psyche of the individual. Resistance to dominant identities is possible only through individual resistance, rather than through the identification of collective identities which may be marginalized or denied by dominant cultural forms. Chodorow cites Patricia Hill Collins' argument that experience is created individually as well as imposed by domination, 'there is always choice, and power to act, no matter how bleak the situation may be' (1990: 237). However, Chodorow's understanding appears to emphasize the individual psychic nature of resistance, rather than its collective potential for political action much more than Hill Collins does. The process may be located within the psyche but any meanings which are implicated must be social.

Nonetheless Chodorow's account of the outer relationship between psychic processes and social, cultural meanings offers some useful insights which can enhance understanding of identity formation. This is especially important in indicating some of the ways in which people have personal investment in an identity position. She uses the notion of animation to describe how cultural categories become endowed with emotional meaning (1995). She cites the example of a patient of hers who is frightened of her own anger. As a woman, the patient, Mrs A feels that women's anger is destructive. In contrast she sees men's anger as 'sudden, violent and explosive but when it is all over, you are still there. If Mrs A could be a man ... she could still express her considerable rage' (p. 227). Chodorow suggests that Mrs A has animated gender struggles and a particular angry struggle with her father in adolescence to reach this understanding of her own anger in adult life. Mrs A has also constructed gender around a male/female polarity and the desire to possess masculine attributes herself. Chodorow traces these feelings back to key moments of animation in her patient's biography including childhood fantasies about images of power, playing king of the mountain and football with neighbourhood boys '... identifications with heroic knights who swashbuckled their way to success, rescuing damsels in distress' (p. 228). Thus Chodorow is able to focus on the psychic processes involved in the formation of gender identity within a specific context, that allows for difference and diversity within particular social and cultural contexts.

Psychoanalytic theories offer strategies for explaining more of the personal dimension of the personal/social identity equation. There are problems in the imbalance that can result from this focus on the psyche. When psychoanalytic theorists attempt to meet the challenge of a fixed universalism and an historical bias they may become too focused on the individual or on the psychic processes at the expense of social, material, cultural and political forces. However, psychoanalytic theories have a great deal to offer in explaining the internal processes whereby identity positions are taken up and the mechanics of identification. The self that emerges from these processes is not whole and unified. However, it remains contradictory and fragmented although analysis may claim to present some accommodation and settlement to the most disruptive of contradictions. Psychoanalytic theories to some extent reinforce the fragmented status of identity, which is characteristic of postmodernism, while presenting some explanation of the desire for unity which is so often the focus of psychoanalysis.

Contemporary accounts of identity, which have been influenced by psycho-analysis vary in the status they afford to the legacy of the relationships of early childhood and there is considerable divergence between those who take a positive approach to the security that can be achieved in adulthood as a result of favourable relationships in childhood and those who stress the uncertainty that can result from problems at this stage of development. For example, Giddens emphasizes the outcome of early childhood as 'ontological security' and a sense of one's own identity and trust in the project of life, so that adults can operate effectively in a world that they know to be fraught with risks, without being overcome by anxiety (1991). Others, such as Ian Craib stress the fragmentation and insecurity of the psyche, which is the psychological inheritance of all adults (1994). Craib suggests that the trauma of infancy leaves everyone with contradictory emotional needs and fear of abandonment and loss.

Ways of knowing

Clinical psychoanalysis involves the observation, analysis and treatment of individuals or groups. The evidence offered in many of the approaches discussed in the latter part of this chapter is based on clinical accounts. Even narrative accounts use such stories of the self which are presented by patients or groups of patients in the clinical encounter or in counselling or psycho-therapy sessions, as data. Other methods adopted include fictionalized or auto/biographical accounts of personal stories. Personal testimony has an important place in the literature on identity, although it also has limitations as such stories present only very small samples. Other theorists support their claims with structured or semi-structured interviews and, increasingly in recent times, with the use of focus groups prior to conducting in-depth interviews. Narrative approaches require the subject to speak and to identify themselves. This can be through texts, through spoken accounts and through the evidence of material culture accessed through ethnography.

The development of theories about identity involves incorporating a wide range of different methodological approaches and interrogating texts across a wide cultural range. The interdisciplinary study of identity has included innovatory studies embracing texts as diverse as poetry, personal testimony, fiction, legal accounts and more conventional qualitative social science data. These different narratives present the evidence that has been offered to support the stories of the self that have been the subject of this chapter.

Conclusion

The focus of this chapter has been on different versions of narrative, told through public stories of technoscience, fiction, psychoanalytic theories, and the personal stories of personal testimony and accounts expressed through psychoanalysis and therapeutic encounters.

Much of the debate has been taken up with the quest for some stability in the securing of identity and the question of how far the subject is actively involved in the constitution of identity. The focus has been on personal stories, although, as I have suggested, these are inextricable in many ways from the public stories through which we attempt to make sense of our own lives. The notion of 'storying the self' and the concept of narrative offer a means of exploring what is involved in the search for some coherence in the construction of identities. Stories can be told in different ways but stories of the self generally have some point, whether they take the form of a linear or a more diffuse narrative, when they revert to childhood experience and some myth of origin. The story of origin may tell us more about present longings than about the past it seeks to recapture, but such stories do represent both a desire for making sense of who we are through piecing the past together, and a focus on the genealogy of family and childhood as a key formative period.

At an historical moment when it seems that new technologies can disrupt certainties about maternity and paternity in the genealogy of family as a source of security, the need to tell such stories about the self seems ever more powerful. However, the links between public stories of technoscience and personal stories are not only intimately connected, but differently inflected. Individuals exercise agency in telling their own stories and in constructing meanings in relation to the public stories of technoscience, such as those made available through developments in assisted reproductive technologies. These technologies make new personal stories possible as well as drawing attention to uncertainties and fragmentation in existing identity stories.

Psychoanalytic accounts provide both examples of personal stories and explanations of the investment people make in the identity stories which they tell. Of course not all stories of the self and narrative accounts employ psychoanalytic explanations, or even incorporate a focus on the unconscious. Holstein and Gubrium (2000) argue that in the twenty-first century, the self has become so fragmented and fluid that its very existence is seriously questioned. They seek to reinstate the self into narratives of identity, in particular through using the concept of narrative to reconstruct a diverse range of stories, which can be told about the self, but do not invoke the insights or the practices of psychoanalysis. Theirs is an empirical self, produced through the 'everyday technology of self construction' (p. 103). This 'everyday technology' fuses the ideas based on ethnomethodology, for example as developed by Harold Garfinkel (1967) with the later work of Michel Foucault and his notion of 'technologies of the self' (1988). While Garfinkel and Foucault may be in many ways very different, they do both, albeit with very different empirical material, focus on the immediacy and relevance of the everyday and upon what is historically and locationally specific. Both focus on descriptions of the detail of the everyday, Garfinkel on the language of routine interactions and the ways in which construct meanings in their exchanges with others and Foucault on the discursive practices through which identities are regulated and re-created. As Trinh Minh-ha has argued, the question of identity is moving away from traditional questions about *who* I am, to transform into questions of *when, where* and *how* I am (1992). It is at the point of this specific transformation that psychoanalytic theorists seek to intervene, to bring the psychic dimensions of *how* identification takes place, into play. It is worth noting that not only do many accounts of the self not include the psychic or the psychoanalytic dimension, but many are actively critical of psychoanalysis in particular. For example Foucault, whose approach has been developed by Nichloas Rose, retained a critical stance which maintained that not only did psychoanalysis not reveal any truths outside discourse, it created the very notion of the unconscious into which repressed desires had been concealed. Psychoanalysis, far from revealing the 'true self' creates a new subject, through its practice and the writings of psychoanalytic theorists, and produces repressed sexuality. Psychoanalysis creates its own 'regime of truth', in that its claims are thought to be true, and thus it becomes part of the regulatory practices that police us (Foucault, 1979).

Arguments such as Holstein's and Gubrium's seek to reinstate agency into the process of constructing the self. However, they omit some of the stories which psychoanalytic theorists argue, offer insights into *why* we might identify as we do. Although some psychoanalytic accounts, in the psycho-social tradition, following on from Erikson and developments within objects relations theories, such as Chodorow's, attempt to meld the cultural and the psychic there are difficulties attached to this endeavour. This is especially the case if one is to accommodate agency, and in particular collective agency, into the story of the self which is produced. Narratives of the self and the idea of constructing meaningful identities through the production of a story permit the notion of the teller of the story, even if it is only as the central character, or even the hero, as Ricoeur suggests, rather than as author. The stories that we tell may move towards satisfying the desire for unity and wholeness, if only temporarily, through making sense of our experience. The stories in this chapter have frequently involved journeys into the self and into the psyche. Another way of making sense of where we are now, and even of who we would like to become, is through looking at the journeys, across space as well as time, which we have travelled in search of finding out who we are, which is the focus of the next chapter.

3   Mapping the self: journeys we take

In Chapter 2, I looked at some of the ways in which identities are constructed through narrative and the stories we tell about ourselves. These stories often take the form of an account which has a starting point; that starting point is often located in childhood or in our family of origin. Not only does the linear narrative have some appeal in the telling of identity stories, but the notion of an origin to which we can relate back has considerable resonance in the retelling and understanding of our own identity stories. Another way of beginning at the beginning is to start with 'home'. Starting points and sources are linked to the idea of 'home' as the place where it all began. Home means different things. Home may connote security and safety or for many people it may be a place of risk danger and violence. Even if migration has taken place because of 'push factors', which force people to leave their homes the place that they have left retains symbolic importance in the construction of identity. At the most extreme, the compulsion which people may experience to leave their home is due to threats of violence. However, the place left retains importance in shaping collective and individual identities.

There is often nostalgia attached to home and people away from their first home may experience homesickness and longing. This is a longing that may have a specific word used to describe it; the longing for home has a particular resonance, which has often been expressed in poetry that seeks to give voice to the strength of these feelings. We often talk about home in a special way. For example, in Wales, the place that is my 'home' in the sense that it is my country of origin, where I was born, although I no longer live there, there is a particular word to express longing for Wales, that is for home. The Welsh language uses 'hiraeth' to express the deep long-ing for Wales, which goes further than patriotism and articulates the desire for home as well as giving voice to feelings in order to retain in one's heart, country, peoples and culture, especially when one is far away. Such expres-sions are often those of diasporic or dispossessed people and are inflected by resistance and sadness, whatever the reason for leaving. As the traditional Welsh song says:

> Hiraeth deep and hiraeth cruel,
> Hiraeth it is that breaks my heart.

Home

> His eyes were wet with weeping, as they always were. Life with its sweetness was ebbing away in the tears he shed for his lost home ... the days found him sitting on the rocks or sands torturing himself with tears, groans and heartache, and looking out with streaming eyes across the watery wilderness (Book 5: 151–3, 156–9).
>
> ...
>
> I long to reach my home and see the day of my return. It is my neverfailing wish (Book 5: 219–20).

This is how those feelings of longing for home are described in Homer's great epic poem *The Odyssey*. Home has a special place in the history of journeys. In the quotation from *The Odyssey* above, in the first extract, the Greek word used for home is *nostos,* which connotes the return journey, whereas 'home' in the second extract uses the word for the household, signifying the material home, the house (*oikos*) to which Odysseus longs to return. In this sense 'home' could be the first home, perhaps the home where a person was brought up as a child or the home they have established as their own in adulthood. There are two dimensions to home here. Firstly, there is the geographical, spatial, territorial location and secondly, there is the private, domestic arena of home. What is translated as 'home' combines the place that is home with the journey by which the homecoming is achieved. Thus 'home' combines the meanings that are attached to the place we have come from and the desire to return, including the whole process of seeking the means to return and contemplating its possibility, even if it is never likely to be accomplished. The longing to return always shapes the present and the ways in which people negotiate their identities in relation to what they might become, as well as what they are.

'Home' may be romanticized, even if that home has been a place of sadness. The idea of home also contributes to the desire to stabilize identity and the expression of longing for home can also be translated as a need to secure the sense of who we are when our spatial location can be seen as compromising that security. Home can be the country or place where we were born, Thus home is set against 'abroad' or 'alien' or 'foreign'. On the other hand, home might represent the tension between the spatial division between the private, domestic arena of the home, and the public arena of commerce and politics; the gap between 'home' and 'work'. Home in this case may be where those in paid employment go to rest and relax, away from the pressures and constraints of the public sphere. As many feminist critics have pointed out (see Woodward, 2002a), this is a most distorted separation, especially for those whose labour is within the home, and whose experience of the public arena is shaped by their association with domestic labour in the home, namely women. The separation of home and paid work that took place with the development of capitalist industrialization, which moved production from the private domestic sphere to large scale production in factories, has contributed to this largely gendered separation. The idea of home is constructed within time and space. There are historically specific constructions of home which have particular resonance. For example, in the west, there were associations between the idea of home as a private domestic space and a particular family form based on traditional familial ideology in the 1950s. This ideology embraced the notion of a heterosexual, married couple and their dependent children in an economic relationship dependent on a male breadwinner and female mother and carer who did not participate in the labour market. This is a largely ideological relationship, which created sets of meanings about home and family that might have harked back to nineteenth century Victorian middle class idealized conceptualizations of home and family. That this might not have accorded with lived experience for everyone is less important than the strength of associated ideas about what constitutes home. The mismatch between dominant discourse and aspects of experience indicates the ways in which such understandings of home change temporally and spatially, advantaging different people at different times. However, this does not detract from the ideological significance of home and its use in a variety of different discursive fields to represent security, rest and respite from the demands and turmoil of the public sphere, even if men have traditionally experienced more rest and leisure in the home than women, who increasingly labour in both spheres. Home has an ideological significance, but it must be understood within the specific contexts that are experienced differently, and marked by differences such as those of ethnicity, gender, disability and generation. There is a reassurance about some articulations of home and a sense that if only we could go home everything would be all right. As the poet Robert Frost said, in his poem, *The death of the hired man*

> Home is the place where, when you have to go there,
> They have to take you in (1914).

The longing for home, even its romanticization may have particular import at a time of rapid change and movement. While the expression of longing that is condensed in the yearning to go home or the reconstruction of 'home' from a different place, may have a long history it has had particular meanings attached to it in the twentieth century and into the twenty-first.

The relationship between desire and reality in relation to home is mediated in different ways and places at different times. There may be disjunctures and fractions between the desires that are experienced and attempts to translate these desires into practice. 'Home' also has particular political meanings attached to it, especially when home is contested and the same territory is read as home by different and often conflicting peoples. 'Home' is grounded. It is an actual territory. Home is Israel and home is Palestine. This contestation has very powerful resonance at this historical moment, when the longing for 'home' and the desire to 'return', in the case of Israel, to what is for Jewish people 'The Promised Land', is translated into a material and physical presence in a place; a place that is also seen as home for the Palestinian people who already live there. Home is not only about longing and desire. 'Home' is conflictingly interpreted as the place that is occupied and the location of belonging by different peoples whose desire and need to be homed, in the sense of having somewhere to live, seems irredeemably antagonistic.

The desire to retain a notion of home, especially when what we call 'home' is far away, suggests the need to belong and has resonance with Benedict Anderson's conceptualization of the nation as an 'imagined community' (1983). Anderson argued that it was necessary to share an idea of what constitutes a national identity in order to have a sense of belonging to that culture. 'Home' is about belonging and about imagining the place that we call home, but there is also a very strong sense of longing as well as of belonging, of a powerful desire to lay claim to an identity that is placed and grounded, as well as imagined. The desire to belong may be part of the processes of the imagination, but there may be more to the experience of longing than the temporary, imaginative construction of continuity in the attempt to make up a place called 'home'. There is a longing to belong and home can be what offers the means of satisfying this need. These feelings may be more strongly expressed at times of rapid change, although if Homer's account is representative of his times, probably eighth century BC, the strength of feeling has a long history! The desire for home is given significance through the movement of peoples, which also has a very long history, in what is called migration.

Migration

Why do people migrate? The movement of peoples and itinerant communities were features of ancient societies. There is some overstatement in the claim that migration is a recent phenomenon. Migration not only has a long history, it has different dimensions. Incentives to migrate often take the form of economic forces. People have long moved to facilitate access to food and resources. Increasingly the motivation to migrate is tied up with economic factors. It can be argued that in the modern period, from the fifteenth century, migration has been closely linked to labour power. The movement of people has been tied to economic factors on a large scale; whether that movement has been the result of coercion or has been the outcome of voluntarily made decisions; the result of 'push' or 'pull' factors. Much of the recent discussion of globalization has centred on the extent of migration across the globe and the developments that have facilitated the speed and frequency of global movements of people. Migrations have taken place across large areas and have involved both the compulsion of 'push' factors, including threats of violence and of starvation, and the draw of 'pull' factors, with economic, social and political incentives. Contemporary debates and media coverage, especially, about refugees seeking asylum in European countries also over-simplify the categories and the motivating factors behind migration, by separating out economic migrants from those who are classified as political refugees. 'Political' refugees, classified as deserving refuge are set apart from economic migrants, who are deemed to be seeking advancement and not deserving of refuge, in a binary logic that underplays the complexity of the operation of 'push' and 'pull' factors and the distinctions between the political and the economic. Political and cultural factors may deny participation in economic life and this can operate in more or less traumatic ways. It has been dramatic as in the case of East African Asian people in Uganda and has been accompanied by violent action as in Afghanistan, the former Yugoslavia and, with catastrophic consequences in Rwanda, but the interplay of different forces is not always so dramatically and publicly enacted. The interpretation of migration as motivated by either push or pull factors can underplay the different experiences among migratory peoples and over-emphasize the homogeneity of any group of people who are leaving their homes to settle in another place. As Lydia Potts argues, some contemporary discussion of migration, in the context of globalization, fails to explore the power imbalances and inequities that are involved, especially those relating to race and gender. A focus on the exploitative dimensions of migration in relation to labour, yields very different understandings of the opportunities for the formation of new identities and for the exercise of some degree of agency in shaping those identities, from some of the more optimistic readings (1990). Potts suggests that, 'Living labour power has been transferred in large quantities and over long distances since the end of the fifteenth century … The journey spans the enslavement of the Indians that followed the conquest of America, the various forms of forced labour and forced migration in Latin America, Asia and Africa, African slavery, the coolie system used to despatch the people of Asia all over the world, and finally present-day labour migration and the brain drain, the exodus of academics from the developing nations' (2002: 440). This movement had impact on the indigenous populations, for example the Indian and Aborigine peoples of Australia and America, and for many of the original residents in Asia and Africa, the arrival of people from outside meant exploitation and even extermination. Material wealth was largely created in the white world. Potts stresses the lack of freedom and choice for most of the people who were involved in these migrations, showing that from the start, the global market for labour power operated according to principles that were exploitative on grounds of race and gender. She cites the example in the case of American Indians of the enslavement of Carib people and those of African descent and hierarchical differentiation between people classified as mixed race or Indians, who were not enslaved (2002). Similarly the effects of migration led to classification and discrimination on grounds of gender.

Migration is differently experienced by women and by men. At many points in the migration of world labour it has been men who have played the major role, for example with men in colonized societies being obliged or compelled to carry out forced labour. The cargoes of slaves from Africa were said to be made up of two-thirds men. However, Potts points out that in the slave owning societies of the Caribbean and the US there was little distinction made between women and men in the work that people were forced to undertake, for example as mine workers and labourers as well as domestic servants. However, there is still limited information on colonized women, another example of women being 'hidden from history', because women had less chance to tell their own stories and were largely classified as dependants. Potts argues that this is still the case today with migrant workers being seen as male or ungendered and very little attention being given to the exploitation of women. Particular aspects of this domination and need to exercise control over women, for example through the desire of colonizers to control the fertility of migrant women, lasted well into the twentieth century and still has some resonance in the moral panics that surround refugees in the west in the twenty-first century. This discussion is offered in part to redress some of the excesses of contemporary debates about migration and movement which stress its newness, as well as to provide some background to debates about globalization which suggest, not only that it is a new phenomenon, but that it is largely liberatory. Migration has different meanings at different historical moments and for different peoples, but it also has a genealogy and a particular history of exploitation that retains meanings in the contemporary context.

Although exile, movement and migration have a long history, they also have particular meanings in recent times. This is expressed in what John Berger called the quintessential experience of the twentieth century: migration (1984). The movement of peoples across the globe does have a long history and certainly cannot be confined to the twentieth century, although during that century it came to achieve a particular status in relation to identity. The movement from one place to another has contributed to the development of 'identity politics' and the notion of 'identity crises'. Migration involves dislocation, between physical place, that is the space one occupies, and the emotional attachment or at least emotional meanings that are attached to the place one has left. Ernesto Laclau uses the idea of dislocation to explain the ways in which he sees modern societies as having no clear centre or core. He argues that social class, hitherto the central, overarching function of economic organization and determinant of all other forms of social relations, which gives meaning to identity has been de-centred. Class has been moved off centre by globalization and dislocation and there are now a multiplicity of centres; a mass of new places from which new identities can emerge (1990). Clearly this has positive as well as negative meanings. The dislocation of class opens up new political allegiances as well as traditional working class trade union activism to encompass other arenas of social conflict, such as those based on gender, ethnicity, race, disability or sexuality. Similarly movement across the globe has both negative and positive outcomes. Refugees are sometimes able to escape the horror of oppressive regimes in their own land and gain sanctuary in a new place and people do move to create more productive lives in more buoyant economies away from their own countries of origin.

Globalization

The impact and extent of globalization is strongly contested, but it clearly has a part to play in the movement of peoples and the dislocation of identities that took place in the twentieth century. How can we define globalization? Given that there is considerable disagreement, what areas of agreement might there be? Globalization involves:

- A multi-faceted process whereby connections between people in different places across the globe are becoming faster and more closely linked
- Movement of people, goods and services and information across the globe, characterized by scope, intensity and velocity.
- An explosion of global trade with the development of new communications and deregulation of markets and, especially within OECD (Organization for Economic Co-operation and Development) states a vast expansion in exports, employment and technology investment, controlled by multinational corporations.
- The reduction of sovereignty of nation states, although there has been a proliferation of the formation of nation states, for example following the break-up of the USSR.

- New relationships between the local and the global being developed through new networks and nodes.
- Global migrations including flows of refugees and asylum seekers on a massive scale.
- Environmental crises on a larger scale than ever before experienced, and there is the exacerbation of the perception of risk.

Globalization is frequently categorized by different dimensions, such as economic and political processes, social relations, the role of technologies or its environmental impact. Discussion of identity in relation to globalization has often focused on the demise of the importance of the nation state or of local cultures in shaping identities, and especially on the role of new technologies in opening up possibilities for the formation of identity. At the basis of this issue are questions about the extent to which it can be possible for people to rethink their identities and exercise any control over defining themselves, in the context of the all-encompassing forces of globalization. The scale and scope of the phenomena associated with globalization suggest that there are imbalances of power and that there might be a much stronger weighting in favour of the agency and control of some parts of the world and on the part of some protagonists. Some debates have focused on the imbalance between the local and the global and there are conceptualizations of the local global tension framed in the language of winners and losers (for further discussion see Held, 2000). Held himself posits an alternative to the extremes of the globalizers who see globalization as imposing enormous economic and political changes, and the opposing traditionalist view that argues that far from being a massive, new phenomenon, globalization has a long history and recent changes have not completely undermined state powers. His view supports the notion that 'globalization is creating new economic, political and social circumstances which are serving to transform state powers and the context in which states operate ... politics is no longer and can no longer be, simply based on nation-states' (2000: 3).

While globalization is clearly multi-facted, some facets have been given greater emphasis than others and those such as 'race' and gender, which are implicated in unequal relationships and contribute more to debates within development studies, have been subsumed or marginalized in the mainstream of globalization (Adam, 2002). Saskia Sassen has argued that gender and race are key components in the global political economy. For example, she shows how, in the global cities that are such crucial sites for the materialization of global processes (1998), most of the daily servicing jobs in the financial sectors are carried out by women, immigrants and people from minority ethnic groups, often all three in the same people, since they are, of course, overlapping groups. This work is an integral part of globalizing processes, although it is not always recognized as such.

There are optimistic and pessimistic approaches to globalization and some argue that its importance has been overestimated (Thompson, 2000). Globalization and the technologies associated with it, necessarily involve the transgression of national boundaries and an increasing transnational dimension to economic, social, political and cultural life. Anthony Giddens has stressed the plurality of globalization and its multi-dimensional processes. What he describes in his 1999 Reith lectures as a 'Runaway World', involves both the erosion of traditional boundaries as well as the increasingly interdependent aspects of globalization. He stresses the ways in which the world has become a single social system as a result of growing ties of interdependence with social, political and economic connections cross-cutting borders between countries and impacting on those living within them. Giddens acknowledges some of the inequities involved in these processes, but argues against the equation of globalization with Americanization and homogeneity and for an optimistic approach to globalization. He claims that processes involved in globalization open up opportunities more than they impose particularly dominant western, US, cultural practices and systems.

The rapid transmission of information across the globe and the spread of corporations, economic systems and cultures across national boundaries open up new networks through which new identities can be forged, as well as new modes of expansion, dominance and exploitation. Time-space compression is a feature of the twentieth and twenty-first centuries that has characterized the globalization of economic activities and the development of cultures of virtual reality through the transformation of communications systems. This happens through the internet and even the telephone, where call centres dealing with customers' queries about their accounts may be based thousands of miles from the customers who call them. In this sense space and time are shrinking. Information technologies facilitate very rapid communications across the globe and people can be physically transported in journeys that cover extensive distances in a very short time. Cultural products, films, music and television programmes are transmitted across the globe so that they are no longer the cultural property of one place. The key question now is not so much in what period in chronological time do we find ourselves, nor in what geographical space, but in what time-space (Bauman and May, 2001). The elision of time and space is a function and a transformative feature of globalization. However, the compression of time and space may, at times, be at the expense of the temporal element in the equation, with greater stress being placed on space and matter and material and monetary resources than on time and generation (Cwerner, 2000). Time in this relationship is the speed of communication, not the human temporality of history and of biography, encompassing birth, life and death; only time over space matters.

Manuel Castells has argued that the concept of the network is crucial to the global process of interconnection, for example through communications networks such as those of information technologies (1997). He suggests that the speed and efficiency of contemporary global communications networks create new power relationships. Networks provide a new material basis that can shape social structures themselves. According to Castells, the power of globally networked financial flows takes precedence over the flows of power (1996). However, there are significant differences between the experiences of different people. For example, taking up Potts' argument about globalized labour markets, women's experience of the networked society in developing countries is not the same as men's. If women are employed at all by trans-national corporations, they are likely to be employed in the most vulnerable posts and at the lowest levels of remuneration. Also, as Barbara Adam argues, for women in developing countries, 'when the torrent of networked financial flows rushes past you in a parallel universe, you may be thrown off balance by the accompanying waves, but for the rest of your life the established flows of power continue to reign supreme' (2002: 8). The point is not only that globalization involves uneven development and inequality, but that inequalities are experienced differently by different people and much of the globalization literature has omitted one of the most strongly experienced areas of difference, namely gender (Visvanathan et al., 1997).

Not everyone has equal access to the most powerful new technologies, although there may be some cultural democracy in the availability of new products and entertainment world-wide. While it may be possible for almost anyone around the world to watch Manchester United on satellite television and indeed to identify themselves as supporters of the club, and purchase ver-sions of the club strip, there are wide discrepancies between those who view and those who decide what is to be seen, and those who buy into the culture and those who make profits from communications networks. So powerful are these networks that it is probably unlikely that anyone reading this will have no idea what Manchester United football team and the whole commercial syn-ergy that accompanies it, are. Men's football offers a particularly good exam-ple of the globalization of culture, with the development of the men's game growing out of the relative autonomy of nation states' regulation and control of their own football associations. The English game, in spite of lack of success by the national team, which is still living, nostalgically off the glory of the 1966 World Cup victory, still plays a significant global role especially through the dominance of particular clubs, like Manchester United, with their associated cultural synergies. Men's football has huge capital investment, and until very recently, up to the crisis of ITV Digital, was cash rich from satellite television with enormous global media coverage, which has built on and massively extended grass roots support. Recent crises are unlikely to have much negative impact on the really big clubs though. By 1998 men's football's global appeal was indicated by the entry of 173 nations in the World Cup that year (Armstrong and Giulianotti, 1999). The 'World Cup' means the men's competition. It is only the Women's World Cup that is gendered in the naming, another indication of the ways in which globalization can appear to be gender neutral and conceal the very different and unequal experiences of women and men in the processes involved.

John Urry has gone further than Castells to refine and extend the language of networks, introducing the idea of scapes and flows. 'Scapes are the networks of machines, technologies and organizations, text and actors that constitute various interconnected nodes along which flows can be relayed' (2000: 35). The scapes include transportation of people and objects, satellites for radio and television, fibre-optic cables for telephone, television and computers. Flows 'consist of peoples, images, information, money and waste, that move within and especially across national borders and which individual societies are often unable to or unwilling to control directly or indirectly' (p. 36). Urry stresses the massive increase in the global flow of information that is playing a key role in restructuring societies at every level. Such technologies are not only available to the multi-nationals and to the west. Indeed it has been noted that computer technologies played a very significant part in the organization of the Al Quaeda terrorist attacks, notably 11 September, 2001 (Urry, 2002).

There has been less emphasis upon some human networks that now traverse the globe than upon those which feature global flows of information. For example the caring networks of women domestic workers has received less coverage and interest. What do these networks mean for the identities of those involved and of other relationships? Will Hutton notes the role of domestic workers, in a discussion on the impact of globalization with Anthony Giddens. Hutton comments that 'the growth in personal household services is the result of the emergence of two-earner households who have to buy in services because the woman is no longer at home' (in Lutz, 2002: 90). Whose identity are they talking about? Hutton makes the assumption that household tasks are women's responsibility and if the woman becomes a wage earner outside the home she has to buy in domestic work. Helma Lutz argues that the focus of the discussion is the white, professional, middle-class woman in the west who 'buys in' services (ibid.) and that Hutton and Giddens ignore the new categories of difference among women, which have arisen through globalization (ibid.: p. 90). Lutz argues that, although the phenomenon of employing domestic servants is a very ancient one, and 'globalization' and the transnationalization of life-courses have transformed these relationships in ways that most globalization and network theories cannot accommodate. While providing home comforts and care for their employers, domestic workers become providers and breadwinners for their own families back home, but issues arise about the care of those workers themselves in their old age, because of the new connections between the global and the local that have emerged. Domestic work is regarded as temporary employment and domestic workers are unlikely to have pension rights in the country where they work. Care workers also develop relationships with the children they look after and multiple identities and differently inflected relationships of caring and working are formed through these processes.

New networks have developed. Although the form and spread may offer new flows, the power relations may remain constant, for example, in the case of domestic service, where 90% of the workers are women (Lutz, 2002). However, in the twenty-first century, new relationships are also formed through the migration of women from postsocialist, Eastern Europe, Asia and South America. Globalized labour market and transnational migration movements feature particular and transforming gender, class and ethnic identities. There are differences within nation states and across Europe, which are also mapped out according to historical patterns that have developed within particular areas, for dealing with migrant workers and the need to recruit sufficient key workers. For example in some European countries there has been interest expressed in providing access, through green cards in Germany for example, for key information technology workers, whereas domestic workers are still recruited via the temporary route. Similarly, in the UK there have been recruitment drives for qualified health care workers and teachers to fill vacancies in these areas. By foregrounding gender, or at least including it in the discussion of globalization and network nodes, it is possible to explore the construction of new gendered identities. The 'push' and 'pull' factors which motivate migration in these global networks are complex. Domestic care workers experience both the push of lack of resources with which to support their families and the 'pull' of some, if limited financial gain; a temporary remedy for problems of the present. Similarly the agency that might be exercised in the shaping of new identities is multi-faceted and complicated. Anne Phizacklea argues that re-constructions of maternal identities that challenge some of the binaries of contemporary western understandings of motherhood, as either 'good' or 'bad' are produced through the migration of domestic workers (1998). When domestic workers leave their own children behind to look after another person's children in a different country, their care for their own children can only be expressed through the financial support that they are then able to provide by sending money home. The bond between mother and children is expressed through material support. The 'good mother' is one who provides for her children, but is not able to provide 'good mothering' on the western model of emotional and physical support, for example through physical contact. In fact the physical contact for domestic workers will be with the children they look after away from their own families. Domestic workers are not allowed to take their own children with them so cannot express closeness through touching and physical care. 'Good mothers' and 'good women' who star as domestic servants overseas may even be rewarded by recognition in their own country of origin, as in the Philippines, where domestic servants are seen as 'soldiers of the nation' (in Lutz: 100). It is not possible to understand the decisions made by care workers in simple terms of coercion or of rational choice, as if these were binary opposites and the one precluded any aspect of the other.

The notion of networks has been taken up in different ways, for example in order to explore the role of agency through actor network theories. Actor network theory uses the metaphor of the network to explore the construction of agency through 'a vision of many semiotic systems, many orderings, jostling together to generate the social' (Law, 1994: 18). In actor network theory, the social world comprises fragmented, intertwining networks. To act it is necessary to mobilize different things that are implicated in these interconnections. Things, other than human agents, such as objects, artefacts and texts can be involved in agency. Actor network theory breaks down the barriers between people and things and attributes what we call agency to things, to material culture. The human becomes de-centred so that it is no longer possible to state that the human is opposite to the non-human. As Bruno Latour says, some of the most firmly entrenched dualisms, animal/human and nature/culture are replaced by new hybrid representations (1993). Agents, who can be large organizations or individual subjects, and which can be things or objects, are relational effects. However, they are not unified effects; they are contingent achievements. As John Law says, 'Agency, if it is anything, is a precarious achievement' (p. 101). Actor network theory extends the metaphor of networks and offers further challenge to the binaries that characterize more grounded theories of identity, although it may also offer its own reification of the processes involved in the interconnections of networks. It is in the poststructuralist tradition in its emphasis on fluidity and contingency, which actor network theory extends to the notion of agency. There can be no essence, no notion of what is human or what constitutes human nature, beyond hybrid representations. Human nature for Latour is 'the set of its delegates and its representations, its figures and its messengers' (1993: 138).

The fluidity of networks offers new ways of addressing agency, providing both an empirical focus on global transformation and new ways of framing theoretical debates about the extent to which, in changing times people are able to shape their own identities and make sense of the changes that are taking place. Agency presents more of a problem for the explanation of some global networks, for example when networks highlight the significance of communications systems and the speed that so characterizes contemporary means of communicating. However, migration is not only about recent developments in communications systems. Our means and systems of understanding and of representing ourselves may have transformed, but there are other aspects involved in migration that are less well developed in network theories.

These theories offer a more limited contribution to the need for people to identify and to locate themselves with any degree of security through transformation and migration. Migration and the information network society involve complex and multi-dimensional relationships which cannot be explained simply in terms of winners and losers as in some theories of globalization. Nor can the over-emphasis on fluidity and the speed of communication flows of some network theories adequately accommodate some of the inequities and imbalances of power that are deeply implicated in globalizing processes. As Saskia Sassen has stressed, race and gender are frequently marginalized in globalization debates. Gender and race are core to the processes involved but also highlight some of the inequalities (1998), for example in care work. Another area of the global labour market that involves the global dislocation of women especially, is due to the creation of the demand for sex work, due to the developments of multiple sites for the operation of international business. It has also been the result of the spread of military bases, although this is not a new phenomenon. Ursula Biemann suggests that 'a new geography is being mapped by the recruitment of women among minorities and slum communities, their transportation along trafficking routes and across borders, abroad and off-shore for labour in the global sex industry. This geography maps the alternative circuits of survival in the margins of a pancapitalist reality' (2002: 86). She notes, however that trafficking operations are not all conducted by powerful syndicates at every level. 'They work in small units, relatives or acquaintances, who recruit girls in slum neighbourhoods, frequently there are bi-national couples who have good contacts to the source country' (ibid.: p. 87) so that the women are able to move to richer countries or to the cities. This is a multi-layered and complex process, which involves exploitation and inequality, but also negotiation within constraints, and denies a simple dualism of agency shaped by the structures of globalization.

As shown in the examples of care work and sex work, gender and ethnicity are part of the strategic nexus between developing economies and western capitalist activities, which are essential to the successful operations of the global processes of corporate capital. Theories of globalization and the network society offer some insights into the ways in which people reform and reconstruct their identities in a changing world, even a 'runaway world', but there are other ways of interpreting change and migration, which provide a different, though complementary focus. Another way of understanding migration, movement and identity, which has a longer history, is the notion of diaspora.

Diaspora identities

In the Jewish Museum in Berlin, there is a child's painting entitled, *Von der Alten Heimat zu Der Neuen Heimat!* Translated into English, this is 'from the old home to the new home'. It was painted by Fritz Freudenheim, when he was twelve, and depicts the journey taken by him and his family when they emigrated from Berlin to Uruguay in 1938. The journey took over a month and during the voyage the boy painted a picture which shows the ship they travelled on occupying the whole of the centre of the picture. This lies between their destination, South America, very large on the left of the painting and Germany, which they had left along the top of the painting, with a large 'Deutchsland' on the right, about the same size as the continent of Africa, at which they called briefly en route, on the bottom right. 'There was a map of the world on the ship and every day an officer marked the spot we had reached with a little flag. This map gave me the idea of doing a drawing, which turned into more of a travel diary', Fritz Freudenheim recalled in 1998 (Stiftung Judiches Museum Berlin, 2001: 49). The painting is about the Jewish diaspora. Freudenheim's painting gives expression to the tension of diaspora; the leaving of the place that was called home and the hope that is expressed in knowing that there will be a new home. Diaspora involves movement and transition, which is clearly represented by the ship, which dominates the picture. Diaspora is symbolized in the movement embodied in the ship. The Jewish Museum in Berlin presents a very particular political and cultural context for the representation of the 2000-year history of German Jewish people. As the director of the museum, Michael Blementhal argues, the museum 'symbolizes a determination to confront the past and to gain a perspective on the societal problems of the present and the future ... This museum is thus the result of the efforts of succeeding generations in Germany to examine the past, knowing that without memory there can be no future' (ibid.: p. 1). The exhibitions and the architecture focus on the opening and closing of cultural borders and the relationship across time between Jewish and non-Jewish peoples in Germany, including the disastrous fractions in that relationship, has particular resonance. The Jewish diaspora is characterized by exile, but the movement is not only a movement *from*, it is a movement *to*; even in the 1930s Jewish people were moving to a new life, as well as leaving, in this case, the threat of death and extermination. The Jewish Museum with its architectural design based around an axis of continuity and cross-cutting axes of exile and of the holocaust, explores the experience of diaspora through the metaphor of the museum building itself. Visitors to the museum are invited to contemplate the experience of diaspora as they walk along the different lines of thinking,

Firstly there is the straight, but fragmented line of the continuity of Jewish history, intersected by the lines of exile and holocaust and interrupted by empty spaces or voids which rise vertically at different points in the museum. Even when the emphasis is on exile and the compulsion to leave home, there is also the hope of making a new life and of finding a new home. The ship as the metaphor for movement and possibility signifies those hopes.

Diasporic identities include those that are formed through movement and the process of dispersal, the scattering of people across the globe. As Stuart Hall has described it:

> Diaspora refers to the scattering and dispersal of people who will never literally be able to return to the places from which they came; who have to make some kind of difficult settlement with the new often oppressive cultures with which they were forced into contact, and who have succeeded in remaking themselves and fashioning new kinds of cultural identity by consciously or unconsciously, drawing on more than one cultural repertoire ... They are people who belong to more than one, speak more than one language (literally and metaphorically); inhabit more than one identity, have more than one home; who have learned to 'negotiate and translate' between cultures and who ... have learned to live with, and indeed to speak from difference. They speak from the in-between of different cultures, always unsettling the assumptions of one culture from the perspective of the other, and thus finding ways of being both the same as and different from the others amongst which they live, Of course, such people bear the marks of the particular cultures, languages, histories and traditions which 'formed' them ...
>
> They represent new kinds of identities ... beginning to think of themselves, of their identities and their relationship to culture and to place in these more open ways (Hall, 1995: 47–8).

Hall argues that this is a new way of looking at Anderson's idea of 'imagined communities'. By using the term 'diaspora' in an open, positive way, Hall suggests that to see diaspora as involving the attempts of dispersed peoples to identify with their country of origin, implies closure. Maintaining the link with the past closes down future reconstructions of identity. Hall challenges both the possibility and the usefulness of hanging onto the desire to return home.

Paul Gilroy has used the metaphor of the ship to indicate the sense of motion that is involved in movement of peoples in the spaces between Europe, America, Africa and the Caribbean. The child leaving Germany might have given the ship priority in his painting, because he was on the ship when he painted the picture, but it also has enormous significance as the means of escape from the one place and the means of reaching the next, the new home. 'The image of a ship – a living micro-cultural, micro-political system in motion – is especially important for historical and theoretical reasons' (1993: 4). As Gilroy argues, 'Ships immediately focus attention on the middle passage, on the various projects for redemptive return to an African homeland' (p. 4). The emphasis is on mobility and fluidity and provides a complex means of exploring the relationship with home for people of the diaspora, without fixity and closure.

However, the stress on movement, fluidity and the moment of transition may underplay the reasons for flight from home having been undertaken in the first place. Dispersal occurs for a variety of reasons, which include both 'push' and 'pull' factors. There are strong economic incentives to move into areas that are seen as more affluent or more productive and as offering more potential for advancement or even in some instances simply a better chance of survival. The notion of diaspora has been reinterpreted from its biblical origins and its basis in the experience of the Jewish diaspora. As the example of the Jewish diaspora showed above, there are historical moments when the threats that trigger exile are so strong that it is hard to imagine that there could still be hope of a new home. Gilroy emphasizes the push factors in this dispersal of peoples, for example in the case of the movement of people from Africa. The modern African diaspora was only achieved through the historical imposition of slavery. As Gilroy argues, 'push factors, like war, famine, enslavement, ethnic cleansing, conquest and political repression, are a dominant influence. The urgency they introduce makes diaspora more than a voguish synonym for wandering or nomadism: life itself is at stake in the way that the word connotes flight following the threat of violence rather than freely chosen experiences of displacement' (1997: 318). Here, the creation of a diaspora consciousness is the result of traumatic experiences of slavery, genocide and pogroms rather than more egalitarian, democratic reconstructions of the self in new common territories. This notion of diasporic consciousness carries considerable weight, especially in its stress on the need for displaced peoples to reconstruct their identities in new places, without ever being able to appeal to the authority and authenticity of some fixed past. However, as Gilroy is aware, the weighting that is given to diasporic identities forged through suffering and exploitation may also carry the burden of victimhood, which it is difficult to combine with the autonomy and strength that should come with newly reconstructed identities. Diaspora has the advantage of offering a more complex mix of factors to underpin movement and change and to permit the reformulation of identities in new spaces, without demanding the necessity of tying identity to the roots of land and blood. Diaspora allows for the dynamism of movement and migration without tying identities down to a primordial, essentialist past, because diaspora includes history and the temporal and spatial specificities of identity formation and the routes that identities travel. While there have been historical moments when it has been necessary to stress the fixity of otherness, there are different meanings attached to this as a strategy, rather than as an appeal to absolute truths of identity. Diaspora offers a means of mapping the self in relation to the places that contribute to the sense of identity. As I have argued identity is closely linked to place, to key places and often to the place that we call home. In this sense the map is a useful metaphor for understanding the formation and representation of identity in relation to location and situation as well as movement and translation.

Maps

Maps chart the journeys we have taken and symbolize places along the routes that we traverse. Maps are abstractions that are constantly being reformulated

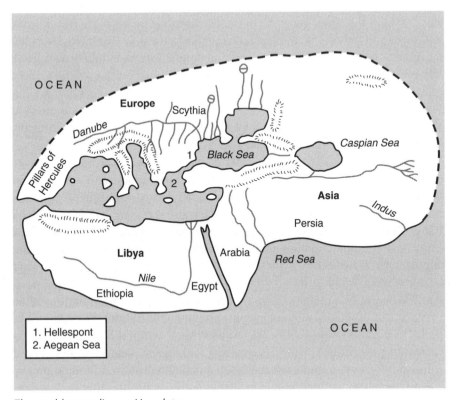

The world according to Herodotus.

in relocating boundaries and political meanings. A map is not a simple reflection. Even the new 'Millennium' maps, which use aerial photographs providing a seemingly representational patchwork of the ground, where the image merges with the symbolic, require translation. They have to be read through symbolic systems. They are not simple uncoded reflections that reproduce what is there. We have to interpret the image, read its code and deconstruct its messages.

Journeys involve movement, yet the map appears as a static representation, fixed at an historical moment, albeit one, which we know can be reconstructed in different circumstances. The map involves selection by the cartographer, as well as interpretation by the map-reader.

The classical historian of antiquity, Herodotus, is accredited with producing this map of the known world in the fifth century before the birth of Christ. The source of the map is unknown but it is based on Herodotus' writings in his *Histories*. It illustrates well the selectivity involved in the production of a map. This map indicates some of the problems of the notion of the 'known world'. In a sense, it is clearly all that was known of the globe to the ancient Greeks. Britain and the Americas had not been 'discovered' so are not included. More significantly, it brings out what was deemed important at the time, the areas in the Mediterranean, what are now known as Greece and Italy are recognizable to the modern eye. Only North Africa has a presence, but the River Nile is clearly of significance, most likely because of the enormous impact which Egyptian civilization had on that of the ancient Greeks. We put in what counts. Martin Bernal, in his book *Black Athena*, has argued that what he calls the 'Aryan model' of ancient Greek civilization as the pure, uncontaminated source of European culture only emerged in the 1840s and 1850s mainly in Germany, but also in other parts of Europe, including the UK. The earlier model of ancient Greek culture, as derived from that of the Egyptians became effaced in the nineteenth century, but is acknowledged in this map attributed to Herodotus. Egypt certainly has a presence in this representation. Certain areas are marked out and named. Herodotus' map may suggest a somewhat crude illustration of the point but the point applies to other, more recent versions. Maps are not simple reflections even of the landmass they represent, but are selective constructions, which offer a path through meanings. Maps have a purpose. It could be political purpose in mapping out the boundaries of nation states, the limits of empire or physical geography or roads, railway lines and flight paths, to provide people with a way of working through their journey. Just as cartographers produce maps in accordance with the political meanings of their time, so peoples construct their identity journeys with pivotal moments and boundaries that have particular resonance for the identities that they seek to reproduce.

Mapping can also be quite explicitly creative, as the following account indicates.

> The Surrealists published an idiosyncratic world map in 1929, enlarging or dwarfing terrain in accordance with their aesthetic principles. The area beneath the equator was for them subliminal and savage, like the human body below the waistline; their cartography favoured places with luridly irrational histories. New Zealand was expanded, because it had earthquakes and cannibals. Easter Island, with its stone totems, grew as big as South America. Australia, boringly British, dwindled to the size of the New Hebrides (Conrad, 2000: 27).

How far can we go in reconstructing space? The wild musings of the Surrealists might be expected, by definition, to be exaggerated and extreme, but this example illustrates the ways in which meanings can be differently weighted through the creation of a map. Peter Conrad, writing about contemporary Australian identity, goes on to translate the Surrealist extravaganza into a present day representation that could reflect cultural reconstructions.

> If this subjective map were redrawn today, Australia would have to be inflated, pushing aside all those upstart Pacific islands. Nicknamed Oz, and situated as far from flat-minded monochrome Kansas as you can get, it has become a magnet for the fantasies of the upper hemisphere (p. 27).

Mapping and its metaphors have profound resonance in many of the ways in which we construct ourselves. Constructing the self is made meaningful through mapping practices that select key moments and pivotal points in the narrative of identity.

Bruno Latour has used the notion of cartography as a means of mobilizing worlds and producing meanings through mapping practices (1987). This is illustrated by Donna Haraway and applied to science. She cites the example of the human genome project which draws on the technologies of cartography. Referring back to the 'Age of Exploration' Haraway cites the practice of drawing on the rhetoric of cartography in the discourses of technoscience. She quotes *Science* magazine,

> Just as the ancient navigators depended on maps and charts to explore the unknown, investigators today are building maps and charts with which to explore new scientific frontiers ([1990] 2000b: 128).

Not only might we seek to understand ourselves through mapping identity, meanings are produced through the mapping metaphors which constitute the identities which are possible. Yet, while maps may change, according to the purpose of those who produce them, they are for a moment fixed and inscribed. Maps can carry the status of objectivity, through formalizing what may be intuitive knowledge (Matless, 1995). Once that knowledge is mapped it becomes subject to codes and regulations and in this way mapping the self goes further than retelling the story and producing narrative accounts of identity. Maps represent another way of attempting to pin down identity, to structure what matters by picking out the key places, the main links and attempting to secure them. Maps chart what matters, where we have been and where we are going.

Changing places; placing changes

On 22 June 1948 a ship called the *Empire Windrush* arrived at Tilbury docks in London from Jamaica; 492 people, the vast majority of whom were men, perhaps there were a dozen women, disembarked. This moment has been seen as symbolic of the transformation of Britain from a mono-cultural, pre-dominantly white society to a multi-racial, multi-cultural one. Of course this is an over-statement. People from the Jewish diaspora, from Africa, Asia, the Arab world and the Caribbean as well as people from different parts of Europe, including Ireland have long since had a presence, especially in the ports and cities of the UK, but *Windrush* carries a symbolic importance. For example, at the time of the 50th anniversary of the arrival of *Windrush* in the UK it was argued that this was a moment when the idea of 'empire' took on new meanings for millions of British people, those already living in the UK and those who had arrived from other places (Lewis and Young, 1998). Whereas 'other places' had meant 'there', from 1948, 'other places' meant 'here'. The arrival of relatively large numbers of British citizens from the Caribbean had an impact on the representation of visible difference in UK. The people who left the *Windrush* could be seen as signifying a different relationship for both those from the Caribbean and those who were already in the UK. For people already in the UK, it meant recognizing the reality of Empire and Common-wealth as part of the UK, embodied and in place. For those arriving it meant a situated understanding of the place that many might have seen as 'home' too as the mother country, as well as their own homes in the Caribbean. This migration could be seen as the start of the opening up of questions about what it meant to be British. Other members of the Commonwealth followed, from Africa and Asia as well as the Caribbean and this can be seen as a pivotal moment in the initiation of the process of reconfiguring Britishness as an iden-tity, in a process whereby some ambiguities and contradictions were made more explicit. Homi Bhabha argues that the arrival of postcolonial peoples within the territory of the colonial power is a crucial moment in shaping identities formed through the reconstruction of the relationship between those who migrate from the peripheries to the colonial metropolitan centre. This forces a rethinking of identity and nation and especially of the limitations of the liberal sense of community (1990: 219).

I would not want to overstate the meanings attached to a particular historical moment but the arrival of those whose migration to the UK was heralded by their disembarking from the *Windrush* can be used as an example, which has particular resonance in the history of migration in the UK, so long as it is remembered that the UK is a very diverse population with a very long and varied history of migration.

Windrush presents a useful illustration of some of the aspects of identity in relation to journeys and mapping the self, which have been considered in this chapter. In this instance there are several different places on the map; there is not a simple passage from the Caribbean to the UK. The Caribbean offers diverse ethnicities and the islands of the Caribbean are also peopled by those who were compelled to travel from other continents, notably Africa. This, like most of the journeys we take in forging identity, is not a simple journey from one fixed location of identity to another. Not only is the 'home' in the Caribbean that has been left a complex, multi-layered construction with a particular history, but there is a strong sense in which those who came to the UK in 1948 (and those who have come since from Commonwealth countries) saw themselves as 'coming home'. Britain was home. In very different circumstances, this is another case of leaving the old home to come to the new, although as the 'mother country' Britain might have not only offered feelings of entitlement, but the security and familiarity of home. Many Commonwealth citizens and colonized peoples were very familiar with the rites and rituals of Britain and the codes and practices through which Britishness was expressed across the globe, and especially within her colonies.

Although migration very often involves push factors so powerful in instigating flight from the home that it is difficult to accommodate pull factors in the equation, for example as experienced in the exile from Africa through slavery, those who left the Caribbean on the *Windrush* had high expectations of the life they could lead in Britain. Indeed some of the people who arrived in London were surprised to see signs of poverty where they had expected universal affluence (Lewis and Young, 1998). The expectations were of belonging because these were subjects of Britain; there was awareness of the legal obligations of the mother country. There were also the pull factors of aspiration to a better life with a higher standard of living as well as expectations of inclusion in British society, although their reception might have been rather more uncertain. David Sibley describes a photograph taken by Roger Mayne of a London street in the late 1940s, which well sums up the contrast between these expectations and the actual experience. It also gives a feeling of the response of the Londoners who might have been puzzled at the new arrivals.

> ... some white working-class children look with obvious curiosity on a group of African Caribbean men in a London street. One of the men turns to the camera but the others walk across the picture, past the children, looking ahead. The street is shabby. The peeling stucco terraces do not bear visible signs of any culture, although other pictures in the collection clearly depict the district as a white working-class neighbourhood, populated by mums in head scarves, children swinging from lamp-posts and posing groups of teenagers with Brylcreemed hair. The photograph presents black men in transit, as if they do not belong, but as a source of curiosity rather than the subject of overt racism (1998: 119).

Sibley contrasts this scene with one depicted 40 years on, of the Chapeltown area of Leeds, which might be classified as the 'black inner city'; a space that combines stereotypical assumptions about 'good' and 'bad' people and the built environment. The scene, with its Caribbean fast food stores and hairdresser's shop is dominated by a CCTV camera. He notes that in the 1990s, this area which had been 'a space secured by black young men in the 1970s and 1980s but [was] now broken up and dispersed by the control apparatus of the state' (ibid.: p. 120). These images contrast. In the first there is bemusement, surprise on the part of those newly arrived and of existing Londoners. The outcome is unknown. The second image tells a particular story of the representation of black identities and appears to exclude the notion of being black and British. Sibley goes on to explore the ways in which space connects with identity and the tension between constructions of the 'black inner city' and the 'idyll of rural sanctuary', with the idealized notion of an unsullied English countryside representing 'true Englishness'. The fixing of this rural space, contrasted with the diversity of the urban context and so strongly associated with Empire, 'in which all heterogeneity and difference is suppressed, signals the exclusion of all racialized minorities (and several others)' (ibid.: p. 127). His aim is to challenge the fixity of identity and especially the racism that is associated with such processes. What Stuart Hall has described as the English identity that was characterized by the image of the white male stiff upper lip (1991) would have been familiar not only to men who had fought in the British military, but also to all people who had lived in the countries colonized in the British Empire. Many of the men who disembarked from the *Windrush* would indeed have fought as British soldiers in the Second World War. The historically and culturally specific identity associated with white, upper-class Englishness is one which has been challenged by recent phases of globalization and in this example was challenged by the arrival of the passengers aboard the *Windrush*. This journey, like all the other identity journeys that have been mapped out has temporal as well as spatial dimensions. The identity journey involved in reconfiguring Britishness takes place over time and in relation to the past, and in particular to past construction of what it meant to be British. There has been an elision between Britishness and Englishness that also forms part of the identity story that has had to be renegotiated. The histories of the nations that make up the British Isles have frequently been subsumed into a national identity that assumes an English dominance. The journeys of multi-culturalism made in the last 50 years of the twentieth century were made alongside those of the reforging of the national identities of the Irish, Northern Irish, Scottish and Welsh people as well as a rethinking of what it meant to be English.

So what has happened to British identity in this period? What light can the *Windrush* example shed on the ways in which Britishness might have been renegotiated? Sibley's depiction of the representation of the city suggests a rather depressing scenario, ranging from initial disappointment to later exclusion. There have been significant changes in British society that the visible presence of so many different people as well as important changes in the formation of cultural identities have effected. There are myriad instances of racism but there have also been key moments of inclusion and the movement towards the possibility of being black and British. There are visible differences in the UK landscape. Equal Opportunities policies in the workplace have replaced the signs of the 1950s that proclaimed 'No blacks, no Irish' in the windows of accommodation available to rent. Contemporary Britain has had to negotiate with its past and there continue to be deeply troubled moments. Extreme acts of racist violence continue alongside the movement towards greater inclusion.

What the *Windrush* signalled was a key historical moment. It also heralds the recognition of multiple identities and of diversity. Although there is a very wide range of different ethnic groups within the UK, having very different identities in many ways there is also a sharing of multiplicity and of heterogeneity that means people are 'in the same boat'. Roshi Naidoo argues for a recognition of the sharing of multiple identities which a celebration of *Windrush* could demonstrate, while allowing for the differences between people. 'To be a member of an "immigrant" community in Britain is to hold together many identity positions at once: for example, one may call oneself "black" at a political rally, Gujerati at a social function, and British at the passport control at Heathrow airport, and not necessarily be tormented by competing subjective voices ... As we reach the end of the millennium, different "black" cultures in Britain are coming of age in many ways. New political imaginings, cultural styles and languages open up the spaces where Britishness intersects with varied diasporic heritages, to create vibrant and resilient identities' (1998: 178–9).

Windrush illustrates the need to reconfigure identities through migration and the movement of people and to renegotiate British identity through the ambiguities of place. This involves re-mapping the self and ourselves. Changing times and changing places mean that this has to be effected through accommodating difference and diversity in a way that leaves space for positive, optimistic readings of multi-cultural, multi-racial identities, like Naidoo's above. The journeys already made cannot be ignored and the experience of racism and exclusion not only have a past, they are part of contemporary life in the UK, as has been experienced on several tragic occasions, including the murder of Stephen Lawrence.

Conclusion

Movement and migration have impact on changing selves and on the different ways in which it becomes possible to represent ourselves. Mass movements of people across the globe are a major feature of contemporary world politics. Mass movements shape international relations and those within communities. Globalization unpacks nation states from within as well as transforming the transnational arena. Migration has a long history and there are continuities in the application of attempts to understand the significance of mobility and movement in the shaping of identity. Migration always has a relationship with home and new identities are formed in some dialogue with home, whatever the reasons for leaving, and however far home is an imaginary construction which tells us more about people's hopes and desires than about any actual experience or history. While the longing for home may appear to represent fixity, stability and the desire for certainty, it may be more about the desire than the location. The journeys we take bridge reality and the imaginary. The notion of 'home' in particular crosses the boundaries between the real and the imagined and between the past, the present and the hoped for future. Home is the place we are going to as well as the place from which we have come. It is because of the strength of the desire to have some notion of a home where we belong that there can be such strong identification with territory and with place, so that identities are more often constructed in relation to the place we have come from than the place we might be going to. When peoples migrate there is always mobility and fluidity, but the over-emphasis on hybridity in some accounts may fail to explain the ways in which identities are forged in the new home.

We are selective about the places that matter and the journeys that make us who we are and who we want to be. The Surrealists' map only draws into relief the fantasies we weave about the journeys we make and the places that are significant in those journeys. More primitive cartography too, illustrates the ways in which there are some places on the map and some points in the journey that assume greater importance in relation to identity than others. However, maps are not only imaginary and identities are not only imagined homelands. Maps also represent land and territory and longing is transformed into belonging to a physical place, in material circumstances that also shape experience. Journeys are made across time and space and many of the appeals that are made to home as a source of identity that supports the authenticity of that which is claimed in the present are linked to histories and the stories we tell about the past. Collective identities as well as those of individuals are supported through history as well, by mapping out the points that support the claims that are made in locating who we are.

Histories are constructed, retold and enacted through narratives and through rituals. As many people who lined the streets of London in April 2002, witnessing the funeral of Queen Elizabeth, the Queen Mother, said, 'We want to be part of history'. This state funeral was perceived as a significant historic event; as one of those moments when the 'imagined community' of the nation comes together through those who watched the funeral cortège, who signed books of remembrance and who watched the television coverage. The rituals of state at such a time draw on past practices and, through symbolic systems and practices construct history, producing meanings about the nation's past. A state funeral draws on particular symbols, notably of military history and practice. The crown that was laid on the Queen Mother's coffin in which the famous Indian Koh-i-Nor diamond was set, was worn by her in 1938 as Empress of India. This suggests that the colonial part has more than a ghostly presence in contemporary rituals. Such symbols are a key part of the means through which the identity of the nation as well as of the individual are represented. Those who participated in various ways by attending the funeral wanted to be 'part of history' and to be represented as well as to see how the nation and its heroes are represented. How do we represent ourselves and what is the role of representation in the formation and presentation of identity? This is the focus of the next chapter.

4 Re-presenting identities

In this chapter I want to look in more detail at some of the ways in which identities are presented and represented. How are identities represented and reproduced symbolically, through the words, images, practices and material culture though which we make sense of who we are? What processes are involved in the construction of meanings through representational systems? The other framing question of this chapter relates to the book's concern with the extent to which people are able to secure and stabilize their identities. Can representational systems offer any certainty in establishing and securing identities? Or, indeed, how can representational systems be used to destablize and subvert the fixity of identity?

It is through representational systems that we make sense both of ourselves and of others. It is through such systems that others make sense of us; representational systems provide the means of classification. People mark themselves out as the same as or different from others, and are so categorized, through the language they use, the way they speak, the words, images and symbols they deploy, including the clothes they wear and the practices, rites and rituals in which they engage. Representation is crucial to the marking of both difference and sameness. It is through all the different aspects of representation, including language, practice, performance and display, that we mark ourselves out as belonging. This is an everyday process, not only one which is part of macro-level exchange, for example which differentiates between nations and cultures. Identities are forged through the cultural practices and symbols through which meanings are made.

As Judith Williamson writes:

> When I rummage through my wardrobe in the morning I am not merely faced with the choice of what to wear. I am faced with the choice of images: the difference between a smart suit and a pair of overalls, a leather skirt and a cotton skirt, is not one of fabric and style, but one of identity. You know perfectly well that you will be seen differently for the whole day,

depending on what you put on; you will appear as a particular kind of woman with one particular identity which excludes others. The black leather skirt rather rules out girlish innocence, oily overalls tend to exclude sophistication … often I have wished I could put them all on together – just to say, 'how dare you think any of these is me'. But also, see, I can be all of them (1986: 91).

This illustrates the way in which our identities are mapped out and re-presented through the material items which we choose to wear and in particular by what they mean in the wider social context. This is an instance of imagining ourselves as we will be seen and considering the social and cultural meanings that these symbols of our identity carry. Choice, of course, is mediated by a whole range of constraints, including the resources we have to fill our wardrobes with different items that might carry different symbolic meanings and represent our identities to others. Cultural, religious and ethnic factors intersect in particular historical contexts, where choice of clothing can have very strong impact, especially for women. As the Moroccan sociologist and writer Fatima Mernissi has argued, in Islamic countries clothing carries powerful meanings. She describes the growing occupation with women's appearance through the 1980s as well as the ways in which Muslim women's groups have embraced the veil as a sign of political protest against western imperialist corruption (1991). Clothes carry considerable weighting in the representation of identities.

The symbols that are deployed in the process of representing ourselves and who we are, involve the minutiae of everyday life as well as the grand signifiers of collective identities, for example as embodied in the flag and the rituals of state and nation. The two levels of the macro and the global and the micro and the more personal are not entirely separate; they are far from distinct and distant. It is often in the minutiae of daily life that the most wide reaching differences of identity are represented.

Michael Ignatieff, in his book *Blood and belonging*, draws on the work of Sigmund Freud to explore some of the contradictions of identity in the late twentieth century conflicts the former Yugoslavia. He describes an exchange between himself and a Serbian militiaman in what he calls a 'village war' between Serbs and Croats. Ignatieff addresses the question of why neighbours, who have known each other all their lives, attended the same schools, eaten the same food, watched the same television programmes and smoked the same brand of cigarettes, are trying to kill each other. Ignatieff tries to account for how the Serb and the Croat conceive their differences. The Serbian man, taking a packet of cigarettes out of his pocket, tells him, 'See this? These are Serbian cigarettes. Over there they smoke Croatian cigarettes' (1994: 1). As Ignatieff comments, 'the smaller the real differences between two groups, the larger such differences are likely to loom in their imagination. Or to put the point in dynamic terms, as real differences between groups diminish, symbolic imagined differences become more salient ... nationalism has turned the imagined differences between them into an abyss which can only be filled by gunfire' (1994: 6). Ignatieff is making a distinction between real and symbolic differences, which might be contested, but the important point here is that he is pointing to the profound meanings that become attached to minor differences between people which are represented symbolically and which take hold of the imagination. 'The differences between Serb and Croat are tiny – when seen from the outside – but from the inside, they are worth dying for *because* someone will kill you for them' (p. 7). The symbolic systems through which these minor differences are imagined are crucial to the process of their magnification, to such an extent that people will indeed kill in the name of these differences, are not only the product of individuals' imaginations, They are public symbols. 'The war in Yugoslavia actually began in the newspapers and television of Zagreb and Belgrade' (p. 10). Ignatieff argues that 'as consumption patterns and life styles converge among human groups, they insist more violently on the marginal differences which divide them' (p. 6). These differences are also part of a global economy of cultural exchange that represents difference in ways that are imagined and experienced in the construction of personal identity.

Broadly we make our own identities and those of others meaningful through representational systems. This may give some indication of how it works. However, it is far from being a simple process! I want to argue, in what has become part of a tradition within cultural studies, that the symbolic systems through which we represent others and ourselves are not simple reflections of some external grounded truth. There is no easy or even possible distinction between the material circumstances in which identities are produced and what it is possible to represent. Symbolic systems are implicated in the process of constructing meaning about who we are.

Meanings may not be shared. The marking of one's own social identity position in opposition to another, which is then classified as 'other' or outsider may involve a complete failure to share meanings. This was illustrated in the example of political rhetoric following 11 September at the start of this book. The experience of differentiation of one collective identity, that of the USA was marked out as different from another identity, that of the terrorist, who at that point could not even be named. There was no shared meaning. The 'enemy' was not only 'the other' – the enemy was incomprehensible. This example illustrates the tension between how we choose to represent ourselves and how others represent us. As was illustrated in Chapters 2 and 3, people seek to negotiate their own identities and to represent others, yet constantly they have to renegotiate or attempt to resist the ways in which they are represented by others, or as 'other' in many cases. The terrain of conflict in the formation and establishment of identities in this chapter is that of representational systems.

A cultural turn

Representational systems are part of culture. Raymond Williams writes about culture as 'the signifying system through which ... a social order is communicated, reproduced, experienced and explored' (1981: 18). For Williams culture is constitutive of other social processes. It does not merely reflect or represent them. Culture is a term that has a variety of meanings and applications, including the distinction between 'high' and 'low' culture. This distinction was somewhat value laden, with those activities, practices and representational systems classified as 'high' culture being more highly valued than those classed as 'low'. This was the sort of distinction that might have claimed that opera was 'high' culture and popular music was 'low'. This was a dichotomy that was challenged by the 'cultural turn' in the social sciences (Hall, 1997). My use here involves more of the anthropological understanding of culture, which includes all that characterizes the way of life of a group of people, whether this is a community, a nation or any other social group. Anthropology is concerned with finding out about how particular groups of people make sense of their lives and the symbols and practices that they deploy that may be distinctive to them and characteristic of their way of life. Culture includes all the ways we have of making sense and of making meanings. Hence, the 'cultural turn' meant asking questions about how people interpret the world and what meanings are given to the things people do and say. This understanding of culture might also appear to stress shared meanings and the ways in which people who share a culture might have a common set of understandings about the world they live in. Language is deeply implicated in the process of making meaning, although culture includes much more, in terms of practices, images, symbols and other sensory experience. Language has a key role in our interpretation of the world, although sharing a language does not necessarily involve sharing a culture. Language is an important means of communication and in the construction of meaning about all aspects of experience.

This makes culture pretty ubiquitous. It would be difficult to position anything outside culture. This is not an uncontested view. The ubiquity of culture could be seen to challenge the material basis of social relations and social divisions. However, Stuart Hall has argued that culture is the 'lived practices' or 'practised ideologies which enable a society, group or class to experience, define interpret and make sense of its conditions of existence' (1982: 7). He maintains that it is possible to hold onto the material basis of social relations while acknowledging that culture is implicated in all such relations. The so-called 'cultural turn' in the social sciences has led to a shift in the kinds of questions that are asked, that can be asked in relation to social relations and experience (Hall, 1997). The emphasis has moved towards a greater concern with meanings and how meanings are produced, rather than taking meanings as fixed and incontrovertible. The cultural turn has also led to a focus on cultural matters which has become far removed from any material base in a Marxist sense or even in the metaphysical sense of a material world as having precedence over the realm of ideas, as we shall see in the discussion of visual culture below. Hall's argument is not that culture replaces the material, but that the material cannot be separated into a 'real' world outside culture that is unmediated by the ways in which people make sense of that world. This argument is well illustrated within the framework of the 'circuit of culture', a device drawn from the work of Richard Johnson (1986) but developed by du Gay, Hall and their co-writers (1997). This circuit includes the key interrelated 'moments' of representation, identity, production, consumption and regulation, all of which are involved in the interrogation of any text or artefact. They take the example of the Sony Walkman and argue that this artefact is represented in particular ways that produce associated identities, which are themselves implicated in the production processes. Again production is influenced by the consumption of the artefact and the whole circuit is subject to regulatory processes. This device of the 'cultural circuit' allows for the development of a cultural theory that incorporates the impact of production but does not prioritize production as the starting point or as the most influential moment in the process. Meanings are created through the interrelationship of these different moments. For example the Sony Walkman is a cultural artefact that is produced through certain technical processes, financed through particular economic systems but made meaningful through the impact of consumption on production and through the ways in which it is represented and regulated. Representational systems play a key part in these processes, especially in relation to the ways in which identities are constituted and experienced. Before going onto to look at some examples of the processes involved in the re-presentation of identity, it is worth revisiting some of the steps along the way and some of the precursors to the 'cultural turn' in order to relate this to the understanding of identity.

The science of signs

Ferdinand de Saussure has been seen as the founder of structural linguistics and as playing a key role in the development of our understanding of the ways in which representational systems operate. His work is particularly relevant here because of his contribution to our understanding of identity formation. His work further compounds the attack on the unified, centred subject of Cartesian thinking. Following Saussure, it can no longer be maintained that individual consciousness is the origin of meaning, knowledge and action. As in psychoanalytic thinking, after Freud the subject is not unitary but split and in Saussure's work this is explained through the ways in which language 'speaks us' rather than our speaking language. Thus it is language, as a symbolic system that speaks or produces meaning through writing and not the author, whether as speaker or writer. Language is crucial to the production of identity for Saussure and the structuralist tradition that followed. It is through language that we are constructed and that we come to know who we are. Language as a key symbolic system locates us in terms of class, ethnicity and gender through the meanings conferred upon these identities. Language is not confined to lexical items but encompasses a symbolic system that includes images as well as words. However, Saussure's focus was on the detailed examination of representation in practice and especially on the more formal aspects of language per se.

Saussurian semiotics have to some extent passed into popular culture in a variety of fields, rather as psychoanalytic concepts such as 'Freudian slips' and the unconscious have become common parlance in many areas of life, from problem pages to films and television and self-help groups. People may not be aware of the specific strategies of Saussurian linguistics, but they are conscious of the ways in which products are promoted through association of ideas. For example, market research and advertising draw heavily, not only on the notion of unconscious desires and feelings, but on the idea of coded meanings, with one object standing for another through the association of ideas. These range from the somewhat crude juxtaposition of the beautiful woman with the car suggesting that the vehicle guarantees particularly successful heterosexual masculinity for the purchaser to much more subtle and complex associations. Advertisers are self-conscious about semiotics, which has become so taken for granted that they play with associations, to which an increasingly sophisticated buying public responds. Sexual signifiers provide the most glamorous associations in the marketing of all sorts of unlikely products, but these have become more self-consciously self-referential and ambivalent in recent years. Calvin Klein plays with androgyny in the promotion of its perfume, quite consciously subverting gendered stereotypes with representations of cool young people of indeterminate gender identities, and French Connection uses the initial letters of its French Connection UK branch to disrupt the perception of the casual viewer, who has to look again to check what they have actually read. Are they really using four-letter words like that to advertise clothes? The letters are not quite in the right order however. This time it is association by words rather than images. Perhaps the most startling fashion advertisements have been those of the Benetton Company, which have drawn on a wide repertoire of seemingly completely unrelated and usually deeply shocking images, such as those of people dying of AIDS and new born babies covered with blood, to promote items of fashion and in particular the 'United Colors of Benetton'. All these meanings combine in a message which Saussure called the sign.

Saussure's work shaped the semiotic approach to representation by emphasizing the distinction between the form of the sign, the actual word, image, picture or photograph, and the idea with which it was associated, that is what it signified, the meaning it has. Although we may talk about signifier and signified as if they were separate, not only do they come together in the sign, they are inseparable. The sign 'is the central fact of language' (Culler, 1976: 19).

Signs do not have essential or fixed meanings according to Saussure; they are in this sense arbitrary. Meanings are relational. For example night has meaning in relation to day. One of the simplest and one could argue, the most crude form of relationship is that of opposition such as expressed in binary opposition, with all the limitations that are involved in excluding shades of meaning between those two polarities. However, Saussure's structuralist contribution has been very important in stressing the primacy of language as a series of signifiers which produce meanings through a system of differences. It is the differences between signifiers that produce meanings. Meanings are not fixed. Language does not reflect reality and meanings can change. Hence it would appear that people can effect changes in the ways in which they represent themselves and how they interpret others. If the speaker/author is de-centred then ambiguities and negotiations become possible. In spite of the possible slippage in the understanding of these meanings that are arbitrary and not fixed, there are still some constraints on human agency in a symbolic system that 'speaks us'. While Saussure's scientific method afforded the benefits of focusing on the detail of language and the specific processes involved in the construction of meanings through language, it did not differentiate between different language users and the often inequitable operation of power that is at play in the production of meanings through language. Saussure's approach has been very influential, which is why I have included this discussion here, but the more scientific specificities of his structural linguistics have largely been abandoned. His greatest contribution has been to the cultural critics who followed him, notably Roland Barthes who shifted the emphasis from language to the wider sphere of culture.

Myths and culture

Barthes has been well known for his analyses of what he calls the mythologies of popular culture; fashion advertising, sport and the mass media transform culture into what appears to be universal, even 'natural'. Barthes' understanding of myth is not that it distorts or hides the truth but that myths are what are taken as true in any particular culture. A myth is thus a way of making sense of the world through 'a complex system of beliefs which a society constructs in order to sustain and authenticate its own sense of being, i.e. the very fabric of its system of meaning' (Hawkes, 1988: 131). Barthes saw mythologies as naturalizing contemporary bourgeois culture so that it appeared that an historically produced society was an expression of nature by obliterating and covering over the contradictions or making them seem 'normal'.

Barthes applied semiotics to popular culture in a way that has much to offer an exploration of the representation of identities in a contemporary consumer society. Barthes 'read' the popular culture of magazines and of consumer products from soap powder to film stars, by focusing on meaning and the messages that were being conveyed by the different aspects of popular culture. For example he takes an advertisement for Panzani Italian food products. The advertisement depicts Panzani (the brand name) spaghetti, cheese, a tin of sauce and some fresh vegetables falling out of a string bag. At one level that is the meaning that is denoted by the picture. Denotation is the first level of descriptive meaning. The second level of meaning, which Barthes claims conveys what he calls 'Italianicity', the Italian qualities that are invoked by the contents of the picture, is connotation. In order to understand the connoted meanings, we have to link the signifiers in the picture, what we can see, to a wider field of meanings and associations with Italian culture. This is a common device adopted in advertisements, which frequently deploy signifiers of national identity to connote associations of Englishness or Frenchness or whatever.

Barthes applies this method of reading culture to all sorts of practices, not just to pictures. For example he looks at wrestling and asks questions, not about who is winning as we might expect the spectator to ask, but about what the spectacle means. He analyses the gestures and actions in terms of their connoted meaning and cultural significance. This, he argues is a grandiloquent, theatrical display not just a sporting contest. 'The function of grandiloquence is indeed the same as that of ancient theatre, whose principal language and props (masks and buskins) concurred in the exaggeratedly visible … The gesture of the vanquished wrestler…far from disguising he emphasizes and holds like a pause in music … In wrestling, as on the stage in antiquity, one is not ashamed of one's suffering, one knows how to cry, one has a liking for tears' (1972: 16). He continues 'The physique of the wrestler constitutes a basic sign' (p. 18). Barthes uses this example to illustrate the ways in which meanings are connoted through actions and gestures as well as through words and images. The example of wrestling is particularly resonant in the elision of theatrical display and performance with competitive sport.

Boxing is another example of such competitive sport, although its rituals may not be quite so explicitly theatrical and there is very real risk of injury for participants. The enactment of the sport is less ritualized and the incidence of physical injury more likely. The following picture is an example of the theatricality of boxing and of the ways in which Barthes' notion of connoted meanings could be applied in a different context. This image resonates more with the circus or with carnival than a serious, competitive and very dangerous sport. The boxer, Prince Naseem conjures up fantastical notions through his entry to the boxing ring, held, supernaturally aloft on a magic carpet. The carpet connotes magic and spectacle.

Barthes' work is in the tradition of structuralist understandings of representation and his approach also involves a de-centring of the subject, affording very limited agency to individuals. It offers an extension of Saussurian linguistics however, which has considerable application in deconstructing some of the ways in which identities are represented and made meaningful and it is an approach which has been very influential within cultural studies as well as having wider social applications.

Prince Naseem Hamed enters the ring to face his opponent Vuyani Bungu. (Reproduced with permission from Empics, Nottingham.)

The semiotic and the psychoanalytic: interpellation

One of the most useful developments of semiotic analyses, which has had particular relevance in the exploration of the links between representation and the formation of identity, lies in the work of the French Marxist Louis Althusser. Althusser identified a significant gap in Marxist thinking, namely the position of the subject in relation to ideology. His work is important in bringing together psychoanalytic theories and semiotics in a Marxist analysis, which still endeavours to foreground the material base of social relations, and the social in the personal, social identity equation. He attempted to use Lacan's reworking of Freud to emphasize the role of language and of symbolic systems in the formation of identity. In spite of the criticism which his work has received, especially for its attempt to distinguish between ideology and some extra-discursive realm of 'truth' and the move away from Marxism by so many cultural critics, Althusser's development of the notion of interpellation continues to have some useful applications. He used this concept to explain the ways in which people are recruited into the subject position, by recognizing themselves – ' "yes, that's me". Interpellation can be imagined in everyday situations by the practice of hailing, "Hey you there!" The hailed individual will turn round. By this mere one-hundred-and-eighty-degree physical conversion, he becomes a subject. Why? Because he has recognized that the hail was "really" addressed to him, and that "it was really him who was hailed" (and not someone else)' (1971: 137). Althusser focuses on that moment of recognition, when we think 'that's me' just as when someone calls out your name and you turn round thinking 'who's calling me?' Through his use of the concept of interpellation, Althusser was able to highlight some of the aspects of the process which links the individual to social processes. This is how individuals are drawn into particular identity positions. He argued that ideology was the process through which individuals are constituted as subjects. Ideology includes sets of ideas, beliefs and practices, not only the grand theories of politics and religion but the ideas through which we make sense of, and practise, our daily lives, Consciousness is not only not free-floating, it is constructed through ideologies. Consciousness is produced through an imaginary subjection. We are subjects in two senses; we are subjected to ideologies and we are also held to be responsible for own actions, as the initiators of action and the subject of the sentence – I and we. 'Subject' and 'subjectivity' are attractive concepts in this sense because, as Michele Barrett argues, they include both conscious aspects of personal experience, what goes on in our heads, but also the unconscious, the dreams and fantasies that are less easy to access (1991).

Althusser's attempt to synthesize psychoanalysis and Marxism was nonetheless beset by problems, not the least of which was Althusser's assumption that the process always works. While the idea of interpellation is useful in exploring what happens when we are recruited successfully into an identity position, for example when we are persuaded to buy certain items, it does not explain the failures or refusals. For Althusser it always works in class interests, which leaves little space for human agency or for resistance to the operation of class based ideologies. However, his initial project was to interrogate the processes in play in the recruitment of subjects into capitalist ideologies, especially what he perceived as the apparent failure of the working classes to attain sufficient self-consciousness to challenge the bourgeois orthodoxies that oppressed them. Much of the work done on the politics of representation in the second half of the twentieth century in Europe also engaged with how subjects are successfully recruited into capitalist, consumer societies to the extent that they come to embody those values.

Consuming identities

Pasi Falk has argued that the modern self (it may in fact be more a feature of the postmodern self) is increasingly the consuming self to the extent that we might paraphrase Descartes' *cogito* into 'I consume, therefore I am' (1994). People in the west, most specifically those with some degree of affluence and access to spending power, are familiar with the notion of 'retail therapy' and the idea that when the going gets tough, the tough go shopping. It may well be more indicative of the parodies of postmodern culture that more traditional, economistic readings of consumption, as determined by the processes of production, which carries much greater weight and significance, have been subverted. Giddens argues that,

> the reflexive project of the self, which consists in the sustaining of coherent, yet continuously revised, biographical narratives, takes place in the context of multiple choice as filtered through abstract systems. In modern life the notion of life style takes on a particular significance. The more tradition loses its hold, and the more daily life is reconstituted in terms of the dialectical interplay of the local and the global, the more individuals are forced to negotiate lifestyle choices among a range of options (1991: 5).

Although Giddens acknowledges the structural factors of capitalist production, he underplays its inequalities. The options for many people across the globe and even within affluent western countries, are not between lifestyle products but about how they can manage to sustain daily life. It is only possible to construct the self through lifestyle choices and patterns of conspicuous consumption, if one has the resources so to do. Poverty and inequality offer significant counter arguments to the claim that we are what we buy and that consuming identities afford greater agency to those who buy into identity positions through consumption of goods and services. There are clearly material constraints to some of these arguments. However, the development of consumption theories and the higher profile awarded to consumption in economic systems in shaping and providing a means of securing and reforming identities are largely intended to counter the under-playing of cultural factors in earlier accounts that prioritized production and the economic base of social relations and divisions.

There are, however, other limitations to the claim that we are free to manage lifestyle identities and exercise autonomy in the process through consumption. How do we make decisions about which lifestyles to buy into? Other approaches to the phenomena implicated in consumption patterns are more cognizant of the ways in which consumers are constrained, not only through lack of resources. Such views emphasize the influence that corporate capital is able to exercise in shaping the decisions that are made by consumers, indicating dependence and lack of autonomy among consumers. We are not simply free agents, floating through the paradise of consumption and fulfilling our desires. Arlie Hochschild has suggested that the feminist proj-ect of increasing women's independence has been curtailed by the images that consumer cultures, for example as promulgated within the women's maga-zine market, use to promote the idea of women using purchasing power to please themselves (1994). This view is challenged and there is also space for the exercise of some independence and autonomy within such consumer cultures, for example women's magazines (Woodward, 1997c). Women read-ers are not simply passive recipients of pre-given identities. They negotiate by accepted or rejecting the identities with which they are presented.

Zygmunt Bauman argues that social skills have become undermined by an excessive concern with individuality and the consumption that people are com-pelled to engage in by the market forces of the capitalist economy in late modernity.

> Unable to cope with the challenges and problems arising from their mutu-al relations men and women turn to marketable goods, services and expert counsel: they need the factory produced tools to imbue their bodies with the socially meaningful 'personalities' medical or psychiatric advice to heal the wounds left by previous – and future defeats, travel services to escape into unfamiliar settings which it is hoped will provide better surround-ings for solution of familiar problems, or simply, factory produced noise (literal and metaphorical) to 'suspend' social time and eliminate the need to negotiate social relations (Bauman, 1987: 164).

Bauman presents a more constraining view of consuming identities than some of the views that express this phenomenon as potentially liberatory and as opening up new, democratic possibilities for forming and representing identities. However, the ironic play on the assumptions and contradictions of consuming identities that has become a part of popular culture in the west, is very much in line with the practices of contemporary capitalism, although consumption can no longer be reduced to a function of the capitalist economy, or a simple outcome of the production process. As Danny Miller argues, consumption is not merely an act of buying goods, it is 'a fundamental process by which we create identity' (1997: 19). Miller sees the process of consumption as creative. Patterns are multi-faceted and diverse, but the main points of his argument are that what we buy and consume contribute to our sense of who we are and that this process is active and creative. Our identities are made up and are represented by the consumer goods which we buy. Consumption is much more than the response and trigger to production; the circuit of production has to include both representation and identity. This is also an active process and consumption is not passively, or crudely, determined by what is produced and how it is marketed.

Pierre Bourdieu retains a materialist class-based analysis, but incorporates taste as exercised by consumers in line with their class identity. The focus on the active process of consumption was taken up by Bourdieu in his work on the ways in which the consumption of goods constitutes the expression of taste. Display of the goods that we have bought, has symbolic significance in demonstrating membership of a particular culture. He suggests that consumption is,

> A stage in the process of communication, that is, an act of deciphering, decoding, which presupposes practical or explicit mastery of a cipher or a code ... taste classifies the classifier. Social subjects, classified by their classifications, distinguish themselves by the distinctions they make, between the beautiful and the ugly, the distinguished and the vulgar, in which their position in the objective classifications is expressed or betrayed (Bourdieu 1984: 2, 6).

Thus identities are organized by their classifications and mark themselves out by the distinctions which they make. This is the way in which class differences are constructed through consumption. This critique is heavily dependent on classificatory systems, which might indicate a rigidity in the marking of identity through consumption. Bourdieu argues that, although patterns of consumption are varied and diverse, they are socially structured. In fact his main analysis was of class as the major social division, paying more limited attention to other social divisions, such as ethnicity and generation; even gender gets only limited coverage. Bourdieu retained an economically based analysis of class, which prioritizes the economic structures which determine social relationships and saw class as the main determinant of consumer behaviour (1984) which is, in Bourdieu's work largely a given, that is formed through the economic structure and the outcome of systems of production and ownership. However, consumption is at the same time material and symbolic. Consumption expresses taste and taste lifestyle and Bourdieu's analysis signifies a shift of focus from production to consumption and onto empirically supported claims that identities are created through the process of consumption.

Falk provides an analysis of the role of consumption in contemporary life with an account of the ways in which the body is implicated in the processes of representing the self. He seeks to reinstate the body into discursive approaches to the body, such as Foucault's, of which he presents an important critique. Falk bases his analysis of consumption on embodiment, whereby he understands the body as sensory and sensual. Thus consumption is linked to sensory experience and to pleasure, for example in his exploration of luxury and conspicuous consumption in the production of contemporary identities (1994). These identities are produced through the interrelationship between the promotion of products and advertising which target the consumer and the body on which such promotions become inscribed.

While Bourdieu retains a strong material base in his analysis, some of the developments of postmodernism have focused more on the discursive and representational systems through which identities are produced. Many postmodernist approaches have stressed the liberatory elements in such approaches. A shift towards greater emphasis on agency and diversity, for example in line with the celebration of diversity, fragmentation and pleasure may open up possibilities for different identities to be created and acknowledged. However, as Lynne Segal has pointed out this can also be disconcerting and in her discussion of the impact of this on feminism she suggests that postmodernism has created 'spaces for more women to flaunt the diverse pleasures, entitlements and self-questioning' (1999: 232) but the narcissism which is complicit in these possibilities may be hostile to political action which in any way counters the interests of late capitalist consumerism. That is to say that the shift in emphasis from the dominance of economic systems and production in shaping identities may itself open up spaces which, while appearing more free and fluid, are equally constraining.

Postmodernist critiques too have focused on the ways in which identities, albeit fragmented and de-centred are signifiers of passivity rather than resistance. Jean Baudrillard, whose early writings were neo-Marxist, moved into a position which prioritized representational systems and the realm of signs and signifiers over any material sources of identity.

Postmodernist readings; sign values

Jean Baudrillard can be seen as part of the postmodernist critique of the grand narratives, the big stories, which offer large scale explanations of the organization of human social relations and historical change, of modernity. Postmodernism can be seen as a cultural expression of the global changes taking place in modes of production and consumption. These changes have been described in a variety of different ways, but there is some agreement that a massive cultural shift has taken place. I have included Baudrillard here because he does make a contribution to the debate, albeit one which seems to me to move into hyperbole and excess, about the ways in which media technologies shape identities and in a sense people become terminals within media systems.

Influenced by Saussure's structural linguistics and Barthes' analyses of popular culture, Baudrillard has argued that commodities are structured into a system of sign values governed by rules, codes and social logic. Baudrillard used the notion of sign values to refer to the socially construct-ed prestige values that are adopted by a range of commodities available in the market. He drew attention to the ways in which commodities, the things we buy and use are not just or the satisfaction of needs, but increasingly indices of social standing. Baudrillard abandoned the material base and notions of exchange value and use value in his later work, arguing that the production of objects has been replaced by the production and proliferation of signs (1976).

Baudrillard has argued that contemporary politics is the equivalent of advertising, sports, fashion, special effects, and in effect what has come to be known as 'spin'. His concept of the simulacrum, whereby the state of replication is so perfect that it becomes indistinguishable from the original, has considerable resonance in contemporary western societies. Technologies employed in the media are capable of reproducing images at high speed and with stunning accuracy at a time when identity is increasingly dependent upon images. The replication of individual, corporate, political and institutional identities is both possible and problematic. The interweaving of simulcra in our daily lives combines different worlds of commodities in time and space. Some contemporary advertising makes Barthes' Panzani advertisement look pretty simplistic, even naive in its form of representation. The time-space com-pression and technological advances in the west in the last 40 or so years have led to a proliferation of sophisticated simulcra, which are difficult if not impossible to deconstruct in order to differentiate between original and copy. However, it can certainly be argued that Baudrillard's vision of the power of space-time compression and the possibilities of technological means of representation is exaggerated in its Euro-American focus, failing to accommodate the experience of those less subject to technologies, whether through exclusion or resistance and through his failure to incorporate power relations into his account.

Discourse and power

Foucault's work also offers a critique of the rational subject of Enlightenment thinking. He breaks down the unified, natural self-reflective subject at the centre of western thought to make way for radically different ways of thinking and of representing the self. In the *Archaeology of knowledge* he demonstrates that the subject, far from being the sole originator of meaning, is actually an illusion. The subject is a by-product of discursive formations (1972). To be a subject is to be subjected. Foucault argued that ideas such as the soul, the psyche and deep inner feelings were the effects of the process of subjection. Foucault moved in his later work to endeavour to address the question of resistance to subjection and developed an 'ethics of the self'. These technologies of the self constitute Foucault's attempt to offer some explanation of resistance to hegemonic forms of identity.

My purpose here is to look at what Foucault's work can contribute to an understanding of the part played by representation in the construction of identity. Foucault's approach to representation is discursive. His aim was to explore 'how human beings understand themselves in our culture within specific historical circumstances'. To some extent Foucault is indebted to Lacan and Barthes (Dreyfus and Rabinow, 1982) although in other ways his work is radically different, especially in his focus on historical contexts. Foucault uses the term discourse to encompass the whole system of representation. Discourse goes much further than language. It includes all the ways in which knowledge is represented at a particular time and 'since all social practices entail *meaning* and meanings shape and influence what we do – our conduct – all practices have a discursive aspect' (Hall, 1992: 291). Discourses can only be comprehended in relation to other discourses and their truth or falsity cannot be determined by reference to some world outside discourse (Foucault, 1978). Meanings are made through discourses (which suggests that anything outside discourse is meaningless). Foucault's social constructionist approach gives high priority to representational systems since they are crucial to the discursive fields though which all meanings are produced. The truth of a discourse is dependent on its acceptance as truth in particular historical circumstances. For example this can be illustrated in the case of sexuality. Foucault argues that what is categorized as 'sexuality', that is a way of defining certain practices, desires and even fantasies was 'put into discourse, and made possible as meaningful at a particular historical moment' (Foucault, 1978). While what is called homosexuality may have been practised for the whole of human history, the person classified as 'homosexual', as a specific subject, was produced, by being 'put into discourse' in the nineteenth century. This was effected by a whole set of interventions in the literature and practice of the law, medicine, psychiatry and morality, all of which produced meanings relating certain acts and relations to a category of person – the homosexual.

Foucault analysed representations of different kinds, including texts and even visual images, such as paintings. The crucial discussion of Velasquez's Las Meninas (1656), which opens *The order of things* (1970) makes an important contribution to debates about the relationship between representation and the subject. He uses the painting which depicts the Spanish royal family in a room where the portrait of the King and Queen, the sitters are being painted but they are not shown, although their image is reflected in a mirror which is shown.

The artist himself is portrayed. The centre of the painting is dominated by the Infanta surrounded by her attendants (Las Meninas). Foucault uses the painting to show how the meaning of the picture is produced through a complex interplay between what is shown or represented, what is present, and what is not represented, what is absent, including the invisible sitters of the portrait depicted, who are reflected or replicated the mirror. What is not represented is as important as what is. This painting has two centres and two subjects in a sense, the King and Queen, whose portrait is the subject and the Infanta who occupies the centre of the actual painting. This supports Foucault's argument that meaning is constructed through a dialogue between the painter/artist and the spectator. It requires a spectator, who is also in a sense subjected to the painting. There are different subject positions produced through the process of representation; here the artist, the subject of the painting, what is shown, and the spectator who is subjected to it. We will return to the relationship between the artist, the subject and the spectator in the discussion of self-portraiture below.

Foucault is hostile to the notion of a rational subject who is the source of meaning. He argues, 'one has to dispense with the constituent subject, to get rid of the subject itself, that's to say, to arrive at an analysis which can account for the constitution of the subject with an historical framework' (Foucault, 1980: 115). In abandoning the autonomous, unified national subject, Foucault attributes great significance to representation in its interplay with 'power in this discursive production' of meaning in historically specific contents.

In his later work Foucault sought to elaborate a theory of resistance to complete subjection, by developing what he referred to as an 'ethics of the self'. This is situated at the level of everyday practices – or techniques of the self, and includes more scope for agency through notions such as reflexity and autonomy. This indicates more of a recognition of his indebtedness to Enlightenment thinking rather than a reversal of his hostility to agency or any suggestion of the reinstatement of the rational subject (McNay, 1994). Foucault's technologies of the self involve the manner in which people 'comply more or less fully with a standard of conduct, the manner in which they obey or resist an interdiction or prescription' (1985: 25). These techniques of the self are situated at the level of ethical practices, ranging from the concrete practices of daily life to the spiritual significance that is attached to them. Foucault uses the example of sexual relations in ancient Greece and Rome to explore

> these intentional and voluntary actions by which men not only set them-
> selves rules of conduct, but also seek to transform themselves, to change
> themselves in their singular being, and to make their life into an oeuvre
> that carries certain aesthetic values and meets stylistic criteria (ibid.: 10–11).

Men (and it is men that Foucault largely focused upon) in the ancient world complied with and interpreted what Foucault calls ethical, rather than moral rules. Moral rules he takes as rigid prescriptions whereas ethics is the actual behaviour of individuals in relation to the rules that are advocated. Hence men interpreted the social mores in relation to their sexual activities with men and with women. For example in ancient Greek society there were rules about sexual behaviour organized around the dualisms of activity/passivity and restraint/excess. The ethical man exercised restraint and was the active partner. It is in the manner of working within these guidelines in the practice of everyday life that Foucault sees the development of the ethical self.

> In economics (marriage) and dietetics [bodily regimen] the voluntary mod-
> eration of the man was based mainly on his relation to himself; in erotics
> [sexual relations with young men], the game was more complicated; it
> implied an ability on the part of the beloved to establish a relation of
> domination over himself; and lastly, it implied a relationship between their
> two moderations, expressed in their deliberate choice of one another
> (1985: 203).

Foucault does offer some rethinking of the ways in which the self is subjected within discursive regimes and his conceptualization of power is not only as a dominating constraining force. While Foucault does include the productive aspects of the power which operates through discourse, seeing power as both constraining and enabling, he develops a theory which prioritizes the visual in the field of control. What he called the panoptic gaze describes the way in which social and political control became institutionized. In

The order of things he outlines the way in which modernity involved a re-ordering of power, knowledge and the visible (1970). The model for this was provided by Jeremy Bentham's panopticon ([1791] 1962). The perception, which was an architectural mechanism, controlled the person who sees and who is seen. The panopticon was a structure devised for use in prison, or factories, hospitals 'a seeing machine … has become a transparent building in which the exercise of power may be supervised by society as a whole' (1979: 207).

When under constant view, the subject of the panopticon gaze, as in the prisoner constantly in the jailer's view, regulation does not have to be corporeal, subjection is mechanical and both seer and seen are implicated. The panoptic model stresses the subjective effects of imagined scrutiny and the permanent visibility of the observed, but Foucault sees the observer as also subjected by the process.

Foucault's work brings historical specificity and more direct engagement with the operation of power to the discussion of representation. His understanding of discourse is wide reaching and covers much more than language, embracing all the ways, including practices and customs through which knowledge is produced and meanings are made. However, in the case of the formation of identity and the representation of the self, there is also a case to be made for the primacy of the visual not only in losing control; visual representations occupy a particular place in the presentation of self to others and in our understanding of the selves which others present.

Jean-Louis Comolli describes the contemporary world as living in a 'frenzy of the visible' (1980) whereby the whole world becomes visible and hence can be appropriated. It has often been alleged that we live in a world dominated by the visual and the visible (Jay, 1998) and there are indeed examples of ways in which to make something visible to know that it is!

Seeing is believing

What does the visual image tell us? What meanings does it produce? Or is there a case for privileging such images as revealing a truth which can be seen as reflecting something which is real, something which presents a faithful reflection of reality?

This image, of the foetus *in utero*, is one that many parents in many parts of the world cherish as the first true reflection of the baby that the woman is carrying. Whereas, prior to the arrival of foetal ultrasound scanning, the proof that a woman was carrying a child would be through her own experience of the movement of the child in her body, endorsed by the experienced hands of a midwife, 'proof' in the twenty-first century, in the Euro-American world

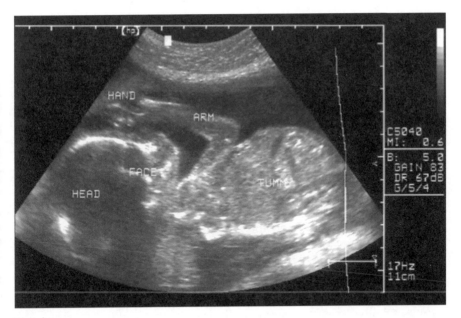

Foetal image.

is visual. The baby would only be seen after delivery. Does the foetus have an identity? Does the mother have an identity? The foetus might be deemed to have an identity having been captured in this visual image. Think about how many occasions there are in the contemporary world when one's identity is secured through a visual image. This could be the photograph on the ID card, the passport photograph, driving licence or security card. People frequently rely on photographic confirmation that they really are who they say they are, even that they exist at all. In the case of foetal ultrasound imaging the picture is proof both that the foetus exists and that the foetus apparently has a separate identity from the mother. This image of the free-floating foetus gives no indication of its dependent symbiotic status. It is possible to provide an image which is separate, suggesting an independent identity too. This suggestion is compounded by the absence of the mother in the image. The mother is not present. We know the foetus is entirely dependent and cannot exist without the mother, but her absence in the image offers the visual evidence of foetal identity but not maternal identity.

Rosalind Petchesky draws on semiotic theory and a feminist discursive approach to deconstruct the image of the apparently 'free-floating' foetus. She uses Barthes' concept of connotation to ask whether this foetal image could be a message without a code, an objective description and something simply denoted. Petchesky (1987) argues that the photographic image was produced through ultrasound scanning, is itself encoded and does connote wider social and cultural meanings. The message encoded in this image is that the foetus is independent, free floating and is a person; it has an identity.

Petchesky uses this example to show the privileging of the visual and the prevalence of the 'male gaze'. This is based on John Berger's claim that 'men act and women appear. They look at women. Women watch themselves being looked at' (Berger, 1974: 47). Her approach also has resonance with Foucault's arguments about the historical development of the medical gaze as a means of discursive control, although his argument does not specifically focus on gender. Petchesky develops the idea of 'foetal personhood' as constructed through the technology that makes possible the representation of an embryo inside the womb and the representation of foetus and mother as separate, independent beings.

The specific example that Petchesky uses is taken from a US anti-abortion film *The silent scream*, which clearly has a particular political position. However, her arguments apply to the privileging of the visual as the primary means of knowledge in western traditions of knowledge. As she says the visual has a peculiar property for detachment and appeared objectivity and creating a distance between the person who sees and what is seen (1987). She cites her chosen example as relying 'on our predisposition to "see" what it wants us to "see" because of the range of influences that are part of the particular culture and history in which we live. The aura of medical authority, the allure of technology, and the cumulative impact of a decade of foetal images … make it credible' (1987/2000: 174).

Petchesky's analysis also focuses on the ways in which images connote other meanings and draw on a range of other associations through different sensory experience. For example the film has a particular voice-over commentary and has background music. Visual representation may have a particular place in constructing identities but they are also closely linked to other discursive fields and senses other than the visual.

Portraying the self

What do you see in this painting? It may depend on whether or not you are familiar with the particular painting. We might even disagree about what is denoted, let alone connoted by the painting. The first time I saw it I thought it was a picture of a woman looking in a shop window. This may indicate something about my own cultural assumptions but I was not alone in this mis-understanding. The art historian Rosemary Betterton similarly misread the painting. She too thought that this was a woman looking in a shop or gallery

Dame Laura Knight. (*Reproduced with permission of Curtis Brown Group Ltd, London on behalf of the Estate of Dame Laura Knight. Copyright Dame Laura Knight.*)

window and did not realize that this was a self-portrait of the artist. Laura Knight chose to paint herself from the back, brush in hand (I missed that first time) contemplating a posed female model whose relation to both the artist and the spectator suggest her removal to the public space of display most often associated with the spectacle of the windows of large department stores (Chadwick, 2001: 13). Shops, that is where you expect to see women, gazing at the items on display in these windows. As Betterton points out, the mistake which many of us make in misreading this picture, and seeing the clothed women as a shopper and not an artist, is revealing of certain cultural assumptions about femininity. While the woman's narcissistic glance in a mirror or a shop window is socially legitimated, her critical investigative gaze is not (1987: 4). Betterton goes on to argue that, while this painting does not represent the voyeurism more common in portrayals of the female nude, neither does it offer the viewer a coherent position. This is partly because it disrupts the more usual relationship between male artist and female model. This normative relationship is upset by the new roles that have a female artist (clothed) and female artist model (naked); the one who looks and the one who is looked at. This version challenges the notion of the male gaze and John Berger's claim that it is men who look and women who are looked at.

> Men look at women. Women watch themselves being looked at. This determines not only most relations between men and women but also the relation of women to themselves. The surveyor of woman in herself is male: the surveyed female. Thus she turns herself into an object – and most particularly an object of vision: a sight (1972: 47).

This self-portrait challenges this reading of the 'male gaze', whatever resonance it has elsewhere in the understanding of women as objects who are subjected to the gaze. As Whitney Chadwick argues 'the painter's incorporation' of the relationship between artist and model and the visual dynamics of working from life in the studio into her self-representation contrasts sharply with many other objectives of studio practice (2001: 13). The painting is also an example of a disruption in the construction of subject positions, as was discussed above in the context of Michel Foucault's critique of *Las Meninas*. The subject of this self-portrait is the artist who painted it. In this sense she has re-created herself. However, the centre of the painting is occupied by the female model whose image is reproduced in the canvas also depicted. The position of the artist or subject to the left of centre, further subjects the viewer to confusion, maybe making it even more likely that we will miss the key signifier of the brush in the artist's hand. To paint oneself from the back, at work, not looking directly out or demurely looking down as was more common in paintings of women was a radical departure from traditional practice. This new formulation further disrupts the gaze of the viewer. This painting brings together some of the conflicts and contradictions inherent in re-presenting the self and highlights the multifaceted dimensions of re-creating identities.

Representing the self through a self-portrait offers insights into the processes that are consciously involved in the construction of identity. The self-portrait brings together the artist, the subject and the spectator in a particularly interesting way, especially since the artist is the subject of the portrait. This is a medium and a genre which allows for some exploration of the role of agency in the construction of the self within the field of visual culture and representational systems. Issues of identity are raised specifically by self-portraiture. The self-portrait is a public statement and involves making visible a portrait of the artist. The genre has different implications for men and for women and there is a tradition within the genre which creates expectations in the minds of spectators. The artist can challenge the conventions or comply with them. The challenge is most evident in the work of women artists since there are very powerful conventions about the representations of women in art and there has been a tradition of male dominance of the genre (Borzello, 2001). Given the constraints of standards of feminine beauty and decorum, self-portraiture, by confronting an individual woman as an artist, is a difficult subject to take on. The self-portrait goes beyond the mirror. It is not a reflection of the self returned only to the self: it is the self made public. However, the metaphor of the mirror, particularly as derived from Lacanian psychoanalytic theory has considerable impact on this experience of representing the self. The identification of the self in the mirror (or in the mother's eyes or the eyes of others) is crucial to ego formation, as the self appears as whole, co-ordinated and complete. The mirrored self offers an illusion of coherence and wholeness which, although it is fantasy, is the point at which the child locates itself in the public world, that is the world outside itself.

The mirror, of course, has considerable significance in later, adult life, perhaps the more so for women because of cultural constructions of what constitutes beauty. The mirror, like the self-portrait, more routinely poses problems for women. These problems relate to the need to negotiate dominant discourse of femininity and representations of female attractiveness. How do women deal with the problem of resistance and develop strategies for representing themselves within this set of conventions? The conventions of self-portraiture suggest that in order to paint themselves women would have to claim that they are worthy of being so represented, that they carry significant status. A self-portrait usually involves a public person of some standing with a particular social position. Such portraits reinforce conventional expectations about the kind of people who should be shown (Borzello, 2001). Women in such portraits are usually shown in relation to a man, reflecting the status of the man with whom they are related. This illustrates one of the key features of the portrait or self-portrait. The portrait is about a public self – the self we seek to show others. Secondly the portrait does reveal something, however reflective about the private self, the 'I' as well as the 'me', although the artist may well seek to present the most favourable 'me' in the self-portrait. Reading the face in the portrait or self-portrait means reading the person, seeing who that person 'really' is. A portrait suggests a knowable self, a unified self rather like the psychoanalytic mirror providing coherence. Not only might we know ourselves, but others might know us too. Lastly the portrait may offer public and private selves brought together to represent some abstract quality, such as honour or courage, modesty or innocence. It is not difficult to align these qualities within the genre of the portrait. Portraiture illustrates this point about social expectations and the conventions attached to representing the self more directly than many other practices, as the Laura Knight self-portrait illustrates. It can be argued that self-portraiture illustrates particularly well the interplay between 'the reflected self-image and the explanation of the social dimensions of lived experience, but self-representation remains crucial to self-understanding' (Chadwick, 2001: 21).

Visual culture

Visual culture opens up a field of vision that extends beyond the immediate understanding of visual images. It addresses the field of vision as a space in which meanings are constituted and debated; a field in which meanings are established and destabilized. In the contemporary world, meanings are produced and re-created visually. What is seen and what is unseen have enormous importance in the process of making meanings. Visual culture incorporates the images that are seen, the means of looking, that is the technologies through which they are viewed and the spectators who look.

Irit Rogoff argues that visual culture opens up a field of 'intertextuality in which images, sounds and spatial delineations are read onto or through one another, lending ever-accruing layers of meanings and of subjective responses to each encounter we might have until film, TV, advertising, artwork, building and urban environments' (1998: 15). This has resonance with Petchesky's earlier critique of foetal imaging.

Visual culture has been developed, along with cultural studies, as an interdisciplinary project which seeks to break down barriers between art and popular culture, between 'high' and 'low' culture, seeing them as inter-dependent. Both are visual systems of representation that reproduce identity positions.

Paul Virilio is one critic who has attempted to go beyond the earlier analysis of the visual analysed by the sign, citing images of class, gender and race. He reformulates his critique in the context of film. In *The vision machine* he focuses on elements of light movement and speed rather than objects (1994). He sees modernity as a constant accelerator in the transmission of messages. Virilio's understanding of postmodernism is that it is the progressive disintegration of faith in perception. He derives his critique from the trauma of the First World War as 'the moment of panic when the mass of Americans and Europeans could no longer believe their eyes, when their faith-perception became spare to the faith in the technical sightline: in other words, the visual field was reduced to the line of fire' (1994: 16–17).

This phenomenon Virilio argues reached its apotheosis in the films of 'smart' weapons in the Gulf War, when targeting replaced perception. He offers a new understanding of visual culture but one which it is often difficult to comprehend and which poses more questions than it answers about the situatedness of the subject. Virilio's work like Baudrillard's subverts all securities in the endeavour to push forward the frontiers of understanding of visual culture, and makes it difficult to escape a relativism that might be too unsettling. Such critiques are also limited in their focus on the power relations that are negotiated in the formation of identity.

Does challenging the unity of the subject as represented and the veracity of visual evidence necessarily mean a collapse of certainty and the insecurity of relativism? Donna Haraway argues for the embodied nature of vision and 'to reclaim the sensory system that has been used to signify a leap out of the naked body and onto a conquering gaze from nowhere' ([1991] in Mirzoeff, 1998: 192). She argues for the specificity of what she calls 'situated knowledge'. Rather than accepting the 'death of the subject' which is implicated in the de-centring of the subject and the denial of both authority and objectivity she argues for the 'opening of generative doubt and a "travelling lens"' (ibid.: pp. 194–5), which the split subject affords. This understanding of the challenge to unity and the 'self-satiated eye of the master subject' (p. 194) is that it opens up new places from which to see and to speak, through what she calls positioning. For Haraway, 'the split and contradictory self is one who can interrogate positionings and be accountable; the one who can construct and form rational conversations and fantastic imaginings that change history' (p. 195). Haraway's situated knowledge offers a far more attractive and positive subjectivity than the deconstructionism that links the author and hence the subject, who is de-centred to the point of disappearance. This perspective brings back the possibility of retrieving the field of visual culture as part of an active project by claiming that 'the only way to find a larger vision is to be somewhere in particular' (p. 198). Haraway is able to do this because she acknowledges her own situated perspective and presents a 'feminist objectivity'; an objectivity that is positioned and can be political.

Conclusion

Representation is a key component in the construction of identities, in their presentation and reception and in the ways in which identity becomes meaningful. It is through language, symbolic systems, rituals and practices that we make sense of who we are, understand who others are and imagine the boundaries that contain the self and mark it off from others. From the work of the early pragmatists such as G.H. Mead, the process of imagining the self symbolically has been seen as an important aspect of the process of identity formation. The focus on representation has been enormously extended, by moving from language to encompass culture and the whole range of practices and texts that constitute discourse. The primacy of visual representations and the privileged place which visual images can be seen as occupying in contemporary western culture has been extended to bring in the whole panoply of visual culture, which nonetheless retains a focus in the techniques, technologies and practices of the field of vision, and of what is involved in seeing and being seen, as well as the other sensory experiences that are all tied up in the field of what is called 'visual culture'.

Underpinning all of the development in theorizing representation is the tension between the personal and the social at the heart of identity. This tension is enacted in two ways; firstly through the debate about the extent to which individuals and groups of human beings are able to shape their own identities. How far can people negotiate the symbolic systems through which they represent themselves and are represented by others and exercise some autonomy even given the constraints of existing systems? While the emphasis of many structuralist theories of semiotics has been placed on being spoken rather than speaking and representing one's own self, the possibility for change is strongly present in critiques which see signification as arbitrary and meanings as fluid and not fixed. The line of vision is not linear and centrifocal, just as the subject is not unified and whole. However, the enthusiasm for change, hybridity and uncertainty which characterizes postmodernism has led to a second aspect of the personal/social relationship within identity which I would like to note.

It is also the case that the focus of analysis of representational systems has increasingly concentrated on the processes that are implicated, that is on the social with the cultural and the symbolic. This has led to even more concern with endeavouring to understand *how* representation works, its techniques and technologies. The social and cultural, as the means whereby images are produced through symbolic systems leaves little space for the material, specific locations of embodied selves and begins to move into an internal space. The desire to stabilize the self, to seek some security in identity and to recognize the specific, material circumstances in which identities are formed and represented does not necessarily require a fixed, coherent identity, nor a complete abandonment of the material, as Donna Haraway has argued. One aspect of materiality in relation to identity, which has also received a great deal of attention in recent years, is embodiment, which is the focus of the next chapter.

5   Embodying identity

In the following extract from her novel *Trumpet,* about the death of a famous jazz trumpeter, Joss Moody, Jackie Kay describes the moment when the trumpeter's son, Colman goes to the funeral parlour after his father's death to pay his respects and say goodbye to the body.

The young son had obviously steeled himself for the occasion and said, 'I've come to see my father, Joss Moody. I spoke to you earlier on the phone. I won't believe he's dead you know, until I see him in the flesh'. Holding [the undertaker] hid his face beneath his handkerchief and coughed awkwardly. 'Yes that's understandable. A lot of people say that.' 'If you don't mind I'd like to get it over with' Joss Moody's son said. 'Yes, indeed,' Mr Holding replied. 'By all means', Holding said, playing for time, 'but there is something I want to say to you first'. 'Can't it wait?' the young Mr Moody said. 'I've got to see him now or I'll lose my nerve.' 'Were you aware ... I mean, did you know that ... I presume in fact that you must be conscious of the fact that ...' 'What are you ranting on about? What's going on? Take me to see my father!' Colman almost shouted. 'What I mean to say,' Holding said, coughing into his fist, 'is that your father is not a man at all, but a woman. In other words he does not possess the male body parts, but instead the person lying through next door that I am given to understand is your father is actually a woman. She is in possession of female body parts'. But somewhere in the middle of his second sentence, the good-looking young man grabbed his collar and started shouting into his ear, 'What's your game? ... Is this some kind of sick joke? Where's your boss?' He shook Holding back and forth, almost lifting him of his feet ... There was nothing for it. He said, 'Are you absolutely positive you want to see her?'

'What are you talking about? Let me see my father? What's wrong with you?' Holding continued to speak quietly, forcing calmness into his voice.

'If you are quite sure you can handle to shock of it, come this way please. You will need to see for yourself'. He took him through and pulled back the white sheet (1998: 115).

The undertaker describes an experience that is totally new to him.

> That look of utter dismay and disbelief. That look of fury and sickness. It was quite an ordeal to witness. All his working life he has assumed that what made a man a man and a woman a woman was the differing sexual organs. Yet today he had a woman who persuaded him, even dead that he was a man, once he had his clothes on. That young man believed his father was a man ... Holding was well used to the business of disguising dead bodies – making them look presentable even when they had suffered quite horrific injuries ... Holding had made many a corpse look stunning in his coffin with his beautiful silk cloths and fine woods. Of course some people could only afford the standard box, but he always did his best for everybody. There was nothing he hadn't seen. Until today. This was a first alright. This was a first (p. 116).

This is a novel, a fictional work, although based on a story about an actual musician. However, it gives expression to a major issue in relation to the securing of identity positions. What is so shocking about this scenario? Is it that the jazz trumpeter, a public figure, was able to deceive so many people? Is it the deception of his son? (In the novel, the young man is aware that he was adopted.) Is it also because someone in such a close relationship has been deceived about something about which they might have expected to be quite certain? There is anger, distress and horror with which it is very possible to empathize, in the reaction of the young man. He sought confirmation of death in the body of his father – 'I won't believe he's dead until I see him in the flesh'. Yet that body is the source of frightening uncertainty. Far from offering stability, it presents terrifying insecurity. One of the seemingly secure anchors of identity, namely gender as marked by sexual difference, has been completely undermined. The situation is exacerbated by the gender of the young man; it is a man who finds out, at this tragic, poignant moment that the first man in his own life, perhaps the primary role model for him, is not a man at all, but a woman. If the young man has developed his own sense of gender identity in relation to his father, this discovery must surely jeopardize the security of that identity.

The source of grounded security which has been challenged here is the sexed body. In endeavouring to secure identity the body might seem to offer a bottom line, a source of security, which offer some fixity in locating our sense of 'who we are'. As Pierre Bourdieu argues the body is the only tangible manifestation of the person (1986). Sex and gender, as shaped by the physical characteristics of our bodies are seen as a key source of identity. At birth, babies are classified by their sex. This is often the first observation of parents and birth attendants and is recorded on the birth certificate. Not only are established, orthodox sources of identity confirmed by categories of sex, people seek the security and certainty of an identity – as a woman and as a man, which is rooted in some corporeal, grounded, material certainty. The body, and in particular the sexed body, may be the source of such certainty. Ambiguity about gender identity, for example as illustrated by transvestism or even transsexualism can be a challenge to certainty, a source of insecurity or a subversion of the fixity of identity. The phenomenon of intersex, where babies are born with contradictory or confusing sexual identities, carrying the genetic blueprint of one sex but the external sexual genital characteristics of the other or ambiguous external sexual characteristics, can cause alarm, confusion and distress in cultures which only permit two sexes. Surgical interventions have been carried out so that the sexual identities of intersex infants are consistent and conform to social and cultural external, visible expectations. As Susanne Kessler argues, although it is largely on the basis of the social implications of uncertainty about sexual categories, the initial observation is made on the basis of features that are visible in the infant body (1998). Why is this? Why do people demand and need some degree of certainty about their identities and why do they see the body as a source of security?

The bodies that we inhabit clearly offer limitations to what is possible, to the identities to which we might like to lay claim. Physical disabilities and the limits to the physical powers and competence of our bodies clearly restrict our potential in certain spheres, for example those of athletic achievement. Physical fragility, impairment or disability will constrain the desire to identify with competitive success as an Olympic sportsman or woman. This may be a particularly dramatic example but there are myriad other instances of the limits which the bodies which we inhabit present to our identification with and occupation of certain identity positions. All sorts of impairments can influence the extent to which we are able to engage in the everyday activities through which our identities are forged. These are the constraints of corporeality, which constantly remind us that we are embodied subjects.

Conversely, the body also offers the more positive aspects of security and certainty about who we are. All societies and cultures have a series of gendered attributes and expectations and practices that are associated with women and with men. These cultural associations vary across societies and across time and space, but they are often (always?) linked to the properties of the sexed body. Being in possession of certain physical features classified as female or male is connected to social, cultural expectations, practices and behaviour. Thus being assigned to a specific gender provides a set of ground rules that govern our behaviour, establishing a cornerstone of identity. One of the first things we may notice about a person we meet for the first time, is their sex and their gender and there may be an assumed connection between sex and gender. We may note clothing and demeanour and immediately categorize a person as female or male. Similarly, ethnicity is often characterized by visible difference, whether of physical features such as skin colour, or clothes that are specific to particular cultures. Disability is not always a visible difference; for example deafness is not immediately apparent, although other disabilities may be more visible. Along with race and disability, gender is the most notable visible difference. Confusion or ambiguity about gender identity is a source of anxiety and can subvert certainty. Assumptions about identity, which are related to our own bodies and those of others, offer security, yet the connection between the body and identity is often assumed but not stated or made explicit.

Where do these ideas about the links between our bodies and who we are come from? In western intellectual thought the body was for a long time either denied or dismissed, as if the thinking subject were disembodied. This western tradition has often taken the form of a dualism expressed as that between mind and body or between body and soul as expressed in Platonic ideals about the transcendence of the soul. Plato's soul/body distinction was integral to his philosophy and this particular dualism has had enormous influence on western thought. In Plato's distinction between body and soul the higher worth is accorded to the soul, and the body becomes subordinate to the elevation of the soul. This is also a gendered distinction. Plato suggests an association between women and the body and states that women have weaker bodies than men. Since the soul is superior to the body this would not in itself be damaging. However, there are many references to the inferiority of women. Plato warns his readers that if they fail to attend to the development of the soul they will end up like women. The worst role model for a young man, who should seek to remain calm and to endure all adversities would be to give in to grief 'like a woman' (*The republic*, p. 605). However, his approach to gender differences is contradictory and his work is not consistently misogynist. In *The republic* he states that there is not social function that belongs to woman because she is a woman nor to a man because he is a man. Natural capacities are distributed alike among both women and men (*The republic*, p. 455).

At several points Plato warns his readers that if they do not have regard for their souls they will end up behaving as if they were women, which suggests both an association between women and the body and the subordination of women in the body/soul hierarchical relationship. Whatever the contradictions within his writing it is these associations that have endured and that have informed later expressions of the dualism (Spelman, 1982). The spiritual qualities of the soul outlive and out-value the embodiment of the flesh. This example is one that has resonance in religious texts, for example, in the proscription against giving in to the weakness of the flesh, the sins of the flesh, in most major world religions. It is women who are linked to the sins of the flesh in many of these major world religions, for example those in the Judaeo Christian traditions. The sins of Eve are the sins of the flesh and of the female body. However, this too is a contradictory story. The status of the body is not always devalued and suppressed. For example in the Christian religion, it is the body and blood of Christ that are celebrated at the Communion service. Christ's ultimate sacrifice is the death of His body on the Cross. Christ's death makes the resurrection possible, in particular the resurrection of the *body*. The traditional Christian marriage service even incorporates some merging of agency and the body in the promise made by men at the ceremony according to the Book of Common Prayer, 'with my body I thee worship'. It may be only men to whom this agency and control of the body is accorded, but it is a powerful expression of human love that combines body and soul.

In the Cartesian divide between mind and body it is the mind that has carried higher status. However, until relatively recently bodies were seen, even by sociologists, as an assumed, taken for granted, *biological* source of certainty. The biological form which human actors inhabit was perceived as separate and distinct from the mind of the thinking subject, but offered its own certainties. Such apparent certainties have their roots in the dualistic tradition of thought that set up and demarcated the polar opposites of mind and body. This dichotomy that characterized Enlightenment thinking was based on a sectarian mind/body split. Along with this binary opposition went the association of men with rationality and the mind, and women with the body and nature.

It is hardly surprising that some of the most influential critiques of the mind/body opposition have come from feminists. Dualisms such as sex/gender, nature/culture, rational/emotional are not evenly weighted, nor are they gender neutral. As the French feminist writer Helene Cixous says:

> Thought has always worked by
> Opposition
> Speech/Writing
> High/low…
> Does this mean something? (1975: 90)

Cixous goes on to present additional illustration of the gendered dichotomies starting with the question:

Where is she?
Activity/passivity,
Sun/Moon,
Culture/Nature,
Day/Night,
Father/Mother,
Head/heart,
Intelligible/sensitive,
Man
Woman (ibid.: p. 90)

Focusing on such gendered dualisms promoted feminist critiques (for example Ortner, 1974) of the ways in which women's bodies have been defined and controlled. Having worked through the more simplistic associations of sex with biology and gender with culture and the social, it became possible for feminists to interrogate the interrelationships and the ways in which gender influenced ways of thinking about bodily differences.

Sex/gender

Sex and gender are frequently conflated. There may be an assumption that the two are interchangeable or that the one can be read off from the other. Not surprisingly, we might expect the undertaker in Jackie Kay's novel to assume that a person classified as 'of the male sex' would be in possession of what he calls 'the male body parts'. Even though the trumpeter has lived his life as male, the possession of female body parts seems to offer a privileged, biological certainty that cannot be denied. So much so, in fact, that the assertion of a biological certainty at his death can override and obscure the identity taken up by the person in life. There is shock that biological sex and what is called gender do not match up in this case.

Debates about the sex/gender relationship within the social sciences have addressed this very problem, namely the hierarchical nature of that relationship when the two are presented as separate concepts. While the mind and the soul might be rated above the body in soul/body, mind/body dualisms, in the sex/gender debate, the embodied sex has higher ranking as a determinant of gender. Liz Stanley (1984) described the argument as being one between *biological essentialism*, which prioritizes biological, embodied sex as the determinant of femininity or of masculinity, and *social constructionism*, which focuses on gender as a social, cultural category. This points to the separation between the two concepts, with sex being associated with biology and embodiment and gender with social and cultural practices. There are two issues here. Firstly, sex and gender have been combined, but there is still the assumption that sex as a biological classification, is privileged over gender as covering social attributes, in terms of the certainty it affords in relation to identity. Secondly, where the two have been explicitly disentangled, the influence of sex upon gender has been awarded priority and higher status than any influence gender as a cultural and social construct might have over sex. There is also a normative claim involved in this hierarchy, namely that sex *should* determine gender.

Gender has become an important concept in the social sciences, although it is only a relatively recent arrival as a key term. It was not until the 1970s that gender played a significant role. In most cases, social scientists studied the world of men and used 'men' and 'man' and the male third person pronouns to encompass humanity. Women were largely rendered invisible, apart from studies of the family and 'sex roles', where women might be mentioned. Gender if recognized at all was female; men stood for humanity. There are exceptions but not many. One particularly perceptive comment showing an awareness of gender was made by the sociologist Georg Simnel, who is usually included in the pantheon of the 'founding fathers' (or maybe 'founding great grandfathers'?) of sociology, although occupying a less prominent place than some of the others.

> The fact that the male sex is not only considered relatively superior to the female, but that it is taken as the universal norm ... is ... based on the power position of the male. ... This fact is evident in the extremely frequent phenomenon that certain judgements, institutions, aims, or interests which we men, naively so to speak, consider purely objective, are felt by women to be thoroughly and characteristically masculine (Simnel, 1911 quoted in Klein, 1946: 82–3).

The tradition of social sciences, especially in sociology, as developed in the nineteenth and early twentieth centuries has had considerable impact on the sex/gender debate. Gender was mostly underplayed within this tradition. In many ways it is Marx and Engels who had the most influence on the feminist work that foregrounded gender in the twentieth century. The Marxist focus on inequality, albeit with an emphasis on class, drew attention to the material inequity and exploitation that was so destructive of working class family life. Engels was more specific about the division of labour that involved gender as well as class and charted the historic exploitation of women by men in the move away from early communist societies to those based on the ownership of private property in *The origins of the family private property and the state* (1972). From the 1970s, feminists, especially Marxist and socialist feminists used the Marxist critique of historical materialism with its focus on reproduction, to incorporate the reproductive work performed by women as well as the reproduction of social and economic relations. In so doing they brought gender into the Marxist analysis.

While Max Weber's conceptualization of patriarchy is one that has resonance for feminist critiques, his contribution to debates about gender was limited. Although he offered a useful definition of patriarchal authority and a focus on the power that men exercise over women, and over younger men and children, he was not critical of the gendered power imbalance and did not question the basic inequality between women and men. However, the concept of patriarchy and its operation across so many societies has proved a useful tool for those who seek to deconstruct and change it.

Emile Durkheim's functionalism allowed limited room for a critique of gender and his consensus based approach provides little focus on conflict and inequality. His work has had less appeal to feminist thinkers who have emphasized gender as a category and gender divisions, largely because of the stress in his work on how societies are integrated and how they hold together successfully. Durkheim saw the increased specialization in the social roles of women and of men, which he witnessed as mainly complementary, with one sex taking responsibility for intellectual functions and the other the more affective roles (1964: 60). In his work on suicide rates he did acknowledge gender differences and interestingly pointed to the disparity between women and men in relation to marriage; married women being more likely to commit suicide than single women or married men, suggesting that there might be more in marriage for men than for women. His explanation of social differences between women and men is largely based on assumed 'natural' differences, for example the calming influence of marriage on men's sexuality, an influence that women do not require given that their sexuality is linked to their reproductive role only.

It was largely feminists of the second wave of the women's movement in the 1970s who made their disquiet explicit and drew attention to these patriarchal assumptions by challenging this androgyny. Gender as a concept was used to provide a focus on the social construction of femininity and masculinity and the importance of social relations and divisions between women and men. Gender included the hierarchical divisions between women and men that were based on social, political and economic practices and institutions. The world was ordered by gender divisions with gender giving meaning to social divisions. Gender was not a separate category but was caught up with other social divisions such as class, race, disability and sexuality. However, what distinguished gender was its emphasis on social and cultural manifestations and, in the 1970s at least, the attempt to disentangle gender as a social construct from sex as a biological one. Ann Oakley (1972) used the terms sex and gender as employed by the US psychiatrist and psychoanalyst

Robert Stoller, who had worked with people whose sexual classification appeared to be ambiguous. Following Stoller (1968), Oakley defined sex as biological and anatomical ('body parts' to quote the undertaker) and gender as the attributes associated with one or other sex in particular societies. Thus sex was seen as residing in the body and was largely immutable, whereas gender was socially and culturally malleable, changing across time and place. Oakley and many other feminists found the distinction useful because it challenged the claims that some of the social attributes associated with women, such as childcare, unpaid domestic labour and the qualities of submission and passivity, were 'natural' outcomes of having a female body. Far from being natural, they were socially imposed practices that could be challenged and changed. While this distinction between sex and gender was well received, especially by feminist critics, it has been seen to be problematic in more recent work. The sex/gender dualism led to extensive interrogation of the category of gender, but largely left 'sex' unexamined.

Post-binaries

Challenges to the sex/gender dichotomy have come from different sources, for example from opposing strands within feminism, the feminism of difference and material feminism. The first is represented by the work of the French feminist Luce Irigaray, who has argued that the notion of gender cannot embrace the specificity of women's embodiment (1985). She demands the recognition of embodied gender difference and presents a powerful, if largely theoretical and philosophical critique of the lack of recognition of women's bodies and women's lives in western culture. Her work is located within the psychoanalytic tradition, the phallocentricity of which she is keen to highlight in her analysis. This involves stressing the psychic and embodied differences between women and men and recognition of the psychic world of women's experience that lies outside society and patriarchal culture. Thus Irigaray's focus is on the pre-Oedipal stage of psychic development, as was discussed in Chapter 2, the stage within psychoanalytic theory that comes before what Lacan called the entry into language and the law of the father. Irigaray prioritizes the female unconscious, rooted in the relationship with the maternal body and the relationship with the mother, rather than the father and the Freudian notion of the paternal phallus or as key signifier of meaning in Lacanian theory. Hers is an embodied conceptualization of identity, grounded in the relationship with the mother. Irigaray develops this embodiment to encompass female sexuality as also rooted in the body and its physical make up (1985), in a manner which has been criticized as essentialist. That is to say that her critique is ultimately reducible to 'body parts' and to a corporeality that is dependent on a dualistic understanding of sexual difference. In fact Irigaray explicitly directs our attention to difference, arguing that it is only by asserting difference and by claiming the specific, embodied experience of women in informing their identities, that we can avoid the marginalization and even elimination of women's experience. She presents a strong counter argument to the phallocentricity, albeit in somewhat different forms, of both Freud and Lacan, but takes a different, more embodied, path from the object relations and Kleinian theorists addressed in Chapter 2, in her challenge to the limitations to psychoanalytic theories.

Theories of sexual difference are themselves challenged by materialist feminists who have developed a critique of the natural and of associated ideas about the primacy of embodied difference which has so frequently been used to justify gender inequalities. Material feminism combined radical feminism with Marxism. Thus the conceptualization of gender, as expressed in the French journal *Questions féministes* in the late 1970s and 1980s, was based on the claim that women and men exist in a class relationship. Men's domination is based on patriarchy and not on some pre-given sexual difference (in Marks and de Cortivron, 1981). Women and men can only be defined in the context of social relations. In a non-patriarchal society there would be non-categories 'women' and 'men', just as in a communist classless society there would be no 'working class' and no bourgeoisie. This approach seems to take us a long way from the body and corporeal experience. However, it does have the advantage of locating sex/gender differences in their social, political and especially their economic circumstances. Sex and gender are clearly too closely interconnected for simple binary oppositions.

Another challenge to the sex/gender distinction derives from earlier work within sociology that was classified as ethnomethodology, discussed in Chapter 1. An interesting example of this is the work of Harold Garfinkel (1967), whose case study of Agnes, a male to female transsexual, focused on how Agnes passed as a woman, even before undergoing gender realignment surgery. Garfinkel argued that the production of a sexed persona is a performance (for everyone, not only transsexuals). Agnes was able to use the information available on acceptable, usual, female behaviour in the appearance of the two (assumed) sexes, to perform appropriately and thus to convince others of the authenticity of the chosen gender role (rather like the jazz trumpeter mentioned in the opening scenario in this chapter). Garfinkel presented his arguments about the performance of sex and sexuality, while not using the term gender, before the developments of 'second wave' feminism. It was also well before poststructuralist and postmodernist explorations of the interconnectedness of sex and gender and Judith Butler's influential work on sexual identity as performativity.

Judith Butler has made very influential contributions to the sex/gender debate and to reconceptualizations of the body. She deconstructs sex and gender, moving from the claim that gender does not simply follow on from sex, to argue that, if that is the case, there is no reason to believe that there are just two genders. Sex is just as culturally constructed as gender (1990: 2). In this case the body does not have a pre-given, essential 'sex'. It is only through the repeated performance of gender that we become gendered. Butler goes further than Garfinkel and Goffman, with whose earlier dramaturgical model of the performance of roles Butler's analysis certainly has some resonance. In *Gender trouble*, Butler explores ways in which particular transgressive performances can subvert the binary male/female, masculine/feminine categories. She argues, for example that the parodic performance of the transvestite shows that femininity cannot be located in women's bodies, nor masculinity in men's.

> The performance of drag plays upon the distinction between the anatomy of the performer and the gender that is being performed. But we are actually in the presence of three contingent dimensions of significant corporeality: anatomical sex, gender identity and gender performance. If the anatomy of the performer is already distinct from the gender of the performer, and both of those are distinct from the gender of the performance, then the performance suggests a dissonance not only between sex and performance, but sex and gender, and gender and performance. As much as drag creates a unified picture of 'woman' (what its critics often oppose), it also reveals the distinctness of those aspects of gender experience which are falsely naturalized as a unity through the regularity fiction of heterosexual coherence. *In imitating gender, drag implicitly reveals the imitative structure of gender itself – as well as its contingency* ... In place of the law of heterosexual coherence we see sex and gender denaturalized by means of a performance which avows their distinctness and dramatizes the cultural mechanism of their fabricated unity (1993: 137–8).

The body clearly has no priority or privilege in shaping gender identity here, although the body is implicated in the practices and customs through which gender identities are performed. Butler uses performativity to describe the processes of repeated 'citation' of past practices, reiterating known customs. She uses the example of 'girling the girl' to describe the way in which the birth of a baby girl is heralded with cries of 'it's a girl', a cry which initiates a plethora of practices, rights and customs including clothes, making physical contact, holding and ways of speaking to and about the child. Butler offers interesting insights into the ways in which performativity works and she effectively subverts the rigidity of two sex classification and the binaries of sex and gender. Her analysis could be very useful in explaining how a woman was able to pass as a man and 'deceive' even his own son. The analysis is weaker on the grounding of the rigid categories that she challenges. She does not go into the inequalities implicit and sometimes explicit in the dualisms that she rejects. As with Foucault, upon whose work she draws, there is limited analysis of the sources of power behind particular 'citations' or of particular locations or any extra discursive sites of the operation of power.

Where does this leave the sex/gender debate? Are we left with a disembodied, socially constructed gender? Is the body reduced to anatomy? The body is invested with sites implicated in the production of meanings about identity, that it would be very difficult to reduce to 'anatomy'. 'With my anatomy I thee worship' lacks the impact of the original! However, the binary of sex and gender has become untenable, but there is a strong case for retaining the term gender rather than sex. As Stevi Jackson and Sue Scott argue, gender focuses on the social aspects of difference between women and men, challenging the natural roots of such divisions, bringing in the possibility of critical analyses of power differentials. They also suggest that sex is a more ambiguous term covering both differences between women and men, and sexuality and sexual practices (2002: 20). They cite former US president Bill Clinton's infamous claim, when challenged about his relationship with Monica Lewinsky, 'I did not have sex with that woman' as illustrative of the limitations of the term 'sex'.

Do identities need bodies?

Can you have an identity without a body? Cyberspace offers the possibility of the increased development of identities in an apparently disembodied space. Changing technologies make it possible to communicate at a distance with an immediacy only possible with physical proximity in the past. The internet might offer a publicly accessible space with the potential for exploring and developing new expressions of identity. New technologies offer the potential of transformation in many areas of experience. One of the main utopian discourses arising out of the development of computer communication is the potential it offers for people to escape the body, especially the constraints of a body which is marked by race, age, gender and corporeal needs, such as eating and sleeping (Lupton, 2000), although, as Lupton points out the virtual body does engage in sexual activity, as the hyperbole about cybersex indicates (p. 480). One of the claims of virtual reality is that it provides the technological possibility of creating identities and forming relationships free from body-based, 'real' identities. Of course, people have presented themselves, without being physically there, by telephone, by telegraph and well before that by letter.

However, the internet offers both very fast communication and a greater security of anonymity than other means of communication. The internet is also largely value free, a democratic space, with equal access afforded to those who want to set up a ramblers' group, or a chat line devoted to the experience of a particular disability, as to those who want to exchange ideas on transgressive sexualities; there are chat rooms even for those supporting consensual incest as well as support groups (Hari, 2002: 98–9). The more positive proponents of virtual reality and computer communication proclaim their liberatory potential especially in transcending the limitations of the traditional separation between body and machine.

Donna Haraway's concept of the cyborg, with its melding of the human body and machine technology provides the means of thinking outside dualisms like that between mind and body, real and virtual and even between the gendered opposition of women and men (Haraway, 1991). Cyberspace presents enormous potential for the growth of cyborg identities that transgress the limitations of oppositions between body and mind and body and machine. The cyborg as developed by Haraway, is a concept that challenges traditional constraining dichotomies and breaks down boundary categorizations and confuses boundary distinction (1991). The cyborg offers a new way of thinking about difference and a new way of conceptualizing the relationship between human beings and machines, people and technoscience and the human and the animal, which can challenge the limitations of essentialism and fixity. Haraway argues that in the late twentieth century there was a breakdown in the distinctions between animals and people, between humans and machines and between science and fiction. This breakdown can be used to construct the concept of the cyborg, which bridges the gap between human and machine. There are myriad examples we might cite of the merging of human and machine. Many of the interventions of reproductive technologies begin the process, even intervening into the uterus carrying the unborn foetus before birth. Our reliance upon and integration with the machine ranges from the almost total dependence on machines for communication as in the case of the physicist Stephen Hawkin, through various forms of mobility support to a reliance on spectacles to remedy visual impairment. Haraway's cyborg is a very optimistic conceptualization of the relationship between people and machines, which seeks to challenge the constraints of the fear that machines will 'take over' and eliminate human agency. The cyborg as described by Haraway is ahistorical, although this has been challenged. She seeks to reformulate traditional hierarchical relationships with new networks. For example, in what she calls the formatics of domination she sets up some alternatives to the comfortable domination in the left-hand column with a new, what she calls, 'scary' formation on the right.

Examples of Haraway's reworking of some traditional hierarchies

Representation	Simulation
Bourgeois novel, realism	Science fiction, postmodernism
Organism	Biotic component
Depth, integrity	Surface, boundary
Heat	Noise
...	...
Eugenics	Population control
...	...
Hygiene	Stress management
Microbiology, tuberculosis	Immunology, AIDS
Organic division of labor	Ergonomics/cybernetics of labor
...	...
Reproduction	Replication
Organic sex role specialization	Optimal genetic strategies
...	...
Family wage	Comparable worth
Public/private	Cyborg citizenship
Nature/culture	Fields of difference
Cooperation	Communications enhancement
...	...
Sex	Genetic engineering
Labor	Robotics
Mind	Artificial intelligence
World War II	Star Wars
White capitalist patriarchy	Informatics of domination

From Haraway (2000a: 53–4).

In the area of reproductive technologies the notion of the cyborg allows us to transcend the ties of kinship and to include those women who have been excluded, for example from minority ethnic groups, lesbians and older women. Women in these groups have often been unable to access assisted reproductive technologies, such as fertility treatment, which might allow them to become mothers. Younger, white, heterosexual women in what are perceived as stable relationships have been more likely to be privileged in benefiting from such treatments and support (in Woodward, 2000b). Haraway's aim is to combine socialist, feminist and technoscientific thinking, but there are still some uncomfortable questions to be asked about the cyborg. Who has the power to construct the cyborg and its representations? Who can benefit from the cyborg and cyborg thinking? Jennifer

Gonzalez argues that the cyborg is historical. It still draws on traditional power relations and fails, ultimately to transcend the constraints of class, gender, race and ethnicity in its representations, even in science fiction (2000). Gonzalez suggests, contrary to Haraway's claims, that far from having no position, the cyborg is indeed 'raced', classed and formed within discourses of contemporary culture.

So, can you really present yourself as having a new identity in cyberspace? Computer-mediated communication provides a space for communication based only on verbal clues. In face to face encounters, 'participants can pick up various social role information such as age, race, nationality. Gender, demeanour, style of dress etc that are absent in computer-mediated communication as any aspect of social role performance, presentation of self and physical appearance are within the written text' (Wiley, 1999: 134–5). So in communication in cyberspace you can present yourself, through the verbal medium as whoever you want to be, with much greater anonymity than other forms of communication. There is less leakage of clues from your physical appearance about who you 'really' are, although computer-mediated talk has its own conventions and codes. Computer communication might offer enormous potential for the elderly, those who are home bound and for people with disabilities who may find on-line communication easy and convenient. It provides easy and fast communication with family and friends, access to informative web sites and the means of accessing a whole range of consumer goods and services, including basic provisions and foodstuff. Mike Featherstone cites examples where, even in the case of those who have extensive physical disabilities, it is possible for the computer user's virtual body to engage in mobility and sensory exploration. You just have to teach the computer a few moves (2000: 612). Virtual reality generates the experience of freedom, rather than just the opportunity to 'escape' the body. 'Body projects' provide myriad opportunities for investing in the 'real' body, for combating the negative effects of ageing, through cosmetic surgery or through working out at the gym or by buying products which will enhance one's appearance (Shilling, 1997). Chris Shilling takes up Anthony Giddens' argument about identity and contemporary forms of intimacy, by showing how the body has become central to our sense of who we are so that the body itself is part of reflexive self-identity; a component to be worked on, as the representation of the self. In the same way, cyberspace provides the means of mixing technology and body and making changes to the body through advances in technoscience. On-line communications involve disclosures about the self which are unmediated by physical clues, even though it is a 'real' body which inputs the communication. On-line, people can reconstruct and create sexual identities. Cyberspace offers a site for the presentation of sexual identities which can be a valuable resource for those who are sexually marginalized (Tsang, 2000). For example coming out on-line can be an important stage in defining sexual identity. Although computer communication offers a public space for the expression of intimate feelings the 'real' embodied person may feel more confident in this disembodied space. This space is still gendered however, and traditional assumptions are made about speaking as a woman or as a man. What has been called 'compu-sex' takes different forms which can be seen as 'a blend of phone sex, computer dating and high tech voyeurism' (Branwyn, 2000: 398). 'Compu-sex' suggests that it is possible for people, most likely men, to achieve some kind of personal sexual satisfaction triggered by an internet exchange. Cyberspace just offers a new space in which to experience sexuality and sexual feelings, possibly through the presentation of a different identity. This may not be very different from the respectable, middle-class man, perhaps a politician or a judge, who presents a straight sexual identity in many areas of his life, including his family, but enacts a gay identity in other spaces. While offering a space for the exploration of new sexual identities or the possibility of greater freedom of expression than are experienced off-line, most bulletin board systems where people communicate involve presentations of the self which draw on existing gender roles. The majority of those who frequent chat rooms in search of compu-sex are men (ibid.). They also involve descriptions of real-world circumstances and the establishment of some spatial context that relates to the 'real' world. Some participants use the cyber communication to express their off-line anxieties, using the bulletin board as a kind of counselling service (ibid.: p. 399). Cyberspace maybe disembodied but it is still 'real' bodies who press the keys and write the scripts. It is 'real' bodies who live off-line. The 'real body' may belong to a man of 47, who is passing as a youth and communicating with a girl of 13 in the privacy of her bedroom. The anonymity of virtual reality is only called into question when the 'real man' attempts to meet up with the child of 13, what is euphemistically called 'off-line' (*The Observer*, 18 March 2001).Cyberspace and virtual reality are both cultural as well as technological spaces (Balsamo, 2000: 495). Cyberspace provides a new space in which to communicate, with potential for transformation of identity, but too great an emphasis on the representational medium can detract from the importance of economic and structural factors for example in access to the medium and in terms of the off-line circumstances which also contribute to the relationships which it is possible to negotiate (Wakeford, 2000: 413). The medium may be new but the subjectivities that are implicated are still embodied.

Body projects

One of the ways in which we attempt to exercise control over our bodies is through the practice of what have been called 'body projects'. As Chris Shilling argues, 'In the affluent west, there is a tendency for the body to be seen as a *project* which should be worked at and accomplished as part of an individual's self-identity' (1997: 69). Shilling distinguishes this contemporary phenomenon from pre-modern practices of decorating and altering the body in line with shared, communal rituals and the expectations of tradition and community. Current practices are more reflexive and involve individualized identity projects. Such projects all involve management and maintenance and the notion that the body is open to reconstruction and can be subject to change and to control. They range from the more extreme commitment of some body builders (Fussell, 1991) and plastic surgery almost on the scale of complete body reconstruction facilitated by modern technological advances, as practised by some media celebrities, to dieting and activity at the health club. In different ways, mastery of the body can be seen as offering a source of certainty in an uncertain world. In spite of traditional western distinctions between mind and body, such body projects indicate strong support for the idea that by taking control of our bodies and presenting an attractive physical image of ourselves we can present an attractive self. As we saw in the last chapter, the visual offers a very powerful medium through which identities are represented. This applies to the bodies that we inhabit as well as to the images we look at. The body is the medium through which messages about identity are conveyed.

Sue Benson takes the example of ideas about fat, using the example of the shift from the middle of the nineteenth century in Europe and the USA towards a very negative view of body fat and a much more positive evaluation of the thin body. She argues that this trend, and the more recent movement towards the valuing of the hard, muscular body, for both women and men, 'is much more than a question of bodily aesthetics. The bad body is fat, slack, uncared for; it demonstrates a lazy and undisciplined "self". The good body is sleek, thin and toned. To have such a body is to project to those around you – as well as to yourself – that you are morally as well as physically in shape' (1997: 123). It seems little wonder that many of us are eager to get down to the gym! However, it is also the case that we also fail in this endeavour and levels of obesity are rising in both the USA and the UK. It is likely that the often confusing and contradictory messages that we receive and the polarization of the fat and the thin body with all this implies for self-image, are just what dooms so many people to failure in this attempt to take control. The ubiquity of body projects and the culture, of which they are part, means that it is not just the case that one has a fat or thin body; it means something about identity.

This movement towards the development of the disciplined body has a longer history. Norbert Elias argues that there has been a civilizing process at work throughout Europe since the Middle Ages (1978). His is a very particular view of social change. He claims that there has been a long-term shift in the incidence, location and expression of violence both in societies and in the personalities of the individuals who make up those societies. The civilized body is able to rationalize and exercise control over the emotions. Civilized bodies perform appropriately according to rules that have been internalized; no more spitting in the street or pushing food into your mouth in an uncouth manner. Certain activities, like having sex and defecating also take place in private. In contrast to the lack of strictures and prohibitions of the Middle Ages, the Renaissance saw the advent of more strictly rule governed behaviour, the exclusion of certain activities into the private arena and greater emotional control, which spread from the court to all levels of society. Court society developed institutionalized codes of practice, based around the body and embodiment, through which people became differentiated in elaborate hierarchies (Elias, 1983). People exercised agency in order to define their embodiment as civilized, that is as distinct from what could be seen as uncivilized, which could be associated with animal rather than human behaviour. The trend towards civilizing bodies involved a socialization process, whereby 'natural' functions are hidden. This also involved rationalization, whereby lines of demarcation are increasingly drawn between impulse and instinct and the control mechanisms that ensure more civilized practice (1978). These processes led to a progressive individualization, where a sense of the self, in control of the body, became increasingly apparent. The key points of Elias' work include the focus on the body as the site of the exercise of this agency and the role of the body in the whole historical civilizing process.

Elias' argument is useful when considering the contemporary trend of body projects including recent developments in emotional control, for example through therapy and counselling, where we are exhorted to control our emotions through greater understanding of them. It could all be seen as part of the civilizing process, along with taking control of our bodies to produce bodies that are both healthy and beautiful.

Elias suggests a relatively smooth if not linear path towards greater civilization. While his thesis may apply to the recent phenomenon of body projects it is difficult to sustain his claims about the ever more civilized body in relation to acts of violence and pugilism, especially given the scale of killing in war during the twentieth century. Elias, however argues that it is not the scale of violence but the form it takes. In recent times, while millions of people have been killed in war and in dreadful acts of genocide and terrorism, fewer individuals have themselves engaged in violent acts, body on body, than in the Middle Ages or in previous centuries. Elias' account is largely one of men's stories. He offers no explanation of men's violence against women or of women's experience of the separation of public and private spheres and how this might impact upon the process of civilizing bodies. Does the notion of civilization explain body projects? Elias' account seems very gendered. His narrative is largely male, but maybe this fits with men's body projects more than with women's.

A sporting diversion

To take an example of a largely male activity, although women have participated in the past and continue to struggle for recognition in this field, would boxing fit the description of a body project and would it be one that could be construed as part of the civilizing process? Boxing is part of 'gym culture'. People engage in the sport as part of a fitness programme as well as seeing it as possible employment, if they turn professional (Woodward, 2002b). Boxing, as a legitimate sport is a highly disciplined activity. It requires dedicated commitment to training and enormous self-control both in training and in the ring. The self-control is demanded in order to comply with the rules of the game and to ensure acceptance, whether as a professional or as an amateur. It is also required in order to avoid physical damage. To be taken off one's guard is to expose oneself to serious injury. As one boxer put it, describing the gym he attended,

> There's no just like free fighting, punching, it's all about learning how to control yourself and ... that's big thing here. ... It's what it's all about – not getting hit (Woodward, 2002b).

Boxing is about self-control; it is also about fighting. This activity would seem to comply with Elias' notion of self-control, but the nature of the activity does seem to contradict Elias' understanding of the move away from individual acts of violence. While the main emphasis of the protagonists might be the avoidance of injury, the main purpose of boxing is to inflict damage through violent body on body contact. While in the gym, in training sparring may not involve injury, the training is directed at damaging one's opponent and learning to achieve the ultimate success of rendering one's opponent unconscious.

Boxing is deeply implicated with masculinity (de Garis, 2000). The involvement with this particular sporting activity has particular resonance for presenting oneself as 'tough' and as a 'real man' in the tradition of a particular form of physical, dominant and dominating masculinity (Oates, 1995). It might be seen as offering a particularly good example of an embodied hegemonic masculinity (Connell, 1985). This is not to say that boxing is not also widely implicated with race and class and location (Early, 1994), but these articulate with masculinity in the production of gendered identities in relation to the sport. As Loic Wacquant observes, 'That boxing is a working class occupation is reflected not only in the physical nature of the activity but also in the social recruitment of its practitioners and in their continuing dependence on blue-collar or unskilled service jobs to support their career in the ring' (1995: 502). This follows Pierre Bourdieu's claim that 'the body is the most indisputable materialization of class taste' (1984: 190). According to Bourdieu different social classes operate with different tastes and lifestyles and have different, and unequal access to cultural capital. (1984). Bourdieu has argued that working-class bodily types constitute a form of physical capital that has a lower exchange value than that which has been developed by the ruling classes (1978). Working-class people have more limited access to the means of converting physical capital into cultural capital and their physical capital is predominantly devalued. Thus boxing could be seen as a largely male, working-class engagement in converting physical capital. Boxing is a sport which has massive capital investment and very high earnings at the top, but for the vast majority of those who are involved at the local level, there are very limited financial returns.

Boxing involves display and spectacle as well as what may at times appear to be a parodic masculinity. It is a good example of the carnivalesque, in its display and parody of masculinity. Bakhtin uses the term carnival to describe hedonistic activities characterized by excess and the symbolic overthrow of hierarchies and social order, such as were experienced in medieval fairs. Such activities included overt sexual displays and excessive consumption of food and drink ([1965] 1984). The display of the fight with the associated trappings of popular culture present an activity that could be construed as contemporary carnival in its excess, if not in its lack of control, although there are myriad stories of excess which result from lack of control in the ring, some of Mike Tyson's heavyweight bouts being good examples. Boxing is also an entertainment, which is attended by a high paying audience, who sometimes enjoy dinner while they watch the display. This highlights the embodiment of class difference and demonstrates starkly the divide in the investment of physical capital by the largely working-class protagonists in the drama of the fight, which at this particular site is viewed by those who are more affluent. Even sparring in the gym is accompanied by popular music, presenting a display not that far removed from the disco (Woodward, 2002b).

Another feature of carnival according to Bakhtin, is the display of grotesque bodies. While boxing is concerned with the display of the perfectly honed, fit, beautiful body it also involves the grotesque body of defeat and serious injury.

Boxing permits what Stallybrass and White identified as an 'alarming conjuncture of the elite and the vulgar' (1986: 135) and can be seen as combining 'the attraction of repulsion (ibid.: p. 140). Boxing carries the mark of civilization. It is heavily regulated yet it permits an alliance of raw

Naseem Hamed: Boxing and the beautiful body. (Reproduced with permission from Empics, Nottingham.)

apprehension, involving flesh on flesh, in the most corporeal of sporting contests, with parodic display. This is entertainment! Boxing is however a form of entertainment that can be explained and positioned within Bakhtin's notion of carnival, as containing a utopian urge (1987). Carnival displaces the normal social hierarchies. Carnival is a spectacle that is also gross and vulgar, repressed in bourgeois culture in the modern period, according to Bakhtin, yet there is also voyeuristic pleasure in carnival even if bourgeois enjoyment of the spectacle is voyeuristic and tinged with guilt. Boxing is a spectacle beset with contradictions and ambiguities enjoyed and reviled in equal proportions, probably at the same time.

Boxing and the broken body. (Reproduced with permission from Empics, Nottingham.)

Boxing may illustrate control, but its practices and its criteria of success challenge this notion of the linear progress of civilizing customers and practices. The enthusiasm of spectators for damage and at least a knock out, also subverts Elias' understanding of the onward march of civilization.

Boxing illustrates some of the contradictions in the formation and presentation of embodied identity. Boxing includes the primacy of gender in relation to identity, but shows that this is a complex connection, which is experienced in different ways and cannot be simply read off as an aberration in the civilizing process. It indicates elements of self-control and of the need to negotiate identity through exercising agency over the body, by taking control, However the body is also subject to its own frailties, even in a sport where human agents seek supremacy over both their own body and that of their opponent. It is embodied frailty that presents one of the limitations to attempts to exercise control and prevents us from fulfilling Aimee Liu's demand:

> I will be master of my own body, if nothing else I vow (in Bordo, 1993: 150).

Imperfect bodies; faulty selves?

How can the body be a project that one seeks to 'master' if that body is frail or impaired in some way? The impaired body presents limits to the extent to which we might seek to exercise control and to perform some transformations by working on the body. The impaired body is also subject to constraining representations and can be stigmatized, suggesting an outside sign of what Erving Goffman has called stimatized identity and 'faulty personhood' (1990). Goffman uses the term stigma as having two aspects. 'A stigma, then, is a special kind of relationship between attribute and stereotype ... does the stigmatized person assume his [*sic.*] difference is known about already or is evident on the spot, or does he assume it is neither known about by those present nor immediately perceivable be them? In the first case one deals with the plight of the *discredited*, in the second of the *discreditable*' (p. 14). Goffman makes a distinction between the body and the human agent who seeks to control and manage that body. He also draws attention to the connection between individuals and their bodies and the society that they inhabit and notes that an individual 'who might have been received easily in ordinary social intercourse possesses a trait that can obtrude itself upon attention and turn those of us whom he meets away from him ... He possesses a stigma, an undesired differentness from what we had anticipated' (p. 15). Just as the slim, athletic body may be used to signify success and an attractive identity, the impaired body may be represented as an indicator of failed identity, quite outside the control of the person who resides in that body. As Tom Shakespeare has argued, non-disabled people project their fears of losing control onto people with disabilities (1994).

Goffman views the body as a material property of individuals, yet they are defined and made meaningful by society. It is this tension, between the person and the society, which is foregrounded in the experience of impairment and disability. Social representations of disability as stigmatized constrain the agency of people with disabilities, but those who give greater emphasis to social construction may marginalize and obscure the very real limitations of the body.

In the latter part of the twentieth century much writing on the subject stressed the ways in which people experiencing some form of disability have been categorized as 'other' by those who are not disabled. In this case, disability has come to be seen as a property of the society rather than the individual or the person who is so classified. For example, campaigns have focused on the ways in which particular contexts, such as the workplace, may be disabling rather than the people who inhabit them being disabled. With appropriate facilities it is possible for a whole range of people to carry out their everyday routines and to participate fully in the workplace as well as in the home. Tom Shakespeare notes the ways in which activists have campaigned, in the tradition of 'identity politics' to enable people with disabilities to participate fully in economic, social and cultural life (1993). From the 1960s onwards, with the development of the disability movement, disabled people became politically active in order to voice their needs. Much of this activism was based on a social constructionist understanding of disability. Difficulties in obtaining employment for disabled people were attributed to discrimination and prejudice and political action has been directed at effecting changes, in legislation and in social attitudes.

However, there have been some difficulties with the all-embracing, overarching social explanation of the experience of people with disabilities. Firstly there is the issue of embodiment. As Shakespeare argues, such political strategies associated with social constructionist approaches have made it difficult for people with disabilities to acknowledge the material experience of embodied impairment. People with disabilities do not constitute a homogeneous group, the members of which all experience similar social exclusion. While social exclusion and the construction of difference and 'otherness', which Goffman calls stigma, are all extremely pertinent, so too are the differences and specificities of bodily experience. There is a need to highlight the importance of the diversity and range of experience. The difficulties of being disabled are often more subtle and more personal than those views which focus on the oppression that results from social organization and structures and upon discrimination. Recent work has indicated the need to move from an emphasis upon the dominance of social structures over the experience of embodiment and to see the two as implicated in a more complex interrelationship (Corker and Shakespeare, 2002). This work draws on some of the developments of postmodernism and poststructuralism and includes critiquing a number of sites at which meanings are produced about disability, showing how disability articulates with other aspects of experience such as gender, race and ethnicity. This requires both engaging with and going beyond the social model. Shelley Tremain argues for the application of Foucauldian discourse analysis, but with the expansion of the discursive space so that disabled people can articulate their lived experiences, including those of corporeality. She offers alternative strategies for disability studies, writing of how disability is categorized as an identity,

> The agenda for a *critical* disability studies should be to expose the disciplinary character of that identity. That is, it should expose the way that disability has been naturalized *as* an impairment by identifying the 'constitutive mechanisms of truth and knowledge' within scientific and social discourses, policy and medico-legal practice which produce it and sustain it ... An interdisciplinary study of 'natural impairment' and 'natural sex' which examines how the disciplinary boundaries of disability studies and gender studies operate to naturalize their own respective 'objects' *and* each other's, might be another way to do this (2002: 44–5).

Those who have campaigned to change views of disability have often argued that, although disabilities are experienced by individuals, disability is a socially imposed restriction. Although the experience is embodied, bodies are simultaneously physical, biological social and psychological. One aspect of the development of the arguments for more sophisticated, poststructuralist under-standings of social constructionism and of the campaigns that are based on it, is a focus on representational systems such as language which position people with disabilities as victims or as damaged. The writer Louis Keith expresses this in her poem 'Tomorrow I'm going to rewrite the English language', in which she draws attention to 'all those ambulist metaphors' of the English language.

> ... I won't have to feel dependent because I can't stand on my own two feet and I'll refuse to feel a failure when I don't stay one step ahead ... (1994: 57).

This illustrates well the way in which people can feel excluded by the ways in which we talk; through the taken-for-granted expressions we use – like 'walk-ing tall', 'advancing in great strides', not to mention the more offensive ways in which people with disabilities are marginalized.

Nasa Begum, in the same collection as Louis Keith's poem, describes the way she was addressed as an Asian British, young person with disabilities.

> I don't remember race being an issue in the hospital where I spent a lot of my childhood and there were so many Asian people where I lived that I did not stand out as being black. It took me a long time to understand why people who did not know me in my neighbourhood

called me 'spastic', 'bandy legs' or 'ironside' and why people with disabilities called me 'paki' or 'nigger'. Eventually I learned that wherever
I went I would stand out as being different from the majority and I had
to be prepared to accept being called either 'paki' or 'bandy legs' and
sometimes both ... But I've come a long way ... I've reclaimed my
identity by refusing to accept a concept of 'normality' which tells me
I must walk, have fair skin and try to blend in by wearing western clothes
(Begum, 1994: 50–1).

This illustrates the ways in which identities are socially constructed, and
historically and socially specific in their formation. Embodiment and disability
are read and experienced in culturally specific ways where 'otherness' is created through aspects of visible difference. Social constructionist theories have
been developed for dealing with exclusion as well as providing a framework
for understanding some aspects of the experience of disabilities.

While some illnesses and examples of impairment may lend themselves
particularly well to a critique that prioritizes stigma and the social construction of 'otherness', others do not. The impact of AIDS in the west cannot be
explained only by its fatal effects. The massive cultural attention paid to the
disease demanded cultural explanations. As Simon Watney claimed, not very
long after the early outbreak of AIDS, 'The HIV virus manifested itself in three
constituencies in the West – blacks, intravenous drug users and gay men. The
presence of AIDS in these groups is generally perceived not as accidental but
as a symbolic extension of some imagined inner essence of being, manifest-
ing itself as disease' (1987: 8).

Susan Wendell describes the over-emphasis on the symbolic and the
cultural construction of 'otherness', as marginalizing the embodied experience
of suffering that can accompany illness and impairment (1996). While
campaigns that have concentrated on a social constructionist approach have
claimed that if only we could create social justice and overcome cultural alien-
ation from the body, the experience of embodiment could be positive and even
pleasant, Wendell uses her own experience of pain to explore the possibility
of reformulating the relationship between consciousness and the body in a
way that acknowledges corporeality more fully.

She suggests that transcendence could be adopted as a strategy for coping
with the exigencies of the impaired body. Rather than denying corporeal
experience as a strategy for coping with pain, she argues for developing an
'observer's' attitude towards the body and accommodating these bodily
sensations, however unpleasant they may be. She argues for attempting to
disengage the self from the body so that she is able to avoid identifying the
self with the body. The body has an independent life and is not simply a
reflector of other processes in Wendell's account. This analysis is useful in

offering an antidote to the excesses of social constructionism, but it seems to be presenting a not that different alternative version of the mind/body split that has been so effectively challenged in recent years.

Maternal bodies; maternal selves

One example of identity where it would be very difficult to fail to have some regard for the body is motherhood. Motherhood might be an identity which at first consideration could be definitely an identity that is rooted in the body; not just one body but two (at least) and at the same time! Motherhood is a contested identity that illustrates well the tensions between essentialist and non-essentialist views. Common sense stories reproduce maternal identity as not only embodied, but as shaped, or even determined, by biology. As Adrienne Rich says 'we are all of woman born' (1977), although not all women are mothers and not all mothers have a biological connection to their children. At some point there has to be a woman's body. Even cloning, which would not necessarily require a man at any point, demands a woman's body for the gestation of the foetus (Woodward, 2000b).

Feminist critiques of the patriarchal control of women's bodies have frequently drawn on claims to an essential female experience (Rich, 1977), whereas other feminist stories distinguish between biological and social motherhood, between the body that carries the foetus to term and the person who rears the child, who may, of course not be the same person (Jagger, 1983). Life in the twenty-first century is more complex! The first woman, the genetic mother, may provide the egg, which is fertilized by a donor sperm (of the genetic father) and implanted in the second woman, the host mother, who carries and gives birth to the baby, at which point a third woman (or it could be a man) adopts the infant and takes responsibility for child care. Cloning would still require a host mother's body, at the time of writing. While fertilization can take place *in vitro*, gestation cannot as yet. A maternal body would be required and the status of this body in relation to identity is one that is socially and culturally mediated. Carrying a child and giving birth are areas of experience that are not without impact on one's sense of identity, however.

Motherhood clearly involves more than carrying a foetus and giving birth, although the stresses, strains and joys of delivery should not be underestimated (Brook, 1976; Oakley, 1980). Adrienne Rich goes further and argues, echoing Irigaray's assertions about the role of the mother in culture and the psychic investment we have in the mother figure, that 'motherhood is the great mesh in which all human relations are entangled, in which lurk our most elemental assumptions about love and power' (1980: 260). Birth is a moment that can combine sensations of physicality, emotion and even spirituality. One of the early proponents of 'natural' childbirth, the obstetrician, Grantley Dick-Read wrote in 1933, 'the birth of a child is an emotional experience which brings with it all the noblest and most loving qualities of men, women and children' (quoted in Brook, 1976: 35). Not everyone's experience indeed, but it captures some of the ways in which birth can be much more than a physical experience and the ways in which the experience combines the corporeal, social and psychic dimensions of motherhood. Some moments in our biographies condense different aspects of human experience, and thus have particularly intensified resonance, more so than other experiences. Birth may be one such moment. Birth is also deeply implicated in the myth of origin as we saw in Chapter 2. In the search for certainty about who we are, knowledge of the birth mother is sought as a means of finding out some 'truth' about our own identity. As one mother put it, 'the desire for motherhood is also about the past. It's the desire to relive my childhood with the mother I desired to have rather than the mother I actually had. Is it the child or the lost mother I want to regain?' (Radford quoted in Gieve, 1989: 137). The position of the mother is mediated by desire and longing.

The intensity of the emotions surrounding birth and the relationship with a child, what Rich describes as the conflicting emotions of 'anger and the tenderness' (1977), may lead to an interpretation which, rather than privileging the moment and the relationship as a pivotal point in the identity story, accords it the status of essential truth. This essentialism is presented as a means of comprehending particularly significant moments rather than locating them along the routes we have travelled; privileged, intense, but at a point in the journey and not the root of 'who we are'. Such moments provide meaning and contribute to our identities, rather than fulfilling the myth of origin.

The intensity of the experience is not the only reason why motherhood has been positioned within an essentialist discourse, even one that offers biological 'truths' about an identity. Irigaray claims that 'the relationship with the mother is mad desire', but it is a relationship which has been repressed and excluded. She argues that motherhood has for a long time been the 'dark continent' of western culture, unspoken and unacknowledged, within the 'shadows of culture' (1991: 35). It is desire for the mother, for the 'imaginary and symbolic relationship with the mother' (quoted in Whitford, 1991: 35). Irigaray prioritizes the female unconscious, rooted in relation to the maternal body, rather than founded on the paternal phallus of Freud or the phallus as key signifier in Lacanian psychoanalysis. Thus the focus of her critique of psychoanalysis is on the pre-Oedipal stage rather than the Oedipal stage as in the work of both Freud and Lacan (Irigaray, 1985).

However, while this approach has the advantage of drawing attention to the different dimensions of motherhood as an identity and of highlighting some of its contradictions, including those related to the psychic investment that the identity carries, motherhood *is* represented, albeit within somewhat constrained categories. Recent research in cultural studies too, has pointed to the

Madonna and Child painted by a follower of Giotto, early fourteenth century. (Ashmolean Museum, Oxford.)

absence of mother figures within popular cultural forms, such as film and even women's magazines (Kaplan, 1992; Woodward, 1997c), where motherhood may be assumed and taken for granted, but absence is not universal. Empirical research has also pointed to the lack of space afforded to maternal voices, for example as indicated by Steph Lawler in her study of the mother–daughter relationship (2000), which seeks to reinstate the stories as told by women as mothers as well as from a daughter's position. Maternal figures are present within representational systems. Motherhood is subject to regulation and discipline, for example through the construction of the 'good' and the 'bad' mother, as categories into which mothers can be positioned. These figures of motherhood are represented within a number of discursive fields, at different sites within cultural systems.

As Marina Warner suggests the Virgin Mary is one of the few women permitted the status of myth. Writing about this painting, Warner claims that the Madonna embodies 'the equivalence between goodness, motherhood, purity, gentleness and submission ... Assumptions about role satisfaction, sexual differences, beauty and goodness are all wondrously compressed in this one icon ... Mary is mother and virgin' (1985: 336). This figure, which combines myth and ideology, embodies motherhood as both natural and idealized, natural and supernatural even, since this is a motherhood that is unsullied by sexuality. The Madonna has carried the infant in her womb and gives birth to Christ's body from her body, but she is not sexual. The cult of the Virgin Mary has significant resonance, beyond the Christian religion, in contributing to one part of the idealized binary between 'good' and 'bad' mothers. However, just as myths can offer idealized images to which we should aspire, so also they can present the antithesis; as Warner also suggests, 'monstrous mothers'. In her 1994 Reith lectures Warner used the example of the film Jurasssic Park to illustrate an aspect of this phenomenon. She describes the female dinosaurs getting out of control as an example of 'naked confrontation between nature coded female and culture coded male' (p. 25). Warner's critique shows how myths have constructed the historical figure of the monstrous mother, which informs contemporary discourses of regulation. From Greek mythology the figure who most frighteningly embodies the 'bad mother' must be Medea who, according to Euripides' tragedy *Medea*, having betrayed and killed for her husband Jason, when he abandoned her, murdered her children. We have contemporary variations on the theme of the bad mother who, even if she does not actually murder her children, is deemed irresponsible and failing in her duty to care for them properly. In the press, television, radio and internet media we are presented with 'bad mothers', welfare mothers of home alone children, lesbian mothers, lone mothers who are not providing their children with appropriate male role models and who are thus responsible for the disaffected young men who have been reared without fathers. Relief is expressed with an air of 'I told you so' when high flying, successful women abandon their careers to look after their families 'properly'.

Motherhood is subject to regulatory practices through the intervention of the state in the Foucauldian language of *biopolitics*. Foucault's notion of bio-politics is used by Jacques Donzelot to describe the process whereby the state, from the eighteenth century onwards intervened in the private lives of individuals, targeting the family, and in particular the body, in the regulation of health, nutrition and hygiene (1980). The figures of the 'good' and the 'bad' mother are also inscribed in the regulatory practices of social policy and of welfare provision. The sources of such knowledge about 'good mothering' have become more diffuse in western cultures where there is a proliferation of expertise and different forms of knowledge, so that, following Ulrich Beck, it might be said that 'expertise' itself is breaking down (1992). Women are bombarded with very diverse expert knowledge about how to look after themselves in pregnancy and their children from birth onwards. This sur-veillance increasingly becomes self-surveillance (Lawler, 2000: 20), however, so that while the responsibility is the mother's, the conditions of the production of different expert knowledges are lost in the rhetoric of choice.

Mothers themselves are part of the process of the production of knowledge about mothering. Women's experiences of pregnancy and childbirth and the work of mothering have also informed women's resistance to the discursive regimes of truth, which have dominated at particular historical periods and have become new sources of knowledge. Childbirth and the demand for control over fertility have significantly been expressed as the need for women to control their own bodies. This control of the body, in particu-lar the control of the reproductive body is of special significance to women because of their role in the reproductive process, notably as having the body that bears the child. Control of the body is closely connected to the agency that we can or cannot exercise over our identities. For women this concerns the choice *not* to be a mother, as well as the circumstances in which they can mother.

Motherhood illustrates well the way that identity is both embodied and socially constructed. The corporeal has particular resonance in the identity of motherhood that encompasses the physicality of birth and of child rearing. Motherhood is especially tied up with conceptualizations of the good and the bad mother and is part of a long tradition that presents a particular, gendered dichotomy in the Madonna and the whore. It is impossible to disentangle the corporeal from the social and cultural, but the corporeal is one of the pivotal points in the narrative of motherhood.

Conclusion

This chapter has covered some of the stories that have emerged within western culture and within the social sciences about the role of the body in relation to identity formation and presentation. One of these stories relates the shift from the absent body, obscured by the supremacy of the mind and the soul, through recognition of the body/mind dichotomy and the disentangling of the two elements, to critiques which stress the interrelationship and inseparability of mind and body in the production of embodied subjectivities. It is a contradictory story. The body emerges in different ways at points in the narrative. At times the body is associated with the flesh and is devalued in relation to the mind, which is seen as the source of human agency. At other times the body is seen to secure certainty, the certainty that comes with scientific knowledge. The body might be seen as the ultimate source of truth about human identity, as in this chapter's opening story. The body is not always devalued; it can be the ultimate sacrifice and an expression of human agency and commitment.

One of the most interesting variants of these stories, is the shift from the idea of separation, for example as represented in the sex/gender binary, to a conceptualization of the interconnectedness of the two, especially in post-structuralist accounts. In this sphere as in the others explored in this book, there are anxieties about the de-stabilizing of identity, which such merging can create. Firstly, the impossibility of disentangling the body from its cultural and social manifestations and inscriptions may lead to a denial of the body and a repression and marginalization of the experience of corporeality. Secondly, an overemphasis on the social construction of identities that are embodied may obscure both the enabling and, more especially, the constraining aspects of corporeality, limiting the recognition that can and should be given to physical needs and wants. There is an expressed desire to acknowledge the body, not just the biological body, but the body as lived by the subject. This means that the body is not only represented and inscribed, it is also experienced and can present enormous restrictions to the range of that experience and to the ways in which we can negotiate our identities. The social sciences, especially sociology, have moved from a disregard of the body to an excess of attention. Yet many poststructuralist and postmodernist accounts offer rather disembodied discussion of the body as inscribed, represented and reproduced through social and cultural practice; the body seems to be everything but corporeal.

It is through the body that we present ourselves to others and make sense of our identities. Even on line we draw on lived bodily experience to represent ourselves and it is embodied subjects who negotiate identities in cyberspace. The material body has a privileged place in the intersection of the personal and the social and the psychic and the social in the negotiation of identity. However, in the different identity journeys in which the body is implicated, there are pivotal moments, at which awareness and experience of corporeality are more important than at others. Some moments offer heightened awareness and a greater intensity of physicality that demand a recognition not available in social constructionist inscriptions. The body is deeply involved in the routes through which identities are forged; this does not mean that the body is the root of identity.

6   Roots and routes

The artistic director of Britain's oldest Asian theatre company Jatinder Verma is asked about his 2002 epic production of the play *Journey to the West*, the story of the migration of Asian people from East Africa in 1968 and their settlement in the UK, 'Is your play about roots?' He replies,

> It depends how you're spelling the word ... I prefer to think of it as r-o-u-t-e-s. Roots lead backwards. Routes are more progressive, leading you to make connections with others. I'm not interested in the particular village in India where my grandfather came from. My identity is located on the road. East Africans are a real conundrum for modern anthropologists because, in some ways, we represent the future, beyond ethnicity. In a truer sense, we are world citizens. I know people who are moving on again, to America. It's as if, having taken the first step out of India, our people are perpetually on the move (in Arnot, 2002).

Verma cites the specific example of East African Asian people and, in this very short quotation, conjures up ideas of movement, routes and diaspora. 'My identity is located on the road', he says. His own autobiography embodies movement. He arrived in the UK from Kenya aged fourteen, his own family of origin having travelled from India to East Africa years before. Verma's *Journey to the West* includes three plays, shown consecutively, at a single sitting (with food breaks!). The first is set in 1901 following the first exodus from Gujerat, which began in the late nineteenth century. The second is set in 1968 and the third in the present in the twenty-first century. Verma's story is one of success and the fluid identities that 'represent the future' and 'move beyond ethnicity' look exciting. Others have used the metaphor 'beyond skin' (used as the title of an Asian fusion music album by Nitin Sawhney) to signify challenges to the fixity of visible difference and reductionist readings of race and blood ties, but moving beyond ethnicity goes further. What does Verma mean by routes? How does this distinction between roots and routes work? The routes he talks about involve the journeys he has taken, the paths which he and other diasporic people have followed and the narratives in which they have been involved. Routes link journeys and stories. Verma's preference for routes rather than roots also attributes more mobility and more potential for change and adaptation to routes. Routes are dynamic. As Verma says people who have already travelled from India to East Africa to the UK might travel elsewhere and create new opportunities and new identities. In this account routes seem to afford more potential for identity being more, or at least as much, about 'becoming' as 'being', as Stuart Hall has argued. Identity 'belongs to the future as much as to the past' (Hall, 1990: 223). It is this potential for change and the desire to look forwards as well as backwards that Verma clearly finds attractive and which makes 'routes a better description than "roots" '. However, the routes he has travelled also relate to his past and provide the inspiration for the plays that he has written. These come from past experience, from the experience of diaspora, but particularly from the journeys which he has travelled, the routes he has already taken. This is what informs the question to which his response is that he prefers routes to roots. Roots tell us about where we have come from; roots are very much involved with the past and with myths of origin. This is not to suggest that a myth is a distortion of truth or a falsehood, but rather that, as in the sense that Roland Barthes has understood myth as discussed in Chapter 5, a myth becomes absorbed into culture, taken for granted and merges with nature. It is clear that Verma has more interest and investment in the dynamics of the present and the future, and the possibilities for change than in tracing his past and his origins in an Indian village, but roots cannot be easily dismissed.

As Madan Sarup suggests 'It is important to know where we come from. All people construct a home, all people have a place to which they feel an attachment, a belongingness. This is in contrast to some postmodernist writers who stress the subject as a nomad, a wanderer, roaming from place to place. We have to understand the power and pull of home' (1996: 181). While movement, change and the possibilities of the new might be attractive, there is also the idea of belonging, of home and of some authentic source of certainty that also has appeal both for individuals and for those seeking to affirm a collective identity, as was argued in Chapter 3.

In Chapter 2, I suggested that individuals often seek the security of a named 'true' parentage that confirms the ties of kinship as well as seeking the revelation of their 'real' 'true' self for example through counselling or psychotherapy; so too do the collectivities of people, whether in ethnic groups or nations. This was discussed in Chapter 3 in the context of the movement of people across the globe. Journeys that are taken so often relate to home, whether it is home as the starting point, to which origins can be traced, or home as the desired point of return. Home is associated with sanctuary and security and may carry the romanticized myth of return, even when it is push factors that have led to exile in the first place. People need a sense of place and of belonging and this is often translated into the desire for roots and some sense of authentic origins, a start to the story so that we can move forward through having laid claim to a myth of origin. The question is whether the notion of identity as rooted and the essentialism that appears to accompany this idea can deliver the security and feeling of groundedness that people may seem to want. Verma acknowledges the pull of India for East African Asian people like himself. Even though he has never lived in India, his birth place being in Nairobi, which was where he lived until he was fourteen, he understands the notion of calling India 'home' even though it is a place where he has only ever been a visitor. In his view the conceptualization of India as 'home' belongs very much in the imaginary. Verma's views in relation to his own identity are also resonant with those of cultural critics and social theorists. Postmodernist, poststructuralist thinking is frequently characterized by its celebration of hybridity, fluidity and contingency, arguing against the apparent rigidity and essentialism of 'roots'.

Gayatri Chakravorty Spivak, an influential literary and cultural theorist, shares Jatinder Verma's view of roots. 'If there is one thing I totally distrust, in fact more than distrust, despise and have contempt for, it is people looking for roots' (Spivak 1990: 93). Spivak's argument is that everyone has roots and there is no need to seek them out. She recognizes the importance of roots, but argues that seeking one's 'roots' is a strategy and a specific tactic that can be deployed at a particular moment. It is a response to the crisis of being excluded and marginalized. Spivak's claim is that the key question does not relate to roots and origins but to who is represented and who is not. She writes about texts, for example those that deal with the history of colonialism. Her argument is that what is required is to expose the slippage between truth and fiction in imperialist histories and to construct counter narratives that allow 'the subaltern to speak'. This means giving voice to those who have been marginalized and who have not been represented; to those who have no explicit presence in the stories that have been told.

Spivak describes herself as the 'post colonial diasporic Indian who seeks to decolonize the mind' (Spivak, 1990: 67). Her aim is to interrogate the imperialism which is inherent, but so often has been unstated, in nineteenth century literary history; to ask questions about who is represented and who is not, in these narratives. Her focus is on the margins and upon those who are not represented, in particular the western construction of the illusion of a homogeneous category of 'Third World Women'. Spivak wants to challenge such dominant signifiers of the outside and of the margins, as being ethnocentric, and as denying the diversity and heterogeneity of those who do 'speak from the margins', if they are permitted to speak at all. This, in part, offers some explanation of Spivak's antagonism to the idea of roots. The search for roots is implicated in an essentialist view of identity that appears to deny diversity and difference, and even a voice to those who are constructed, without specificity, as 'other'.

Looking for certainties: the problem of essentialism

What do we mean by essentialism? At an historical time that is characterized by uncertainty, fast change and transformation (Beck, 1992; Giddens, 1992), it is hardly surprising that people have turned to sources of security in the context of the affirmation of identity that is grounded in some essential 'truth'. As was discussed in Chapter 3, much of the recent debate about globalization has focused on the speed and scale of change and the perception of risk in the 'information society'. Even if many people now have much longer life expectancy than in the past, especially in the continents of North America, Europe and Australia, there is a much higher awareness of the possibilities of risk. This takes the form of anxieties about food, the external environment and health, and in the more affluent areas of the world there is enormous emphasis on taking responsibility for taking care of the self. The search for stability and 'truth' operates at the level of the individual, in relation to the body and psychological well-being as well as in the global arena.

This search for stability may take the form of appeals to genetic certainties, such as proof of parenthood or the revelation of 'who I really am' through psychoanalysis or therapy, as I suggested in Chapter 2. It may be the political certainty of securing sexual identity by appealing to a natural source, for example as some gay men have done, by arguing that they have always known they were gay, in order to counter arguments that homosexuality might somehow be socially constructed, for example by being 'promoted' in schools through sex education lessons. Far from being learned or socially produced, they argue their sexuality is natural, a part of who they really are. In order to give emphasis to the strength of personal and collective investment in an identity position, such as sexual identity, we may claim that it is natural and rooted in biology. It is not something that can be changed. Such apparently essentialist claims have been widely implicated in what were called 'new' social movements when they emerged in the west in the 1960s. Identity politics, giving voice to claims made by marginalized or oppressed groups and drawing on identity to mobilize into political action, has involved appeals to the unique and essential qualities of those sharing particular identities. For example some elements of the women's movement have argued for a celebration of the qualities shared by women, which men, per se cannot possess (Woodward,

1997a). These might be to some biological exclusivity shared by all women or to a history of oppression, 'herstory' as Mary Daly has described women's shared experience through time (1979). What has been called radical feminism and its political offshoots, which have included the advocacy of separatist tactics, have been implicated in assertions that difference rests on such essentialist claims.

Other appeals are to the certainty of a shared past and of belonging to a kinship group which can be identified by its essential qualities. This may take the form of constructing narratives of origin of a people, retelling stories of battles, fought and heroic tales, which condense to 'reveal the truth' of a shared past. The rituals of state often reinforce the successful accomplishment of such identities which become fixed through such reconstructions of a shared, authentic history. Rituals play a crucial part in sustaining the collective memory and reinstating notions of collective identity. Such rituals may have religious and secular aspects. As Emile Durkheim argued, despite differences in content there are few functional differences between religious, national and secular rituals and ceremonies because their aims and their outcomes are remarkably similar (1915). This has been especially marked in England and Wales, where the monarch is both head of state and head of the Anglican church and the Church of England in Wales, whereby as the established church, it still plays a significant role in rituals ranging from state events such as the opening of Parliament and state funerals to memorial and commemorative events.

Secular occasions such as the Football Association Cup Final even may employ quasi-religious songs and hymns and serve a very similar function in bringing people together for moments of shared national identification. Drawing on the language of religion and the history of the state, rituals serve to confirm and establish notions of a British way of life and national identity. Such rituals, especially those that involve the state and its dignitaries as well as the monarch, often draw on historical narratives and the authority of archaic practices, historic costumes and often the use of Latin phrases to lend the status of the past and of past glories to current re-enactments. The military may also be involved. For example Remembrance Sunday constructs a particular view of belonging to the nation which invokes a military past where the identity of the nation is closely linked to military endeavours and associations of self-sacrifice and heroism. The state funeral provides a site for the enactment of the glorious past of the individual who has died in the context of the nation's past. This was particularly resonant at the funeral of Winston Churchill, the British war time leader of the Second World War, who died in 1965. On this occasion the military had a very dominant presence, and even though this point can be seen as marking the end of Empire there was a parade of dignitaries and officers of state signifying the past that was. This was a traditional funeral, attended by dignitaries of state, Commonwealth and other world political leaders, the monarchy and the aristocracy. Thousands of people lined the streets, largely deferentially, as British subjects. The funeral of Diana Princess of Wales, in 1997, was in many ways very different. As one observer remarked, people were there as 'British citizens', rather than as British subjects, as at Churchill's funeral (Woodward, 2000c). 'Citizenship' might imply some possibility of active involvement and even control over the shaping of events, rather than the passivity of the spectator. Diana's funeral saw a break with protocol, the flag at half mast at Buckingham Palace, the Queen responding to the 'people's' demands and the presence of a more diverse range of people, including media stars and Diana's friends. Whereas in 1965, the global presence at Churchill's funeral was that of political leaders, and the largely elderly, white, male colonial order, by 1997 there appeared to be a more diverse, inclusive representation. The ritual of state in 1997 was characterized by expressions of emotions and the presence of numerous media stars, with the popular singer Elton John singing at the funeral service itself in Westminster Abbey, although many of the traditional rituals of state were maintained (Woodward, 2000c). By 1997 Britishness could be seen to have been reformulated as more diverse, more inclusive with some representation of women and minority ethnic people for example. Such rituals offer defining moments in the narrative of the nation. Through a recognized enactment of particular practices, incorporating dignitaries and heroes (even newly constructed popular heroes, as in the case of Diana's funeral), they retell the nation's history in specific ways that re-present dramatic accounts of national identity, and thus compound people's investment, both in a particular narrative and in a myth of origin; a specific story of the nation's 'true' past.

At the local level, those seeking to assert their own ethnic identities make similar appeals to the past. For example in the 1980s in the conflict in the former Yugoslavia, the Serbs reconstructed their past of warlords and storytellers, the Guslars of the Middle Ages, as a means of consolidating their identity. As Michael Ignatieff noted following his own stay in the Balkans, outsiders are told 'you have to understand our history… Twenty minutes later you were still being told about King Lazar, the Turks and the battle of Kosova' (1993: 240). At moments of conflict and crisis appeals to the authenticity of a time past that can be revealed and restated are a key component of securing identity in the present. In order to cope with fragmentation and uncertainty some communities do seek a return to a lost past or even to a 'golden age' 'coordinated … by "legends and landscapes"; by stories of golden ages, enduring traditions, heroic deeds and dramatic destinies located in promised homelands with hallowed sites and scenery' (Daniels, 1993: 5).

Essentialism involves security, but that means fixity and a containment that may limit change. Essentialism can also be seen as the binary opposite of nonessentialism. An essentialist view of identity may imply a dualistic approach whereby identity is constructed only through oppositions, such as those for example of nature and culture, and mind and body, which were discussed in Chapter 5. While there is an attraction in securing boundaries, and thus establishing clear ideas about our own identities, there are also limitations. Binaries permit no ambiguity or ambivalence, no middle ground of managing difference, although they are part of the desire for unity and wholeness, which requires clear boundaries. Especially at moments of crisis it may be very important to have coherent guidelines to mark out 'us' from 'them', and to provide a clear idea of our own story. Such moments may be most marked at times of war when a nation and its people may feel threatened. However, the retreat to essentialism, or its celebration, depending on the position taken, can also be marked when individuals need to be able to assert their own personal identities.

Another aspect of this identity story is one that seeks to explain the process of inclusion and exclusion, to offer a history of the positioning of 'us' and 'them' and more especially of the insiders and the outsiders. Edward Said's influential work on the western colonialization of Asian societies, *Orientalism*, explores the ways in which representations and discourses of colonized peoples as 'Other' and thus as different or inferior, are both a condition of, and an integral part of political economic colonialism. His claim is that representational systems in the west produced the idea that the diverse nations of the near and far east can be homogenized into a single civilization, namely 'the Orient'. Thus the 'Orient' becomes the binary opposite to the west – the 'Occident', against which the Orient is defined as backward, despotic and undeveloped as well as mysterious and exotic. Thus intervention by the west in such societies becomes justified. Said's argument was that the 'Orient' was not discovered but *made* (1978). He argued that 'a very large mass of writers, among them are poets, novelists, philosophers, political theorists, economists and imperial administrators, have accepted the basic distinction between East and West as the starting point for elaborate theories, epics, novels social descriptions and political accounts concerning the Orient, its people, customs, "mind", destiny and so on' (in Bayoumi and Rubin, 2000: 69). In *Orientalism*, Said's aim was to use Foucauldian discourse theory, based on the meanings that are produced through discursive fields, to deconstruct this whole thought system and to expose its power relations and structures, in order to challenge the hegemony of western thought. He sought to liberate intellectuals from the shackles of systems of thought like Orientalism (p. 65). Said challenges the equation of western knowledge with objectivity and shows how deeply implicated are the practices and representational systems through which such knowledge is produced in the interplay of power between west and east. The identities so produced through these processes are polarized as are the 'Orient' and the 'Occident'.

In his later work, Edward Said has incorporated his own experience of exile, and especially the experience of the Palestinian people into his writing on the processes that are involved in the creation of exclusion and displacement. He is concerned with those exiles who have not always been accommodated, 'Palestinians or the new Muslim immigrants in continental Europe, or West Indian and African blacks in England whose presence complicates the presumed homogeneity of the new societies in which they live' (in Bayoumi and Rubin, 2001: 372). Said links the experiences of individuals to the social, political and economic conditions which create the exiled subject and the identity of the 'other. As Said has written 'Exile is one of the saddest fates' (ibid.: p. 369). However, these oppositions are not lived exclusively as if there were just the one or the other, as if people were included or excluded in a simple binary. The exile is not permanently cut off because the exile retains constant reminders of the place that has been left; 'the exile lives in a median state, neither completely at one with the new setting nor fully disencumbered of the old, beset with half involvements and half detachments, nostalgic and sentimental on one level, an adept mimic or a secret outcast on another' (ibid.: pp. 370–1).

Homi Bhabha has been critical of the fixity of colonial discourse and his work suggests that the relationship between east and west as expounded in *Orientalism* may fail to accommodate the ambivalence of the relationship between colonizer and colonized. Bhabha argues that the colonizer expresses both repression and repulsion for the colonized, towards whom there may also be feelings of sympathy or even attraction. He also argues that colonized people do not simply reject the culture of the colonial power. They may also absorb that culture, which creates ambivalence and hybridity on the part of colonized people. Bhabha suggests that Said's initial argument could be extended to accommodate the interrelationship between colonizers and colonized and to engage with the alterity and ambivalence of orientalist discourse. He seeks to go beyond what he sees as Said's 'introducing a binarism within the argument which, in initially setting up an opposition between these two discursive scenes, finally allows them to be correlated as a congruent system of representation that is unified' (in Seidman and Alexander, 2001: 392). Bhabha attempts to avoid the essentialism in which he sees Said's earlier account in *Orientalism* as being implicated through his own emphasis on ambivalence rather than opposition.

What are the main problems with essentialism? Firstly the counterpoint to greater security seems to be fixity and lack of scope for change. Reducing sexual identity to biology might appear to offer strength to some arguments which seek to counter homophobia or other hostilities, but it carries the risk of overemphasizing one dimension of sexual identity at the expense of others, notably cultural aspects, and to limit the range and forms of expression of sexuality. An important limitation of essentialism is its articulation through binary oppositions, for example the dichotomies of nature and culture, or 'insiders' and 'outsiders'. Boundaries are firmly fixed, one or the other where interrelationship and ambiguities cannot be accommodated. Such dichotomies may construct the outsider as the 'other' in a fixed static relationship, rather like the photographic image, which appears to capture the moment, as if it were a message without a code. Part of this image is a fixed past with a single linear story line that accommodates no divergence, change or flexibility and no differently inflected moments as we reconstruct our identities.

Paul Gilroy goes further and argues for the historical specificity of identity to be recognized as a means of making political action possible (1997). He distinguishes between collective identities and individual identities, arguing that individual identity in the contemporary world is seen as constantly being negotiated, redefined and reconstructed. Gilroy's suggestion is that 'in the market and consumer economies, individual identity is worked upon by the cultural industries and in localized institutions and settings like schools, neighbourhood and workplaces' (ibid.: p. 311). Consuming identities and the body projects that people work on in order to re-present themselves, which were discussed in Chapter 5, are indeed seen as fluid and constantly changing. However, on the other hand, he sees collective identities as becoming increasingly primordial, which is how he characterizes essentialist perspectives. He rejects appeals to collective identity which 'conceive it as so fundamental and immutable, represent a turning away, a retreat inwards, from the difficult political and moral questions which the issue of identity poses ... If identity is indeed fixed, primordial and immutable, then politics is irrelevant in the face of the deeper, more fundamental forces – biological or cultural inheritance, kinship, homeland – which really, in this view regulate human conduct ... If identity and difference are essential and substantially unchanging, then they are not amenable to being changed by political methods ... To live with difference is viewed as living in jeopardy' (p. 310). If difference is disruptive, sameness might seem to offer a security. However, Gilroy cites the disastrous destruction of lives both in Bosnia and in Rwanda in the 1990s as illustration of the dire outcomes of what he calls the dismal logic of essentialist sameness which can only end in 'separation or slaughter' (p. 311). He cites the desire to fix identity in the body, for example through visible signs of difference, such as colour, height features and hair, as necessarily contradictory and hence doomed to failure and disaster. In the case of the genocide in Rwanda, people were classified into 'tribal types', which resulted in either death or deliverance. As African Rights reported, Tutsi people were killed because they were so classified by 'tribal type' on their ID cards. People were even killed because they 'looked' like a Tutsi, having the expected tall stature and straight nose characteristics (1994). Gilroy uses this evidence to warn against the dire consequences of fixing or essentializing identity. He does, however, recognize the ways in which identity might appeal, 'in the turbulent waters of de-industrialization and the large-scale patterns of planetary reconstruction that are hesitantly called "globalization" and "late modernity"' (p. 312). He acknowledges that recovering a sense of identity might indeed be a means of warding off the more disturbing aspects of rapid change and uncertainty at this time in history, but his warnings against essentialism are strongly expressed.

Where do you come from?

Tracing our roots may be important to us as a source of our own sense of who we are, but it is also what we do in identifying who others are. Roots offer a means of marking ourselves out as different from others and the same as those who share the same stories of origin; those who have investment in the same narratives of roots and sources. As I argued in Chapter 4, sources of identity may be inferred from the clues that others present to us and this is how we are identified by others. Not only do visible differences signify identity, they also indicate sources of that identity. This can be through the way we speak, language or accents, how we dress, and the visible differences of skin colour or some forms of disability. The writer Jackie Kay, whose novel was cited in Chapter 5, has written extensively about the matter of identity. As a black, lesbian woman, the child of a Nigerian student and a white Scottish woman, who was adopted by a Scottish couple and brought up in Glasgow, she has several stories to tell. In her poem, '*So you think I'm a mule*' (1991) she addresses the issue of making assumptions about the roots of identity from visible appearance and the problem of hybridity. While others may make their own judgements about 'who we are' from outward appearances, seeking to fix us in a position that we reject, it does not solve the problem of the need to belong. While the set of 'roots' offered to us by others may be unacceptable, there is still the problem that each of us faces in finding where we think we belong (Woodward, 2000a). In the poem Kay is asked the question, 'Where do you come from?' by a white woman. The woman is not satisfied with the response that the poet is from Glasgow, and presses for a reply to where she *really* comes from, meaning what are her roots, her place of origin. Kay's response is hostile to the fluidity of hybridity, which she reads negatively

> 'If you Dare mutter mulatto
> hover around hybrid
> hobble on half caste'

Kay equates hybridity, not with fluidity and change, but with claims of impurity, of miscegenation and all that is associated with 'mulatto' and 'half caste', as if these mixes were tainted because they lack unity and wholeness. This approach challenges the celebration of hybridity that characterizes many cultural critiques and the political action Kay recommends is an identification with her black sisters, through an alliance with political blackness that identifies positively with being black. Rather than adopting a fixed essentialist position though, this could be interpreted as what Spivak calls 'strategic essentialism' (1990).

Spivak is critical of those who make statements, as in the case of intellectuals, but who do not commit themselves to a specific position. She claims that many people may try to protect their theoretical purity by repudiating essentialism, but taking up essentialist positions at times is both necessary and specific. Spivak herself admits to being an essentialist from time to time, by suggesting that there are different ways in which one might adopt such a position. 'Strategically, one can look at essentialisms, not as descriptions of the way things are, but as something one must adopt to produce a critique of anything' (1990: 51). That is to say one does not have to take total, universalist position, but that frequently it is necessary for dominated, marginalized groups of people to appeal to bonds of cultural experience in order to take action and to be represented. Spivak's concept of strategic essentialism goes some way towards addressing the dilemma expressed in Kay's poem. How do we negotiate identity when roots are transformed and belonging becomes troubled? Strategic essentialism offers the possibility of translating key moments along the routes we have travelled and of privileging points along the way, rather than resorting to the one moment, the starting point in the myth of origin. The following discussion of whiteness employs a specific example to illustrate the tension between roots and routes in order to consider how identities can be reframed and reconstructed to retain the notion of belonging.

Whiteness and identity

Much of the discussion that has taken place about ethnicity and identity has focused on otherness as marked by visible difference. Even the very term 'ethnic' is sometimes used to signify otherness. This suggests that some people are implicated in ethnicity and bear ethnic identities, because they are different, as if there were human beings who did not carry ethnicity; rather in the way that 'ethnic food' is used to connote food from different cultures as if English or British food, for example, was not specific to a culture in any way. In this sense ethnicity has been associated with not being white. However, the concept of ethnicity has been adopted as preferable to that of race, at some points within the social sciences, as a way of marking difference, which is not tied to reductionist unchanging foundations. Ethnicity, with is focus on culture and social relations permits change and adaptation in a way that the biologically reductionist category of race does not. Ethnicity marks cultural and social differences between groups of people, rather than invoking spurious biological fixity where visible and embodied differences might be seen to determine and circumscribe identity. Race, with its essentialist implications and grounding in biology and genetic inheritance has also been so strongly associated with the devaluing and repression of those who have been classified as non-white. Some critics however prefer the notion of 'race', using the quotation marks to challenge any notions of fixity but to retain the political dimensions of race that can be obscured by the more democratic idea of ethnicity. The culturally based notion of ethnicity, in which all groups in human society must be involved, may marginalize the impact of the inequalities and oppressions that have been borne of raciology and racism.

Social scientists and cultural critics often debate essentialism and berate the limitations of fixity in the context of diaspora identities and the constraints of the racism that emerge from essentialist readings of identity. Fixity, especially that which is based on visible and embodied differences, might indeed feed racism. What happens when you turn it around and apply the same debates to whiteness? Is whiteness an identity? What does it mean to be white British? Is whiteness assumed in postcolonial countries of the west so that it is taken for granted as 'normal' and unproblematic, rather like being a man, where only women are marked as gendered?

Debates about whiteness have frequently focused on the way in which whiteness is assumed, not only as a tabula rasa upon which the world is written, but as the norm. Visible features are not transparent as signifiers of difference. As Donna Haraway argues whiteness is largely unseen, its invisibility a sign of its dominance and hegemonic status (1992). Race is not simply located in nature, we have to learn to see racial difference; its categories are socially constructed. Is it possible to represent whiteness as an identity and what would this involve? If we confront the privilege of whiteness, with all its assumptions of 'normality', what could be the next stage? Is it possible to retain a critique of privilege while challenging the homogeneity of a 'white identity'? The idea of categorizing people according to visible difference and skin colour seems somewhat unusual when we attempt to do it for whiteness. What could there be that would link together all people as Caucasians, who have a white skin? The other reason it may seem strange is because we are much more familiar with categories of non-white identities, for example on the census form and in ethnic monitoring forms, than we are with subdivisions of whiteness. As Paul Gilroy has argued, raciology closes down difference and diversity; it prioritizes race over all the other aspects of identity. Raciology is based on the power of race as a means of classifying into racial commonality, 'transmuting heterogeneity into homogeneity', by appealing to 'the lore of blood, bodies and fantasies of absolute cultural identity' (2000: 82–3). In the discourses of everyday life and in academic critiques we may not be so accustomed to doing this with white people. However, it is clearly deeply problematic to lay claim to being white. Such an adherence would be haunted by the ghosts of fascism and white racist supremacy or, as Alistair Bonnett had argued, at the other extreme, result in white guilt and an excess of confessional anguish over being in such a position of privilege (1998). White offers a very troubling identity.

Once we start to interrogate whiteness and to call it into question what do we find? If whiteness could be an identity it would seem inevitably tarred with the brush of racism and assertions, not so much of normality, but of superiority. What ways might there be for understanding the relationship between whiteness and identity, which might go beyond not only what is taken for granted, but also the oppositions that so characterize our understanding of difference? A key opposition that underpins the production of difference, involves a tension between essentialism and social construction. This is the essentialism that draws on the rhetoric of roots and of a fixed reading of identity, which is set in opposition to the discourses that are now almost ubiquitous in cultural studies, of hybridity and fluidity and of mobile fragmentation (Araeen, 2000). What alternatives are there to these dualistic modes of thinking and how might other readings assist both in our understanding of whiteness and in addressing some of the problems which existing critiques have presented? In order to engage with this question, it is necessary to explore the dilemma arising from the desire to establish roots and to locate identity and, in this case to apply the question to whiteness and its relationship to identity.

Identity links the inside and the outside; the personal and social. However in stories of the self that circulate in the west there may have been an increasing introspection and concern with the self as an individual, which might have led to an over-emphasis on the inside at the expense of external factors and upon individualism rather than collective agency. This can be criticized for reducing the impact of collective action and narrowing the focus of identification (Gilroy, 1997). Identity offers a means of locating ourselves and others. However, it is the notion of 'others' that creates tension, opposition and exclusion. In order to lay claim to an identity there seems to be some necessity to say what or who I am not; by stating where we do belong we mark ourselves off from those to whom we do not belong.

There are two elements in this definition of identity that this discussion invokes. One is the appeal to the past and its authority, whether in stories of past achievements, a shared history of a people, or of stories of origins – roots – or on some essential biological foundation, which can be used to authenticate the present and shape identity and its aspirations for the future. The second is the marking of difference, especially the way in which identities are marked by what we share with those who are like 'us' and what differentiates 'us' from 'them'. Nowhere is this more highlighted than in the binary of black and white, except that between men and women, with all the attributes which these dualisms invoke. Race thinking is one of the strategies people deploy in differentiating, in telling people apart.

What do we mean by whiteness and how is it represented? In changing times, when, as was shown in Chapter 3, there has been increasing consciousness of the need to combat racism, most anti-racists would argue for the heterogeneity and hybridity of black and diaspora identities. White can, however be classified within anti-racist discourse as a single identity. As Alistair Bonnett argues, there are problems in stabilizing a white identity. White racial identities were produced through the nineteenth and twentieth centuries and through contemporary policies by two routes. Firstly, as expressed through the confessional and the idea that white people experience guilt at the privileges of being white, for example as expressed by liberal discourses and secondly, through historical geographies of whiteness, as made manifest at particular times and in particular places. Bonnett argues for anti-essentialist readings of whiteness which retain its political dimensions. Whiteness has to be both recognized and resisted. In order to recognize whiteness and its specificities, what Bonnett calls its historical geographies, it is important to look at how whiteness is both classified and represented. What are some of the routes that white identities have travelled?

Representations of whiteness

What does 'white' connote? There is a whole string of associations ranging from purity to the blank space – nothing. Recent interrogations of the use of white in representational systems suggest that white too is complex and multi-faceted and cannot be read in a single way (Tercier, 2000). Richard Dyer has argued that 'White as a hue is an unstable category', but that the 'idea of whiteness as neutrality already suggests its usefulness for designating a social group that is to be taken for the human ordinary' (1997: 47). Whiteness has become the subject of intellectual investigation so that whiteness too becomes visible, across a whole range of disciplines and discursive practices and through multifarious systems of representation. Whiteness is not arbitrary. As John Tercier argues, 'within certain bounds, and at certain levels of function, arbitrary choice ceases and whiteness itself, what it is and what it has become, inscribes on its own blank surface the reality of the ideal of the immaculately white' (2000: 17).

White images take different forms. White can encompass differences, notably the binary opposition between black and white. This is the most crude representation of whiteness although it may not operate at the most explicit and direct levels. This is an opposition that is more often assumed rather than stated. Whiteness is deeply implicated in gendered discourses. It can connote purity. As Dyer has argued, in the symbolic systems of fine art and of cinematic representation, whiteness is associated with purity that is inflected through gender. White women are represented as 'whiter than white'; even more white than white men, who may bear a more ruddy complexion (1997). It is through symbolic systems that meanings about whiteness are constructed. Dyer argues that whiteness is created as a 'culture of light' and that the claim to racial superiority to which whiteness is heir is requires both visibility, whites have to be seen to be whites, and the invisibility that constitutes the watcher as well as the person seen (p. 44). Purity signifies perfection and idealization which is carried by the whiteness of the image. Whiteness connotes sexual purity for example through the virginal bridal dress and the unsullied whiteness of so many representations of white women. White may signify purity, but it also creates the open space and the blank page. For example the purity of pristine whiteness characterizes the open space of the art gallery (Tercier, 2000). Mary Kelly's *Post partum document* shown at the ICA in 1976, is a creative artwork of a display of soiled babies' nappies, which can be seen to violate the purity of the gallery and to cast a slur on its purity. White, by establishing purity, invites violation. Mary Kelly's display pollutes the white space.

The 'purity' of whiteness can be subverted by contradiction. In Isak Dinesen's story *The blank page* he suggests that although white appears as blank page, white speaks. Dinesen retells a traditional tale, handed down from mother to daughter, told by an old woman. The story is used to illustrate how 'where the story teller is loyal ... silence will speak'. It also illustrates a different version of whiteness from the pristine, the pure, blank page. The story is about a convent in medieval Portugal where the nuns span the flax for the bed linen of the royal house. After the wedding night of the royal princes and their brides the blood stained sheets were hung on the balcony of the palace to proclaim the 'purity and virginity' of the bride. The nuns' privilege extended to their being allowed to display a square cut from each sheet, in a gold frame in a gallery in the convent, each bearing the 'faded markings' of the wedding night (1975: 103). In the midst of the long row of frames, each labelled with a plate bearing the pure bride's name, there was one plate with no name, 'and the linen within the frame is snow-white from corner to corner, a blank page' (p. 104). Gayle Greene and Coppelia Kahn argue that the story, like the linen, 'is woven from the fabric of western patriarchy' (1985: 6). Their purpose, like Dinesen's is to link the blood-stained sheets to the printed page, mine is to use this as an example of the ambiguity of white. Whiteness carries the potential for its own contradiction. The apparent purity of whiteness can be subverted and challenged in different ways.

White might even involve a joke. It is not chance that Yasmina Reza chose a white painting for her play *Art*. In the play one member of a group of three male friends spends a huge amount of money on an oil painting, which his friends, when they see it are somewhat surprised to find is more or less just a large white canvas. The play explores the relationships between the men in a specific cultural, historical context, employing the vehicle of the painting to focus on debates about what constitutes 'art'. It is often amusing as well as instructive about contemporary aspirations and cultural hierarchies but it is interesting that Reza chooses a white painting as the focus of the play. There is some discussion about *how* white the picture actually is. (Is it properly white? A bit cream?) The denouement of the play involves the ultimate defamation of the expensive, prestigious painting with the amusing addition of a little skier with a jolly red bobble hat, crayoned, as graffiti, onto the 'work of art'.

White is part of representational systems with all the connotations of purity and pollution, and the blank page and the illumination of the white light. Whiteness constructs categories, which position people and identify them in relation to particular meanings of whiteness. This applies to people who are categorized by visible difference as well as to paintings. Amy Pagnozzi, an Italian American (1991) cites a visit to New Zealand where she describes the people as 'very white, not New York white (i.e. ethnic, blended, beige) but naked, pasty, underdone; white white'. She relates an encounter with a New Zealand woman who is amazed to find that Pagnozzi is 'white' in the States; 'well you wouldn't be here' she said (ibid.: p. 130).

One of the routes through which meanings are produced about whiteness is through classificatory systems such as the categories to classify persons in a variety of places. The census offers one example of a site at which people as recorded as belonging to particular ethnic categories, which have raciologist connections. Censuses provide a means of racial categorization. Policy decisions are made on the bases of census data. Although people may be invited to categorize themselves, the categories provided are determined by others, by those who design the questions. The census does not just classify race, it also decides what counts. For example, Sharon Lee, using the US census, has demonstrated that census categories have suggested that any proportion of 'black', 10%, 20% makes the person black, rather than 90% or 80% white (1993). Census categories have altered in recent years, although categories of non-white people have changed more than those of white people, with changing times. In the case of the US census, some categories remained constant, notably that of 'white' at the top of the list for 200 years, since 1850 in fact. The US census changed to include Irish as whites, whereas they had previously been categorized as 'black' (Warren and Twine, 1997). In the early nineteenth century Celts and other European migrants were classified as 'black' in the USA but all, along with the Irish became white by the end of the nineteenth century. Categories may be used for political purposes, for example 'black' may be used as a political category, whereas white can be seen as an assumed class without differences. In the 2001 UK census a question on religion was introduced to ascertain more information about the diversity of respondents in the 'Asian' category. However, there have been those who bear the visible difference of whiteness yet who are not classified as white. This has been the case with the Irish, who have been a key 'other' for the British, or rather the English. The Irish have been racialized even more than the Welsh and negatively characterized by particular stereotypical features. It has been argued that the Irish provided a model for slavery and colonialism, and that in British race-thinking the Irish represented the 'missing evolutionary link between the "bestiality" of Black slaves and that of the English worker' (Cohen, 1988: 74). In this sense they were 'white negroes'. What Donna Haraway has called the 'simianization' (or ape-like representation) of the Irish is important because it demonstrates the relationship between 'people of color ... constructed as objects of knowledge as "primitives", more closely connected to the apes than the white "race"' (Haraway, 1992: 153). More recently, Roddy Doyle in his novel and film, *The commitments*, has a character claim that the 'Irish are the blacks of Europe'. At different times people are differently classified and there may be 'degrees of whiteness'.

However, so powerful are the oppositional elements of the black/white dichotomy that it might be seen as the dualism that overrides all others. It is seen as at least on a par with gender with all the associated attributes that line up on each side. This binary, like that of the man/woman gender dualism goes beyond visible difference and suggests far reaching and essential differences between people based on the differences that can be observed. As Frantz Fanon argued, the excessive, even fetishistic, stress on skin colour and visible appearance, what he called 'epidermalization', brought together visible difference and underlying, imagined features. In the past and even in very recent times, this has led to scientific investigation into brain size, physical and athletic capabilities, all linked to 'race' in the 'science' of raciology. Variants of psychoanalytic theory suggest whiteness is the key signifier of difference – the phallus of race. This illustrates the dynamic of difference and the way in which 'black' as some homogeneous source of otherness is constructed in relation to white. This has led some to some explanations of the desirability of whiteness seeing white as the ultimate signifier, as a racial parallel to the phallus. Whiteness is a master signifier (a signifier without a signified, not a physical property which is invoked, just as the phallic signifier is used to explain sexual difference). Kalpana Seshadri-Crooks uses the Lacanian theory of sexual difference to explore the ways in which whiteness is represented and desired in order to offer an explanation of how it is that whiteness has been associated with purity and has been so privileged within symbolic systems. Thus she employs Lacanian psychoanalysis to explain how race thinking and the privileging of whiteness operates, rather as some feminists have used psychoanalytic thinking to critique patriarchy (Mitchell, 1975). Mitchell's aim in her work was not to justify patriarchal privilege but to offer an explanation of how and why such power relations have become entrenched even at the level of the unconscious. Similarly Seshadri-Crooks applies psychoanalytic critiques to an interrogation of what she defines as the desiring of whiteness. Rather than being a physical property manifest in visible difference such as skin colour, whiteness is the signifier through which all other meanings are produced. This offers some explanation of how whiteness might have come to connote purity and superiority and also to create racist meanings. As Dyer suggests white people are not literally white, nor do they themselves signify whiteness, whiteness is a property outside those who might appear to carry it. Psychoanalytic theories attempt to provide an explanatory framework for how this works. While the shift of emphasis from observable practices and political and institutional power structures, plays a useful part in critiques of whiteness, there is a danger that the focus on the unconscious may reinforce the idea of a homogeneous whiteness, without differences and diversity.

The recent focus on whiteness and the interrogation of what whiteness means and how it is represented, in many areas of academic work, combine to present a useful antidote to the widely held view that race and difference do not concern white people. Whiteness carries different meanings and tells different stories. Stories of white identities include those of white supremacy and colonial, racist discourses, as well as those of the marginalization and oppression of particular sections within the category white. Whiteness carries its own potential for violation and for contradiction. While the dominant narrative and what might be seen as the 'regime of truth' about whiteness is the story of privilege and of racialization of those classified as non-white, there are internal contradictions, which, if ignored, might lead to a reinforcement of the racism that derives from privilege. Whiteness contains an internalization of its own 'other', which a homogeneous reading of whiteness, as only encompassing privilege, denies at its peril. An investigation of whiteness also involves addressing the disempowered, disenfranchised category of whiteness, notably as represented by disaffected young white men in western cities. For example, disturbances in several cities across Yorkshire and the north west of England in 2001 involved deep seated hostility on the part of disadvantaged white as well as black people, especially the young white men who could be seen to have been most badly affected by job losses resulting from the decline in coal mining and heavy manufacturing industry at the end of the twentieth century. Whiteness has to be addressed in a way that transcends the binary logic of black and white so that it becomes possible to accommodate differences and heterogeneity and the slippages of meaning to which difference is necessarily subject. This also requires thinking outside the notion that essentialism can only be countered with its opposite, non-essentialism, or perhaps even that one has to opt for roots or routes.

Beyond essentialism?

In order to move beyond the binary logic that constructs oppositional categories of gender and race, Donna Haraway argues that the mix which non-essentialist, cyborg thinking offers, suggests all sorts of new possibilities, especially for those who have been dispossessed, the developing world in relation to the developed world, women in relation to men. The cyborg reproaches and challenges hegemonies that are unreflective and even shocks through language and cultural practices. The cyborg has no roots, no origins and through its amalgamation of human and machine avoids the stage of original unity, or identification with nature in the western sense (2000a). Cyborg thinking demands what Haraway calls a 'situated knowledge', a scholarly consciousness of science. She argues that 'the cyborg incorporates text, machine, body and metaphor, which are interrelated and theorized in practice in terms of communication' (Haraway, 2000a). The promise of cyborgs is 'the promise of monsters' with its interconnection of human and animal and of body and machine.

One of the ways in which this thinking can be illustrated is to use the example of two visual images, which Haraway employs in her article, 'The virtual speculum, in the New World Order' (1997). She cites the example of Anne Kelly's cartoon, which Haraway labels *The virtual speculum* as illustrative of feminist 'reproductive freedom'. The cartoon depicts an image based on Michelangelo's *Creation of Adam* from the Sistine Chapel in Rome. The entire ceiling of the Sistine chapel was painted in the early part of the sixteenth century. Michelangelo's painting is a familiar icon within the canon of western Christian art, depicting God in the heavens surrounded by angels stretching out his hand to Adam the first man, who lies, unclothed on the left of the painting gazing adoringly at his creator. Haraway points out that these images in the Sistine Chapel can be seen as a very important moment in the 'eruption of salvation history into a newly powerful visual narrative medium' (p. 28). Although specifically Christian, it has also become part of a humanist tradition in its celebration of the human body and in the production of a particular narrative about the realization of 'man', making possible the development of the apparatus of science and the notion of 'modern man'.

In Kelly's version, a female nude is in the position of Adam, whose hand is extended to the creative interface with, not God the Father, but a keyboard for a computer whose display screen shows the global digital foetus in its amniotic sac. A female Adam, the young nude woman is in the position of the first man. Kelly's figure is not Eve, who was made from Adam and in relation to his need. In the *Virtual speculum* the woman is 'in direct relation to the source itself' (1997: 25). Kelly's cartoon works for those who understand the contemporary notion that the foetus exists, because it has been visualized, as was demonstrated in the discussion of Rosalind Petchesky's work in Chapter 4. Identity is created through the presence of the visual image, the one that confirms the existence of the child and thus by implication confirms the maternal status of the mother. The foetal image on the screen is one that we have to learn to read, since it would be very difficult (it is very difficult) to make out the human form from the image displayed. Haraway uses the two images to explore how visualization techniques and communication technologies construct and re-craft bodies and identities. Haraway's main concern in these examples is with gendered bodies and the potential for constructing a politics that encompasses difference and challenges the constraints of existing boundaries. By employing the codes of the canonical image it becomes possible to subvert them and to tell a different story. The same cartoon illustrates both cyborg thinking and the need to examine the stories that are told and the routes travelled in this representation of whiteness. The cartoon draws on an assumed white story being told. In order to subvert the patriarchal imagery, the cartoon has to deploy its codes and re-present white patriarchy. This image of Kelly's is both subversive of the assumptions of a genre and of patriarchal thinking and positive in its recognition of women and the need for women to participate actively in the engagement with reproductive technologies.

However, it is also important to incorporate the *story* into the critique; to look at the routes that the representation has travelled and to seek explanation in that journey rather than only in seeking what the image aims to produce in the present and in the future. The woman in the image is white and re-produced within the constraints of a very particular genre. She has to be in order to provide the subversive reading that is suggested. However, the focus on the repertoires upon which the image draws also permits acknowledgement of the privileging of whiteness. This is the component that too much emphasis on hybridity and the transcendence of boundaries through cyborg thinking might marginalize. Critiques of representations of whiteness and the deconstruction of its images have to include those stories that have privileged readings. Routes allow us to pick out those key moments, whether these are significant formative moments in personal or collective biographies or privileged points, which include the particular historical moments which have created specific privileging of whiteness.

The combination of cyborg thinking with its challenge to dualistic, oppositional thinking and an interrogation of the stories which are told through the routes which have been travelled, permits a challenge to essentialism which does not leave us stranded between what Pnina Werbner has called the Scylla of universalism and the Charybdis of differentialism (Werbner and Modood, 1998). This combination can offer a 'situated knowledge' which permits the location of power, and privilege, and avoids an over-emphasis on the fluidity of hybridity which could marginalize the reality of racism.

Not only might the excessive concern with fluidity and contingency in the formation of identities that are mobile and in flux, lead to a relativism which marginalizes difference and especially inequalities, hybridity might present its own limitations. Hybrid identities may limit our understanding of racialization, or they might even institute news forms of racism. The endeavour to combat the constraints of essentialism may set up new, equally constraining orthodoxies. Debates about multi-culturalism have been concerned with the notion that, while anti-essentialist positions have challenged the fixity of such understandings of identity, multi-culturalism may have set its own, equally limiting agenda. Rasheed Araeen suggests that 'the triumph of the hybrid is in fact a triumph of neo-liberal multi-culturalism, a part of the triumph of global capitalism' (2000: 15). He supports the argument that multi-culturalism merely supports liberal attempts 'to contain and displace the struggle of the deprived and the oppressed ... [in] a new form of racism' (p. 16). His arguments are largely centred on the ways in which arguments about the fluidity and contingency of identity have been deployed within fields of artistic activity. He is concerned to indicate some of the ways in which such explanations can be seen to be more repressive than liberating especially for black and Asian artists, for example because they have been compelled to identify with their culture 'of origin', with their roots in fact. He argues that multi-culturalism, far from being supportive of the equality of all cultures, represents the ways in which the dominant culture accommodates 'those who have no power in such a way that the power of the dominant is preserved' (ibid.: p. 16). Araeen is most critical of Homi Bhabha whose arguments about hybridity, he argues, have created a separation between white and non-white peoples. So, for example, while white artists can draw on any cultural inspiration, when non-white artists create cultural forms they are expected to display signs of their 'otherness'. Alternatives to essentialism present their own problems, especially if hybridity is defined as 'other'. A hybrid other is perhaps just a bit more complicated than any 'other' and the principle of exclusion remains intact.

The stories we tell involve the routes we have travelled, the journeys that we negotiated. The idea of 'routes' enables us to prioritize particular moments on the journey in order to highlight the moments that matter, the ones that have been formative. Vital elements in the construction of national identities relate to myths of origins. These stories are told through symbolic systems – the flag, representations of past heroes, buildings and symbols of past greatness (often military greatness). However, the nation, like the individual and the communities to which we belong have travelled diverse paths. The weight of history is not linear, nor deriving only from one source. The inclusion of routes enables us to prioritize moments along the way and to include recognition of those who are allowed to tell their stories and those who are not, viz. to include power and privilege. We pass through different places along the way, stopping off at some that are more interesting or more important than others. What's important is not just the first place, the place we came from but the routes we have travelled. As the cultural critic and sociologist Stuart Hall argues, we are the product of the routes we have traversed, rather than a product which can be traced back to a single source. Indeed for many people (all people?) that source is not singular. Hall argues that his own place of birth, Jamaica, is itself a product of different elements; even if he could say that was his source, the island itself is not a single place fixed in time. The culture, i.e. all the meanings that shape who we are and involves a social place in our heads, through which we make sense of our pasts, present and what we want to become involves taking up your social, cultural place. Social positions offer different ways of being at different times and within different spaces.

We need to retell the stories, to re-remember the places we have been and how we have been, how we are and what we want to become. Often roots and the search for roots tell us more about what we want to become than about what we actually were or where we came from, and more about how we wanted to redefine ourselves than about our actual past. In telling ourselves stories we can say 'that was me ten years ago' and now I am the sum of all that – we are the sum of that past of all those stages in the narrative. We are, have been and will be different in relation to different social contexts.

Conclusion

The notion of identity as rooted in some primordial past, in the stories we tell either about ourselves as individuals or as part of a group, nation or class or even in the bodies we inhabit, is beset with problems. While rootedness may satisfy some of our desires to belong, to be able to lay claim to an identity which marks us out as sharing culture and experience with those with whom we identify, the risk of 'otherness' and the exclusion, exile and racialization that can accompany such dualisms are too limiting and constraining. Within the discourse of roots and routes the latter idea appears to offer a far more fruitful means of negotiating identities in the twenty-first century. Routes combine the stories through which identities are constructed and presented with the journeys we have travelled, both literally in a world characterized by global migration and transnationalism, and metaphorically through the imaginary constructions of place, and especially of home, that play so large a part in the formation of identities in exile. Attempts to stabilize understanding of the self in relation to embodiment, as explored in Chapter 5 also form sites in mapping the self.

However, the notion of roots and routes, like the binary of essentialism and non-essentialism may be yet another dualism which constructs its own boundaries and is not such a liberatory discourse through which identities can be understood as might at first appear. Routes are associated with a rejection of the limitations of essentialist fixities. Non-essentialist readings of identity produce categories of hybridity and contingency, which may not only fail to fulfil desires to stabilize our sense of who we are, but present their own problems. Hybridity may establish new and constraining binaries, which close off innovation and change outside those dualisms. How are people marked out as hybrid? If we are all hybrids, who are we? An excess of fluidity and movement, which classifies identity as hybrid may leave us with no meaningful ways of placing ourselves. In order to mark out difference hybridity may enforce an identification with the place of origin among those who are classified as 'hybrid'. However, as I have attempted to suggest in the discussion of routes in relation to the construction of identity, through an awareness of the temporal and spatial dimensions in the formation and representation of identity, it is possible to accommodate an understanding of the pivotal moments, places and stages which map out the self. Some moments are more important than others are. Routes permit an understanding of the points in the journey that are more significant and the places that have been selected in mapping the self. Routes do not alone provide explanations of why some moments are more important than others, nor do they provide insights into the personal investment we have in points along the way. The process of identification is thus described rather than unravelled. However, the notion of a route permits the inclusion of situated knowledge about identity; one that belongs in place and time and has material meanings. Routes do not necessarily involve a linear narrative and thus provide the means of incorporating change and transformation. As Verma said in the opening quotation to this chapter, routes are dynamic and about the future, and about becoming as well as belonging.

7 Conclusion

The identity stories explored in this book have involved revisiting some of the narratives of identity which have produced meanings about who we are and who we could be. These stories are widely implicated in what we were and in the stories of the past, which influence the present and reconstruct the future. Identity is troubling. Just at the moment when you might think that you have a handle on it the narrative is reframed and its structure becomes uncertain. The more we seek fixity and certainty the more troubling identity becomes. Identity matters, but perhaps it matters because it is so troubling and so difficult, if not impossible to contain.

This book has followed a narrative that involves telling some of the identity stories which have particular resonance and which can be used to address some of the most important questions about identity and its articulation in the contemporary world. In order to construct this narrative I have revisited some of the earlier accounts of identity, many of which carry considerable weight in more current explanatory frameworks that have been propounded to deal with more recent stories of 'identity crises'. Identity is certainly not a new story, although it may have particular impact on contemporary debates. The concept of identity has the advantage of bringing together different academic disciplines, which have produced some imaginative and creative analyses that also contribute to the development of interdisciplinarity, for example within cultural studies, feminist critiques and those arising from post-colonial and transnational studies.

Identity is at issue at this point in the twenty-first century, as was illustrated by the introductory example of 11 September 2001. Such contemporary instances of situations where identities are at stake in the conflicts that feature at global, local and personal levels, permeate this book. The book began by setting out some of the problems of reworking and reconfiguring some of the traditional dualisms that have underpinned the understanding of identity. Many of the theories that form part of the identity stories that have been addressed in this book, have involved attempts to set boundaries and to circumscribe and to classify different dimensions of identity. This often involves definitions that are founded on different relationships, one of which is that based on oppositions and dualisms. In some ways this is one of the starting points that has had to be renegotiated. The relationships between sameness and difference, structure and agency, the natural and the social and that between essentialist and non-essentialist perspectives, which are imbricated in each of the other interconnections, are widely implicated in discussion of identity. Throughout the chapters in this book I have endeavoured to show that, while such dualisms have the advantage of clarity, they are impossible to disentangle and coherence may well be at the expense of the complexity, subtlety and multi-layered textures that are that are vital to an engagement with identity. An opposition framed in the language of 'us' and 'them' is deeply problematic, if understandable at particular historical moments, because of the polarization it imposes upon social relations. It is more useful to understand these apparent dualisms as interrelationships and to seek out the connections rather than the oppositions in order to think beyond a polarity between seeing identity as rooted, grounded and fixed on the one hand or fluid, contingent and hybrid on the other. The stark oppositions that confront many people in the twenty-first century also encompass complexity and internal differences that cannot be reduced to simple dualisms, however traumatic and confrontational some of the hostilities may seem at one level. Strength of feeling and the investment people make in identity positions provide a different focus and require an understanding of the social, psychic, embodied and specifically historical situations in which these are experienced. This more complex understanding of the interrelationship does not rule out adopting a political position or even assuming a strategic essentialism, as Spivak has suggested.

The body is the site of the construction of meanings about difference and is frequently the mark of visible difference, but it is also experienced and inhabited and offers possibilities and constraints for the negotiation of identity positions. The body too has been the focus of dualistic thinking, for example in the distinctions between mind and body, the natural and the social and between sex and gender. Feminist critiques have offered ways of thinking that transcend such binary logic but retain the primacy of the body as the site of experience. For example, the idea of embodiment, which denies a distinction between mind and body, has been revisited through Judith Butler's understanding of performativity, which develops an understanding based on the idea that social agents constitute reality through social practice. Thus it becomes possible to conceive of identities such as those of gender, race and disability as corporeal styles which permit an interrogation into how individuals live in their bodies and constitute categories such as gender, race and disability in social relations.

In challenging dualistic thinking one of the major problems that has been encountered is the problem of retaining the possibility of political action and of engaging with the very strongly held investment that can be made in identity positions. An excess of flexibility and fluidity might suggest that it is not possible to take up a grounded political position and, as was argued in Chapter 6, theories of identity based on hybridity can construct their own rigidity oppositions, which might be just as constraining as those they sought to avoid.

The book's own story has built up ways of rethinking the problem of identity by developing ideas about different ways of reframing the debate. This development has been organized through the exploration of narratives of the self and the personal journeys which include those that are implicated in psychoanalytical accounts of the subject, which led on to wider perspectives on mapping the self as were addressed in Chapter 3. Identity involves attempts at securing some degree, however momentary, of certainty, through tracing sources and origins, whether into the psyche and personal experience, family, kinship or the history of the nation. These stories are represented and given meaning through symbolic systems and practices. The symbolic arena is one of contestation as well as presentation as was demonstrated in Chapter 4, and theories of representation and discourse analysis have contributed greatly to debates about identity. Processes of representation are widely imbricated in the formation and presentation of identities, especially in the marking of difference and sameness. Difference is marked in particularly powerful ways in relation to the body and the body could be seen as carrying specific importance as a site upon which identities are inscribed, as well as offering some degree of certainty, albeit sometimes in the form of constraints and restrictions, in the exercise of agency and autonomy in defining the self. Chapter 5 took up some of these claims and interrogated the extent to which the body can afford some certainty.

Embodiment is crucial to the construction of identity, although theoretical perspectives range from those that perceive the body as purely discursive to those which secure certainty through essentialist readings of the body. Essentialism was the focus of Chapter 6 in the discussion of the tension between understandings of identity that are based on roots and the search for certainty through myths of origin and the more dynamic notion of routes. While the two might be presented dualistically it is more helpful to deploy the notion of routes to encompass the desire for home and for belonging, than to see the two as mutually exclusive. The understanding of identity as hybrid and constantly changing and fluid can breed its own limitations through establishing a new orthodoxy that cannot accommodate the strength of feeling about belonging and about the pivotal moments in the routes of identity.

The discussion began with the identity stories that people tell at the personal level, which are linked to the public stories of academic research, technoscience and politics. In Chapter 2, I suggested that narrative can provide a very useful means of reconceptualizing identity matters, which holds onto the investment that people make in their own identities as well as providing a means of exploring some of the interconnections between the personal and the social. The structure of narrative raises issues about place and family of origin and the notion of storying the self in relation to the roots of childhood experience.

The narratives of psychoanalysis involve an emphasis on the primacy of early childhood experience and yield examples of this form of constructing and understanding identity. Psychoanalytic theory permits greater understanding of the identification processes that are necessary in the taking up of an identity and in recruitment into identity positions. While this terrain is much debated and contested, there has to be some interrogation of what could be called inner space in order to address what lies within the psychic and unconscious involvement in adopting an identity; in making it your own in an active sense. The psychoanalytic offers a way into an understanding of how and why people take up particular identities, whatever the limitations of such discourses in terms of their claims to universal revelations about the 'true self'. There have been many reworkings of psycho-social approaches to identity and some notion of investment at the level of the unconscious is a feature of many different critiques. There are however also hostilities, especially to the claims that psychoanalytic theories are said to make about accessing some realm of truth which operates outside the conscious and the rational areas of experience. Critiques in the Foucauldian tradition offer powerful counter arguments and construe the claims of psychoanalysis as constitutive rather than revelationary. This does not necessarily invalidate the discursive regimes through which psychic meanings and psychoanalytic understandings are made, nor deny the notion of inner space or energy in the process of identification, but it does challenge their claims to extra discursive truth. There is also a tension to be negotiated between the application of psychoanalysis and psychotherapy in revealing and uncovering meanings and even truths about the self that were indiscernible prior to the analysis or therapy, and the notion that it is the analysis itself that creates these understandings of the self.

One of the other areas in which we seek certainty and security is through the articulation of home, as the place we belong. Belonging has emerged as an important aspect of identity. This might be through idealized, romanticized conceptualizations, for the imagined community that we reconstruct at times of uncertainty. On the other hand it might be more material and occur through the longing for the safety that can be afforded by occupation of a material place that constitutes home. Home has an important place in the understanding of raced and gendered identities, in the context of migration. While migration and the movement of peoples has a long history it has had particular resonance in the twentieth and into the twenty-first centuries, in the context of the phenomenon of globalization. Again this concept too is strongly contested, but few would argue that changing patterns of mobility and the change of economic and cultural globalization and the speed of communications systems and networks have had no impact on identity. However, while much of the debate has focused on the relative impact of globalization and the extent to which its outcomes are positive or negative, within some critiques there has been more limited concern with the gender relationships and inequalities upon which globalization has impacted. It is not only in narratives of the self, personal identities and in the primacy given to sexuality and gendered identity in psychoanalytic theories that gender counts. I have tried to demonstrate more widely the articulation of gender and race, in particular in the theorizing of identity. Race, gender and understanding of the body permeate the conceptualization of identity and are not separate categories which can be disassociated from other dimensions of the self. Nor are they the preserve of those who can be marked, for example as if gender were the concern of women and not of men, or race a matter for black people and not white.

The ways in which difference, as a key component of identity, is articulated draw upon theories of representation such as those involving semiotics and discursive critiques. What I have taken to be included within the sphere of representational systems, as is the case with visual culture, involves diverse practices, images, rituals and symbols. Although there is a strong case for the primacy of the visual, for example as illustrated by Rosalind Petchesky, the visual embraces a whole range of sensory experiences, which articulate in the production of meaning and the discursive field goes far beyond words and images. Not only do symbolic systems provide the terrain for the representation of identity, but they are contested. It is through representation that meanings change and are reformulated. Representation offers an appropriate vehicle for the interrogation of the relationship between the personal and the social in the construction of identity. The emphasis of much of the theory that seeks to present explanatory frameworks for the operation of symbolic processes, is on the constraints of structuralism and in many cases poststructuralism. The language speaks us rather than the other way around. One of the dilemmas within the field is to explore ways in which people might represent themselves and seek a voice. The most useful approaches have been those which have been developed, for example within feminism and postcolonial theory, to explore how it could be possible to speak from the margins.

One of the structural constraints, which must present limitations to the exercise of agency in shaping identity, is that of the material body that each of us inhabits. From having been largely excluded from sociological critiques the body has, in recent years occupied a central place in the understanding of identity. Embodiment and the body have become ubiquitous. However, it is often a most incorporeal body that has occupied that space. The body has been written as discursive product, rather than one which eats, sleeps, has babies and dies. (This is not an exclusive list!) One of the concerns of academic critiques has been to reinstate the body. This has been worked through identity politics, for example through the work of people with disabilities and those for whom the material body plays a central role (as it must surely for everyone to varying degrees) in the shaping of identity. Embodied identities permit the extension of explanatory frameworks to encompass difference and diversity and to challenge some of the assumptions about normality and unity. A concern with the body as a crucial site for the representation and enactment of identity provides a significant challenge to the natural/social binary, but also makes it possible to retain a materiality that subverts some of the excesses of fluidity and contingency. The body is socially and culturally made meaningful in space and time, but it also carries a material dimension that cannot be subject to discursive, social construction only.

The relationship between roots and routes in providing understanding of identity brings together the different strands in the narrative of this book. Roots, in investigating and establishing sources and myths of origin, trace the story of who we are back to where we have come from. Roots lay claim to certainties that can be revealed, whether through the histories of kinship, nation and ethnicity or of sexuality and gender within the biographies and biologies of individuals. Roots seek a starting point to the narrative of the self. Routes recount the whole story, but nonetheless have to identify key points and pivotal moments in mapping the self.

This focus on the specificities of identity formation is indicative of both theoretical and methodological shifts within the study of identity. Methodologies have focused more on the minutiae of everyday life and the ways in which subjects construct meanings about themselves. The impact of phenomenological approaches, which give high priority to description of direct experience, has in many ways superseded the creation of theories that posit causal explanations of how identities form. Social scientists have increasingly focused on the world as their subjects of enquiry present it to them. This has required empirical research, in some fields involving the analysis of discourse, although this has taken many different forms, ranging from the interrogation of texts, practice and legislation in Foucauldian approaches to the close analysis of scripts of interviews and of conversations in social psychological approaches. The discursive field of enquiry also embraces a whole range of texts, including first person testimony, fictional accounts, internet communications and cinematic and other media representations. However, the impact of phenomenology has been to direct attention to empirical investigations of the ways in which social actors constitute themselves.

Theory and methods also overlap and interconnect. The theories that generate and derive from more empirical approaches to investigation have also moved from the overarching meta-narratives of the nineteenth and twentieth centuries. These theoretical positions have been classified, perhaps because of their reaction to what has gone before and their dialectical relationship with the grand theories that prefigure them, post-modernism and poststructuralism.

Postmodernism and poststructuralism: different ways of thinking identity?

Postmodernism and poststructuralism have haunted the discussion throughout this book, although they have not on the whole been compartmentalized or labelled as specific discursive fields. They can be distinguished by certain features, many of which will have emerged in the exploration of identity offered in the book. At its best, and most useful, postmodernism allows the 'others' to speak, by challenging the certainty of grand narratives and global explanatory theories. It has presented troubling alternatives. For example, understanding of social divisions has been expanded to include race ethnicity, gender, sexuality, disability and generation. An emphasis on certainty is replaced by an ontological focus on uncertainty, instability, hybridity and reflexivity. The subject and the social world have been de-centred through concerns with language, discourse and culture. New versions of 'truth' and 'reality' have taken the places of the meta-historical narratives and critiques of Enlightenment coherence. Some approaches have combined inner and outer worlds in an incorporation of psychoanalytical theories into social and cultural theories.

Poststructuralist thinking has demonstrated the limitations of dualisms and sought to indicate the complex interrelationship between some traditional binaries. Rather than seeing meanings as produced through oppositional relationships, such as the 'us' and 'them', which were already seen as problematic in the initial illustration at the beginning of the book, poststructuralist theorists have explored the connections and the ways in which difference is internal as well as external. We have to manage the differences among ourselves, as well as construct differences between ourselves and others. While some of the polarized and oppositional relationships of structuralism provide a useful starting point for thinking about identity, later critiques have exposed their limitations. For example, early second wave feminists demonstrated the weaknesses of seeing gender as simply read off from biological sex and sought to differentiate between the two, categorizing sex as a biological category rooted in the body and gender as a cultural, social expression of identity. Later feminist work broke away from the distinction between the 'reality' of sex and the 'appearance' of gender. Butler's work stresses the ways in which gender is an expressive act, part of the ritualized practice by which discourse produces the outcome that it names. It is impossible to distinguish between some category of embodied sex that could be unrelated to and separate from gender.

Similar poststructuralist themes engaging with such critiques have been developed by postcolonial theorists such as Gayatri Chakravorty Spivak and Homi Bhabha. According to Spivak, the production of identities and especially of writing historical identities, which always involve contested and conflicting versions of the story, challenges the idea of hegemony. Conflicts are intrinsically part of the struggle for inclusion on the part of minority, subaltern identities. Bhabha too aims to disrupt settled stories of identity, by focusing on the multiple ways in which the nation can be constructed. He endeavours to open up a space between those who are included and those who are excluded, those who have power and those who do not. Within such theoretical approaches, ethnic identity is bound up with dynamic and changing relations of political power and domination, cultural and social inheritance.

However, while postmodernism and poststructuralism open up possibilities and new ways of thinking, they can also involve difficulties, no less daunting than in the theories they seek to replace and challenge. Not only are some such works expressed in a language that can be opaque and can obfuscate more than it illuminates, they may establish new certainties and new orthodoxies, through the new conceptualizations they offer to constitute our understanding of identity. One of the most serious criticisms of such theories is the omission of a considered political position that engages with the material requirements of political action. For example Butler can be seen as offering most valuable challenges to the constraints of determinism and complex insights into the practice of gender, but in the final analysis what she presents is description, that cannot go beyond the practices that are described and does not offer a critique of the power relations that might operate more widely, nor does she prescribe any action. In seeking to avoid the limitations of structuralist binaries, theorists who critique them have addressed complexity and specificity, but lack the necessary commitment to taking a position which structuralist approaches imply and even necessitate. If the positions are 'us' or 'them', we are positioned. Most significantly in the past, positioning has been in class terms, for example within the Marxist paradigm, however, and one of the main contributions of postmodernist and poststructuralist critiques is to admit those who are not included in the dialectic of class analyses. They introduce new dialectics, which encompass differences of, for example gender, sexuality, race ethnicity, dis/ability and the diversity of embodiment. Some aspects of these critiques have been associated with political commitment and an analysis of the operation of power, which locates inequality, for example within identity politics, although in many cases, the opening up of spaces within which to speak and be heard has led to an overemphasis on contingency and hybridity, within which it is difficult to locate the sources of power and inequality.

Another aspect of the cultural turn and the developments of identity politics is that, in foregrounding culture in order to counter economic determinism, the material and the economic disappear from the explanatory framework, although they clearly do not disappear from people's lives. It has been an important contribution of some accounts that they have managed to incorporate the ways in which the economic organization of the social world articulates with other influences on the formation of identities, for example in the work of Pierre Bourdieu, and in showing that culture mediates the production of meaning but cannot be disassociated from material factors and economic structures as in the work of Stuart Hall.

Donna Haraway has linked these poststructuralist critiques to more widely based social changes, including those manifest in globalization, the information society and the developments made possible through the advances of technoscience. She offers an alternative challenge to the constraints of classificatory systems that depend on oppositions, by suggesting that social, scientific, technological (what she calls technoscientific) changes make it possible to break down the barriers between humans and machines and people and animals in a transformed and imaginative understanding of cyborg thinking. One of the advantages of Haraway's approach is that she situates her exposition in a materiality that accommodates and embraces political action and the scope for commitment and takes into account material, economic inequalities.

Revisiting the dimensions of identity

In the introduction to the book I suggested that identity could be defined as having several different dimensions. Of these it is the interrelationship between the personal and the social, which I would emphasize as most important in distinguishing the concept of identity. These two areas interconnect, but it has also been useful to explore some of the ways in which the social lives within the personal and the personal in the social. This has been illustrated in different ways. While psychoanalysis may privilege the personal through its focus on the psyche, it is impossible to conceptualize the personal, psychic space outside the social world that gives it meaning. This is implicated in the process of identification, which actively links the personal to the social, through the recruitment of subjects. We only become subjects through this process, although there are varying degrees of emphasis afforded to the activity on the part of the subject who is recruited into an identity position. The move away from an oversocialization of identity may have led to an excessive concern with the psychic processes at the expense of the social constraints as well as the social opportunities. It is also important to note that the social aspect of the identity puzzle presents opportunities for action and for reconfiguring social relationships and collective identities as well as personal identities. The personal social relationship offers the chance to remake ourselves and remake social relations, as class action and more recently identity politics have illustrated.

Difference is another key dimension of identity that has been explored at several different points in the book. Identity is marked by difference and the ways in which we distinguish between ourselves and others. It would be hard to envisage an understanding of identity that did not necessitate an exploration of difference and include the concept as fundamental to a grasp of what identity means. However, as I have suggested, difference is strongly tied up with the operation of power and frequently involves the devaluing of one part of the equation. The differences that have been explored relate to gender, race, ethnicity and disability. Gender has a particularly embodied and historical dimension in relation to the marking of difference and along with race and in some cases disability bears the mark of visible difference, which provides particular inflections that are imbricated in the valuing and devaluing of identities.

Difference and sameness involve the marking of boundaries and the identity story is characterized by the moments at which boundaries are drawn, redrawn and transgressed. This is part of the dynamic of identity. Rather than fixing boundaries, it is necessary to redraw them through the political action with which the formation and establishment, especially of identities are necessarily implicated. These processes are historically specific and located in different places at different times. The ways in which boundaries are drawn depend on the symbolic systems that are utilized in the process as well as on the multi-faceted dimensions of identity. While it is possible to privilege some aspects at particular moments and in particular places, the material, the economic, the body, place, location, all have to be represented – we have to make sense of them through symbolic, discursive systems.

These discursive terrains are also contested as has been argued above. There may be some slippage in the form which conflict over identities takes but some form of discursive contestation is always implicated. The body has been cited as a site of inscription and symbolic representation, produced through discursive regimes within some accounts. Another contested site is the conceptualization of home in the mapping of identity. Not only is the physical location of home contested, it is a place that involves a wide range of different meanings expressed through different representational systems.

Identity travels, but it is about belonging. Roots are important, but an insistence on fixity and essential sources makes change difficult and stultifies development. Keeping in mind the journeys we have made and would like to make, and holding onto the moments that matter, make routes a more useful concept. We need to remember, in order to know where we have come from, so that we can create new stories of the self, while not losing sight of belonging.

References

Adam, B. 2002. The gendered time politics of globalization: of shadowlands and elusive justices. *Feminist Review*, **70**, 3–29, London: Palgrave.

African Rights. 1994. *Rwanda: death, despair and defiance*, London: African Rights.

Althusser, L. 1971. *Lenin and philosophy and other essays*, London: New Left Books.

Anderson, B. 1983. *Imagined communities: reflections on the origins and spread of nationalism*. London: Verso.

Araeen, R. 2000. A new beginning. Beyond postcolonial cultural theory and identity politics. *Third Text*, 50, Spring, 3–20.

Armstrong, G. and Giulianotti, R. 1999. *Football cultures and identities*, Basingstoke: Macmillan.

Arnot, C. 2002. Staging a survival. In *The Guardian G2*, 18 March, 5.

Bakhtin, M. [1965] 1984. *Rabelais and this world*, Bloomington, IN: Indiana University Press.

Balsamo, A. 2000. The virtual body in cyberspace. In Bell, D. and Kennedy, N. (eds), *The cybercultures reader*, London: Routledge.

Barrett, M. 1991. *The politics of truth from Marx to Foucault*, Cambridge: Polity Press.

Barthes, R. 1972. *Mythologies*, London: Cape.

Baudrillard, J. 1976. *L'echange symbolique et la mort*, Paris: Gallimard.

Bauman, Z. 1987. *Legislators and interpreters. On modernity, postmodernity and intellectuals*, Cambridge: Polity.

Bauman, Z. 1992. Survival as a social construct theory. *Culture and Society*, **9**, 1–36.

Bauman, Z. and May, T. 2001. *Thinking sociologically*, Oxford: Blackwell.

Bayoumi, M. and Rubin, A. (eds) 2001. *The Edward Said Reader*, London: Granta.

Beck, U. 1992. *Risk society: towards a new modernity*, London: Sage.

Begum, N. 1994. Snow White. In Keith, L. (ed.), *I mustn't grumble: writing by disabled women*, London: Women's Press.

Bellah, R.N., Madsen, R., Sullivan, W.M., Swindler, A. and Tipton, S.M. 1985. *Habits of the heart: individualism and commitment in American life*, Berkeley: University of California Press.

Benson, S. 1997. The body, health and eating disorders. In Woodward, K. (ed.), *Identity and difference*, London: Sage.

Bentham, J. 1962. *Panopticon, Works of Jeremy Bentham published under the superintendence of his executor John Bowring,* 11 Vols, New York: Russell and Russell.

Berger, J. 1974. *Ways of seeing,* Harmondsworth: Penguin.

Berger, J. 1984. *And our faces, my heart, brief as photos,* London: Writers and Readers.

Berger, P., Berger, B. and Kellner, H. 1973. *The homeless mind,* New York: Random House.

Betterton, R. 1987. *Looking on,* London: Pandora.

Bhabha, H. 1990. The third space: interviews with Homi Bhabha. In Routledge, J. (ed.), *Identity: community culture, difference,* London: Lawrence and Wishart.

Biemann, U. 2002. Remotely sensed: a topography of the global sex trade. *Feminist Review,* **70,** 75–88.

Bonnett, A. 1998. Constructions of whiteness in European and American anti racism. In Werbner, P. and Modood, T. (eds), *Debating cultural hybridity,* London: Zed Books.

Bordo, S. 1993. *Unbearable weight: feminism, western culture and the body,* Berkeley: University of California.

Borzello, F. 2001. Behind the image. In Ridel, L. *Mirror mirror,* London: National Portrait Gallery.

Bourdieu, P. 1978. Sport and social class. *Social Sciences Information,* **17,** 6, 819–40.

Bourdieu, P. 1984. *Distinction: a social critique of the judgement of taste,* London: Routledge.

Braid, M. 2002. Your daddy was a donor. *The Observer,* 20 January, 1.

Branwyn, G. 2000. *Compu-sex erotica for cybernauts.* In Bell, D. and Kennedy, B.M. (eds), *The cybercultures reader,* London: Routledge.

Brook, D. 1976. *Naturebirth,* Harmondsworth: Penguin.

Butler, J. 1990. *Gender trouble: feminism and the subversion of identity,* New York: Routledge.

Butler, J. 1993. *Bodies that matter,* New York: Routledge.

Castells, M. 1996. *The rise of the network society,* Oxford: Blackwell.

Castells, M. 1997. *The power of identity,* Oxford: Blackwell.

Chadwick, W. 2001. How do I look? In Riddel, C. *Mirror mirror,* London: National Portrait Gallery.

Chodorow, N.J. 1978. *The reproduction of mothering,* Berkeley: University of California Press.

Chodorow, N.J. 1995. Gender as a person and cultural construction. In Leslett, B. and Joeres, R.B. (eds), *The second signs reader,* Chicago: University of Chicago Press.

Cixous, H. 1975. Sorties. In *La jeune née,* English translation in Marks, E. and de Courtivron, I. (eds) 1980. *New French feminisms: an anthology,* Amherst: The University of Massachusetts Press.

Cohen, P. 1988. The perversions of inheritance. In Cohen, P. and Bains, H. (eds), *Multiracist Britain,* Basingstoke: Macmillan.

Collins, P. Hill, 1990. *Black feminist thought, knowledge, consciousness and the politics of empowerment,* New York: Routledge.

Comolli, J.L. 1980. Mechanics of the visible. In Heath, S. and de Lauretis, T. (eds), *The cinematic apparatus,* New York: St. Martin's Press.

Connell, R.W. 1985. *Masculinities*, Berkeley: University of California.

Conrad, P. 2000. New new world. *Granta*, **70**, 11–37.

Cooley, C.H. [1902] 1964. *Human nature and the social order*, New York: Scribener's.

Corker, M. and Shakespeare, T. 2002. *Disability/postmodernism: embodying disability theory*, London: Continuum.

Craib, I. 1994. *The importance of disappointment*, London: Routledge

Culler, J. 1976. *Saussure*, London: Fontana.

Cwerner, S. 2000. The cosmopolitan ideal: time belonging and globalization. *Time and Society*, **9**, 2 and 3, 331–45.

Daly, M. 1979. *Gyn/ecology: the metaethics of radical feminism*, London: Women's Press.

Daniels, S. 1993. *Fields of vision: landscape imagery and national identity in England and the United States*, Cambridge: Polity Press.

De Garis, L. 2000. Be a buddy to your buddy. In McKay, J., Messner, M. and Sabo, D. (eds), *Masculinities, gender relations and sport*, London: Sage.

Dinesen, I. 1975. *Lost tales*, New York: Vantage.

Donzelot, J. 1980. *The policing of families*, London: Hutchinson.

Dreyfus, H. and Rabinow, P. (eds), 1982. *Michel Foucault: beyond structuralism and hermeneutics*, Brighton: Harvester.

Du Gay, P., Hall, S., Janes, L., Mackay, H. and Negus, K. (eds), 1997. *Doing cultural studies*, Buckingham: Open University Press.

Durkheim, E. 1915. *The elementary forms of the religious life: a study in religious sociology*, translated by Swain, J., London: Allen and Unwin.

Durkheim, E. 1964. *The division of labour in society*, New York: Free Press.

Dyer, R. 1997. *White*, London: Routledge.

Early, G. 1994. *The culture of bruising: essays on prizefighting, literature and modern American culture*, Hopewell, NJ: ECCO.

Eichenbaum, L. and Orbach, S. 1982. *Outside in inside out*, Harmondsworth: Penguin.

Elias, N. 1978. *The civilizing process*, Vol. 1, *The history of manners*, New York: Pantheon Books.

Elias, N. 1983. *The court society*, Oxford: Basil Blackwell.

Engels, F. 1972. *The origins of the family, private property and the state*, New York: International Publishers.

Erikson, E. 1968. *Identity, youth and crisis*, New York: W.W. Norton.

Falk, P. 1994. *The consuming body*, London: Sage.

Fanon, F. 1968. *Black skins white masks*, translated by Markmann, L., New York: Grove Press.

Featherstone, M. 2000. Post-bodies, ageing and virtual reality. In Bell, D. and Kennedy, B.M. (eds), *The cybercultures reader*, London: Routledge.

Feffer, A. 1993. *The Chicago pragmatists and American progressivism*, Ithaca: Cornell University Press.

Foucault, M. 1970. *The order of things: an archaeology of the human sciences*, translator anonymous, London: Tavistock Publications.

Foucault, M. 1972. *The archaeology of knowledge*, translated by Sheridan-Smith, A.M., London: Tavistock Publications.

Foucault, M. 1973. *Madness and civilization: a history of insanity in the age of reason,* New York: Vintage.

Foucault, M. 1978. *The history of sexuality,* Vol. 1, New York: Vintage.

Foucault, M. 1979. *Discipline and punish, the birth of the prison,* New York: Vintage.

Foucault, M. 1980. *Power/knowledge: selected interviews and other writings: 1972.*

Foucault, M. 1985. *The use of pleasure,* Vol. 2, translated by Hurley, R., Harmondsworth: Penguin.

Foucault, M. 1988. *Technologies of the self,* Amherst: University of Massachusetts Press.

France, L. 2002. For better for worse. In *The Observer,* 3 March, *Magazine,* pp. 18–27, London.

Fraser, M. 1984. *In search of a past: the manor house, Amnersfield, 1933–1945,* London: Verso.

Freud, S. [1900] 1965. *The interpretation of dreams,* translated by Strachey, J., 1965: New York: Avon Books.

Freud, S. [1905] 1953. Fragments of an analysis of hysteria. In Strachey, J. (ed.), *The standard edition of the collected works of Sigmund Freud,* Vol. 7, London: Hogarth Press.

Freud, S. 1923. *The ego and the id, Standard edition,* Vol. 19, London: Hogarth Press.

Fussell, S.W. 1991. *Muscle: confessions of an unlikely body builder,* New York: Poseidon Press.

Garfinkel, H. 1967. *Studies in ethnomethodology,* Englewood Cliffs: Prentice-Hall.

Giddens, A. 1991. *Modernity and self-identity: self and society in the late modern age,* Oxford: Polity Press.

Giddens, A. 1992. *The transformation of intimacy: sexuality, love and eroticism in modern societies,* Sandford University Press.

Giddens, A. 1999. *Runaway world.* The BBC Reith Lectures, BBC Radio 4, BBC Education.

Gilroy, P. 1993. *The black Atlantic: modernity and double consciousness,* London: Verso.

Gilroy, P. 1997. Diaspora and the detours of identity. In Woodward, K. (ed.), *Identity and difference,* London: Sage.

Gilroy, P. 2000. *Between camps,* London: Allen Lane.

Gieve, 1989. *Balancing acts: on being a mother,* London: Virago.

Goffman, E. 1974. *Frame analysis,* New York: Harper and Row.

Goffman, E. 1959. *The presentation of self in everyday life,* New York: Doubleday.

Goffman, E. 1961. *Asylums,* New York: Doubleday.

Goffman, E. 1990. *Stigma. Notes on the management of spoiled identity,* Harmondsworth: Penguin.

Gonzalez, J. 2000. Envisioning cyborg bodies: notes from research. In Kirkup, G., Janes, L., Hovendon, F. and Woodward, K. (eds), *The gendered cyborg,* London: Routledge.

Greene, G. and Kahn, C. (eds) 1985. *Making a difference. Feminist literary criticism,* London: Routledge.

Hall, S. 1982. Culture and the state. In *The state and popular culture,* Milton Keynes: Open University.

Hall, S. 1990. Cultural identity and diaspora. In Rutherford, J. (ed.), *Identity, community, culture, difference*, London: Lawrence and Wishart.

Hall, S. 1991. The local and the global. In King, A.D. (ed.), *Culture, globalisation and the world system*, London: Macmillan.

Hall, S. 1992a. The west and the rest. In Hall, S. and Gieben, B. (eds), *Formation of modernity*, Cambridge: Polity Press; Milton Keynes: Open University.

Hall, S. 1992b. The question of cultural identity. In Hall, S., Held, D.D. and McGrew, T. (eds), *Modernity and its futures*, Cambridge: Polity with Blackwell Publishers and the Open University.

Hall, S. 1995. New culture for old. In Massey, D. and Jess, P. (eds), *A place in the world: places, culture and globalization*, Oxford: Oxford University Press.

Hall, S. 1997. The work of representation. In Hall, S. (ed.), *Representation: cultural representation and signifying practices*, London: Sage.

Hari, J. 2002. Forbidden love. In *The Manchester Guardian*, 9 January, pp. 8–9.

Haraway, D. 1991. *Simions cyborgs and women: the reinvention of nature*, London: Free Association Books.

Haraway, D. 1992. *Primate visions*, London: Verso.

Haraway, D. 1997. The virtual speculum in the New World Order. *Feminist Review*, No. 55, Spring, London: Routledge.

Haraway, D. 1998. The persistence of vision. In Mirzoeff, N. (ed.), *Visual culture reader*, London: Routledge.

Haraway, D. 2000a. A manifesto for cyborgs. In Kirkup, G., Janes, L., Hovendon, F. and Woodward, K. (eds), *The gendered cyborg*, London: Routledge.

Haraway, D. 2000b. Deanimations: maps and portraits of life itself. In Brah, A. and Coombes, A. (eds), *Hybridity and its discontents politics, science, culture*, London: Routledge.

Hawkes, T. 1998. *Structuralism and semiotics*, London: Routledge.

Held, D. (ed.) 2000. *A globalizing world? Culture, economics, politics*, London: Routledge.

Hochschild, A. 1994. The commercial spirit of intimate life and the abduction of feminism: signs from women's advice books. *Theory Culture and Society*, 11, 1–24.

Holstein, J. and Gubruim, J. 2000. *The self we live by*, Oxford: Oxford University Press.

Ignatieff, M. 1993. The highway of brotherhood and unity, *Granta*, 45, 225–43.

Ignatieff, M. 1994. *Nationism and the narcissism of minor differences*, Milton Keynes: Open University Pavis Centre Paper.

Irigaray, L. 1985. *This sex which is not one*, translated by Porter, C. and Burke, C., Ithaca: Cornell University Press.

Irigaray, L. 1991. This sex is not one. In Whitford, M. (ed.), *The Irigaray reader*, Oxford: Blackwell.

Jackson, S. and Scott, S. (eds) 2002. *Gender: a sociological reader*, London: Routledge.

Jagger, A. 1983. *Feminist politics and human nature*, Totowa: Rowman and Allanheld.

Jamieson, L. 1998. *Intimacy: personal relationships in modern societies*, Cambridge: Polity Press.

James, W. [1892] 1961. *Psychology: the briefer course*, New York: Harper and Brothers.

Jay, A. 1998. Scopic regimes of modernity. In Mirzoeff, N. (ed.), *Visual culture reader*, London: Routledge.

Johnson, R. 1986. The story so far: and for the transformations. In Puntere, D. (ed.), *Introduction to contemporary cultural studies*, London: Longman.

Kaplan, E.A. 1992. *Motherhood and representation: the mother in popular culture and melodrama*, London: Routledge.

Kay, J. 1991. *A dangerous knowing*, London: Sheba.

Kay, J. 1998. *Trumpet*, London: Macmillan.

Keith, L. (ed.) 1994. *I mustn't grumble: writing by disabled women*, London: Women's Press.

Kessler, S.J. 1998. *Lessons from the intersexed*, Rutgens: Rutgens University Press.

Klein, M. 1986. Early stages of the Oedipus conflict. In Mitchell, J. (ed.), *The selected Melanie Klein*, Harmondsworth: Penguin.

Lacan, J. 1977. *Ecrits; a selection*, London: Tavistock.

Laclau, E. 1990. *New reflections on the revolution of our time*, London: Verso.

Laplanche, J. and Pontalis, P. 1973. *The language of psycho-analysis*, London: Hogarth Press.

Latour, B. 1987. *Science in action*, Cambridge, MA: Harvard University Press.

Latour, B. 1993. *We have never been modern*, Hemel Hempstead: Harvester Wheatsheaf.

Law, J. 1994. *Organising modernity*, London: Blackwell.

Lawler, S. 2000. *Mothering the self, mothers, daughters, subjects*, London: Routledge.

Lee, S. 1993. Racial classifications in the US census 1890–1990. *Ethnic and Racial Studies*, **16**, 1, 75–94.

Lewis, G. and Young, L. 1998. *Windrush* echoes. *Soundings*, **10**, Autumn, 78–85, London: Lawrence and Wishart.

Locke, J. [1690] 1964. Woozley, A.D. (ed.), *An essay concerning human understanding*, London: Collins.

Lupton, D. 2000. *The embodied computer/user*. In Bell, D. and Kennedy, B. (eds), *The cybercultures reader*, London: Routledge.

Lutz, H. 2002. At your service madam? The globalization of domestic service. *Feminist Review*, **70**, 89–104.

Marks, E. and de Courtivron, I. (eds) 1981. *New French feminisms*, Brighton: Harvester.

Matless, D. 1995. The art of right living. In Pile, S. and Thrift, N. (eds), *Mapping the subject*, London: Routledge.

McNay, L. 1994. *Foucault: a critical introduction*, Cambridge: Polity Press.

Mead, G.H. 1934. *Mind, self and society*, Chicago: University of Chicago Press.

Mercer, K. 1990. Welcome to the jungle. In Rutherford, J. (ed.), *Identity, community culture, difference*, London: Lawrence and Wishhart.

Merleau-Ponty, M. 1962. *Phenomenology of perception*, New York: Routledge.

Mernissi, F. 1991. *The veil and the male elite: a feminist interpretation of women's rights in Islam*, translated by Lakeland, M.J., New York: Addison-Wesley.

Miller, D. 1997. Consumption and its consequences. In Mackay, H. (ed.), *Consumption and everyday life*, London: Sage.

Mirzoeff, N. (ed.) 1998. *Visual culture reader*, London: Routledge.

Mitchell, J. 1975. *Psychoanalysis and feminism,* Harmondsworth: Penguin.

Moore, H. 1994. *A passion for difference: essays in anthropology and gender,* Cambridge: Polity.

Naidoo, R. 1998. All in the same boat? *Soundings,* 10, 172–79.

Oakley, A. 1972. *Sex, gender and society,* London: Temple Smith.

Oakley, A. 1980. *Women confined,* Oxford: Martin Robertson.

Oates, J.C. 1995. *On boxing,* Hopewel: ECCD.

Ortner, S. 1974. *Is female to male as nature is to culture?* In Rosaldo, M.Z. and Lamphere, L. (eds), *Women, culture and society,* Stanford: Stanford University Press.

Pagnozzi, A. 1991. September, race in America: mixing it up, Marbella, 130–34. In Warren, J.W. and Twine, F.W. 1997. White Americans: the new minority? *Journal of Black Studies,* **28**, 2, November, 200–18.

Petchesky, R. 1987. Foetal images: power of visual culture in the politics of reproduction. In Stanworth, M. (ed.), *Reproductive technologies: gender, motherhood and medicine,* Oxford: Polity with Basil Blackwell.

Petchesky, R. 2000. Foetal images: power of visual culture in the politics of reproduction. In: Kirkup, G., Janes, L., Woodward, K. and Hovendon, F. (eds), *The gendered cyborg: a reader,* London: Routledge.

Phillips, A. 2000. *Promises promises: essays a literature and psychoanalysis,* London: Faber and Faber.

Phillips, A. 2001. The end of identity. In *The Times,* 20 November, pp. 2–3.

Phizacklea, A. 1998. Migration and globalization, a feminist perspective. In Koser K. and Lutz, H. (eds), *The new migration in Europe, social construction and social realities,* London: Macmillan.

Plato, 1955. *The republic,* translated by Lee, H.D.P., Harmondsworth: Penguin.

Polkinghorne, D. 1988. *Narrative knowing and the human sciences,* Albany: State University of New York.

Potts, L. 1990. *The world labour market: a history of migration,* translated by Bond, T., London: Zed Books.

Potts, L. 2002. *The world labour market: a history of migration,* translated by Bond, T., London: Zed Books.

Questions Feministes Collective, 1981. Variations on a common theme. In Marks, E.M. and de Courtivron, I. (eds), *New French feminisms, an anthology,* Brighton: Harvester.

Reich, W. 1951. *The sexual revolution,* London: Vision Press.

Reich, W. 1970. *The mass psychology of fascism,* New York: Simon and Shuster.

Reza, Y. 1996. *Art,* translated by Hampton, C., London: Faber.

Rich, A. 1977. *Of woman born,* London: Virago.

Rich, A. 1980. *On lies secrets & silence, selected prose,* 1966–1978, London: Virago.

Ricoeur, P. 1991. Narrative identity, translated by Wood, D. In Wood, D. (ed.), *On Paul Ricoeur: narrative and interpretation,* London: Routledge.

Riesman, D. 1950. *The lonely crowd: a study of the changing American character,* New Haven: Yale University Press.

Rogoff, I. 1998. Studying visual culture. In Mirzoeff, N. (ed.), *Visual culture reader,* London: Routledge.

Rose, N. 1991. *Governing the soul: the shaping of the private self*, London: Routledge.

Rose, N. 1996. *Identity, genealogy, wishing*. In Hall, S. and du Gay, P. (eds), *Questions of cultural identity*, London: Sage.

Rustin, M. 1991. *The global society and the inner world*, London: Verso.

Said, E. 1978. *Orientalism*, Harmondsworth: Penguin.

Sarup, M. 1996. *Identity, culture and the postmodern world*, Edinburgh: Edinburgh University Press.

Sassen, S. 1998. *Globalization and the discontents: essays on the new mobilities of people and money*, New York: The New Press.

Segal, L. 1999. *Why feminism?* Oxford: Polity Press.

Seidman, S. and Alexander, J. (eds) 2001. *The new social theory reader*, London: Routledge.

Seshadri-Crooks, R. 2000. *Desiring whiteness, a lacanian analysis of race*, London: Routledge.

Shakespeare, T. 1993. Disabled people's self-organization: a new social movement? *Disability and Society*, **9**, 3, 283–264.

Shakespeare, T. 1994. Cultural representation of disabled people: dustbins for disavowel? *Disability and Society*, **9**, 3, 183–99.

Shilling, C. 1997. *The body and difference*. In Woodward, K. (ed.), *Identity and difference*, London: Sage.

Sibley, D. 1998. The racialisation of space in British cities. *Soundings*, **10**, Autumn, 119–27, London: Lawrence and Wishart.

Spelman, E. 1982. Women as body: ancient and contemporary views? *Feminist Studies*, **8**, 1, Spring, 109–31.

Spivak, G.C. 1990. In Haraym, S. (ed.), *The post-colonial critic: interviews, strategies, dialogues*, London: Routledge.

Stallybrass, P. and White, A. 1986. *The politics and poetics of transgression*, London: Methuen.

Stanley, L. 1984. Should 'sex' really be 'gender' or 'gender' really be 'sex'? In Anderson, R. and Sharrock, W. (eds), *Applied sociology*, London: Allen and Unwin.

Steedman, C. 1986. *Landscape for a good woman: a story of two lives*, London: Virago.

Stiftung Judiches Museum, Berlin, 2001. *Discovering the Jewish museum Berlin*.

Stoller, R. 1968. *Sex and gender*, New York: Aronson.

Taylor, C. 1989. *Sources of the self: the making of the modern identity*, Cambridge, MA: Harvard University Press.

Tercier, J. (ed.) 2000. *Whiteness*, Vol. 1, No. 1, Room 5, London: The London Consortium.

Thompson, G. 2000. Economic globalization? In Held, D. (ed.), *A globalizing world? Culture, economics, politics*, London: Routledge.

Tremain S. 2002. On the subject of impairment. In Corker, M. and Shakespeare, T. (eds), *Disability/postmodernism: embodying disability theory*, London: Continuum.

Trinh Minh-Ha 1992. *Framer framed*, New York: Routledge.

Tsang, D. 2000. Notes on queer 'n' Asian virtual sex. In Bell, D. and Kennedy, B.M. (eds), *The cybercultures reader*, London: Routledge.

Urry, J. 2002: The media and the war on terrorism. In *Pain's Lecture*, Milton Keynes: Open University.

Urry, J. 2000. *Sociology beyond societies: mobilities for the twenty-first century,* London: Routledge.

Virilio, P. 1994. *The vision machine,* London: British Film Institute.

Visvanathan, N. Duggan, Nisonoff, L. and Weigersman, 1997. (eds), *The women, gender and development reader,* London: Zed Books.

Wacquant, L. 1995. The pugilistic point of view: how boxers think and feel about their trade. *Theory and Society,* **24**, 4, 489–535.

Wakeford, N. 2000. Cyberqueer. In Bell, D. and Kennedy, B.M. (eds), *The cybercultures reader,* London: Routledge.

Warner, M. 1985. *Alone of all her sex: the myth and cult of the Virgin Mary,* London: Picador.

Warner, M. 1994. Managing monsters: six myths of our time. *The Reith lectures,* London: Vintage.

Warren, J.W. and Twine, F.W. 1997. White Americans: the new minority? *Journal of Black Studies,* **28**, 2, November, 200–18.

Watney, S. 1987. *Policing desire: pornography, AIDS and the media,* London: Methuen.

Wendell, S. 1996. *The rejected body,* New York: Routledge.

Werbner, P. and Modood, T. (eds) 1998. *Debating cultural hybridity,* London: Zed Books.

Whitford, M. (ed.) *The Irigaray reader,* Oxford: Blackwell.

Wiley, J. 1999. Nobody is doing it: cybersexuality. In Price, J. and Shildrick, M. (eds), *Feminist theory and the body,* Edinburgh: Edinburgh University Press.

Williams, R. 1981. *Culture,* Glasgow: Fontana.

Williamson, J. 1986. *Consuming passions,* London: Marion Boyars.

Wittgenstein, L. [1953] 1973. In Anscombe, G.E.M. (ed.), *Philosophical investigations,* Oxford: Blackwell.

Woodward, K. 1997a. *Identity and difference,* London: Sage.

Woodward, K. 1997b. *Concepts of identity and difference.* In Woodward, K. (ed.), *Identity and difference,* London: Sage.

Woodward, K. 1997c. *Motherhood: meanings and myths.* In Woodward, K. (ed.), *Identity and difference,* London: Sage.

Woodward, K. 2000a. *Questioning identity,* London: Routledge.

Woodward, K. 2000b. Representing reproduction: reproducing representation. In Kirkup, G., Janes, L., Woodward, K. and Hovendon, F. (eds), *The gendered cyborg,* London: Routledge.

Woodward, K. 2000c. *Defining moments,* BBC, Open University TV programme.

Woodward, K. 2002a. Up close and personal: the changing face of intimacy. In Jordan, T. and Pile, S. (eds), *Social change,* Oxford: Blackwell.

Woodward, K. 2002b. On the ropes: masculinity, men and boxing, Pavis Centre Paper, Milton Keynes: Open University.

Wrong, D.J. 1961. The oversocialized conception of man in modern sociology, *American Sociological Review,* **26**, 2, April, 183–93.

Index

DATE DUE

AUG		
MAY		
DEC		
JUL 1 2 2006		